Justice for All

"Justice, justice shall you pursue."
(Deuteronomy 16:20)

In gratitude to the Honorable Norma L. Shapiro (z"l) for her devotion to justice and her unfailing support of The Jewish Publication Society.

University of Nebraska Press
Lincoln

Justice for All

How the Jewish Bible Revolutionized Ethics

JEREMIAH UNTERMAN

The Jewish Publication Society
Philadelphia

Library of Congress Cataloging-in-Publication Data
Names: Unterman, Jeremiah, author.
Title: Justice for all: How the Jewish Bible revolutionized
ethics / Jeremiah Unterman.
Description: Philadelphia: Jewish Publication Society;
Lincoln: University of Nebraska Press, [2016] | Series: JPS
essential Judaism series | Includes bibliographical refer-
ences and index.
Identifiers: LCCN 2016038361 (print)
LCCN 2016039040 (ebook)
ISBN 9780827612709 (cloth: alk. paper)
ISBN 9780827613263 (epub)
ISBN 9780827613270 (mobi)
ISBN 9780827613287 (pdf)
Subjects: LCSH: Ethics in the Bible. | Jewish ethics—
Biblical teaching. | Bible. Old Testament—Criticism,
interpretation, etc.
Classification: LCC BS1199.E8 U58 2017 (print) |
LCC BS1199.E8 (ebook) | DDC 296.3/6—dc23
LC record available at https://lccn.loc.gov/2016038361

Set in Minion Pro by Rachel Gould.

To my grandchildren and their descendants.
May they all be ethical and devout Jews.

Contents

Acknowledgments

I owe a debt of gratitude to a number of individuals who encouraged and aided me in the research and writing of this book.

First and foremost, I must thank the superb Hebrew Bible scholar Yair Zakovitch, Professor Emeritus at the Hebrew University of Jerusalem, Israel, who has been an incomparable friend since we met as graduate students in the late 1960s. Not only was he the first to encourage me to write this book, but he was the only one to read and critique every section immediately after a first draft was printed out. If the interested layperson finds this book readable, it is primarily due to his efforts to convince me to stylize it properly. Further, his numerous substantive comments challenged several of my ideas and forced me to sharpen my thinking as well as to write with greater clarity. This book would not be what it has become without his help.

Special thanks go also to another extraordinary scholar and friend, Shalom Paul, also Professor Emeritus of Hebrew Bible at the Hebrew University. I had the honor of being his teacher assistant in the early 1970s, and his teachings appear often in both the text and endnotes of this book. He generously volunteered to be my sounding board during the research and writing of this work. Over countless coffees and meetings at his office, he questioned me on my progress and discoveries, referred me to particular scholarship and ancient texts, occasionally double-checked key Akkadian terms, permitted me to take home books from his personal library—frequently driving me to and from the University, and commended the book to a publisher. I will never be able to repay his many kindnesses.

Three other dear friends deserve particular mention for reading and commenting on advanced drafts of each chapter: prolific scholar Marvin Sweeney, Professor of Hebrew Bible at the Claremont School of Theology, took considerable time to write a great many judicious notes on the work; Associate Professor of Biblical Studies Dru Johnson of the King's College (New York) brought fresh ideas to the substance and pedagogical aspects of the book (especially after he introduced some of the material to his students); Simon May, well-known author and Professor of Philosophy at King's College (London), not only opened up my thinking with his unique perspectives but spent hours in conversation with me that helped refine my concepts. All recommended the book to publishers. My deep appreciation to all.

One unparalleled friend must be thanked for his unique contributions: Ari Kellen not only continuously encouraged me to write this book (and read it with great interest despite his extremely time-consuming and responsible position), but also—without being asked—provided much needed support. To him (and his wonderful family), I owe more than I can say.

A number of individuals read one or more parts of the book and were kind enough to make comments. In particular, Nechama Unterman, a professional copy editor, voluntarily made extensive notes on several chapters, and Yael Kellen read much of the book and gave me a college student's viewpoint. Rabbi Raymond Apple, Professor Moshe Soller, Steven Bramlett, David Waren, Benny Muchawsky, Velvel Pasternak, José Carp, Danny Siegel, and Professor Ed Greenstein all made comments on at least a portion of the book. Yoram Hazony of the Herzl Institute (Jerusalem) gave me a forum for presenting several of the chapters. My gratitude to all.

My thanks also go to Hebrew Bible scholars Michael Segal, Nili Wazana, and Shimon Gesundheit who, as successive chairs of the Hebrew

University Bible Department, arranged for me to acquire library privileges at the university, where I did the vast majority of my research. I also wish to express my appreciation to the staff of the Hebrew Union College library in Jerusalem for also granting me library privileges.

I am very grateful to the Jewish Publication Society's director, Barry Schwartz, and managing editors, Carol Hupping and Joy Weinberg, for their enthusiasm and assistance in shepherding the book to publication. Further appreciation goes to Ann Baker and Elaine Durham Otto of the University of Nebraska Press for their editorial work on the book.

Many thanks to all those who have befriended me, and with praise to the Holy One, blessed be He, who has given me the strength and time to write this book. May it be a *kiddush HaShem*, a sanctification of His name.

Introduction

In the late 1960s and early 1970s, when I was a graduate student in the
Bible Department of the Hebrew University of Jerusalem in Israel, I
became very excited about certain academic studies on biblical ethics
that I was reading, as well as by certain courses I was attending which
dealt with biblical teachings on morality. At the same time, I was dis-
appointed that these studies were not being made available to the general public but were mostly hidden away in academic journals or dense
books virtually inaccessible to all but university scholars. One day I
approached a visiting professor from the University of California, Berkeley, Jacob Milgrom, who was writing some of these fascinating ethical
studies, and confronted him on why he wasn't translating them into
reader-friendly language geared to the interested layperson. He
responded, "You do it!"[1]

Well, I was a bit taken aback. After all, I was a mere graduate student,
and I didn't feel worthy of that task. However, I kept the project in mind,
maintained my enthusiasm for it, and never forgot about it. This book
is my attempt to fulfill both my original wish and my teacher's directive.

Why I felt that it was necessary to write this book, however, goes back
to an earlier historical period. Once upon a time, indeed, until the nine-

teenth century, the Hebrew Bible, as the Old Testament, had an honored place within western civilization. Even after Christianity lost its political power, the stories of Genesis, the Exodus from Egypt, the revelation of the Ten Commandments on Mount Sinai, and other biblical texts too numerous to mention still held powerful sway over American and European imagination. It made little difference whether one believed in the Hebrew Bible as God's word or Divinely inspired, or even if one was an atheist. The Hebrew Bible was viewed as a fount of unparalleled wisdom, values, history, and spirituality that was not duplicated in the only other ancient foundational literatures of the West, that of Greece and Rome. It is not for nothing that the crest of Yale University contains the Hebrew words *Urim* and *Thummim*, the oracle of the breastplate of the Israelite High Priest, or that the crest of Princeton University states in Latin, "Old and New Testament," or that the seal of Dartmouth College has the Hebrew words *El Shaddai* (a biblical name of God).[2]

However, during the nineteenth century, archaeological discoveries of ancient Egyptian and Mesopotamian artifacts and inscriptions began to capture the imagination of Europe and America. Quickly the traditionalists, predisposed as they were to the superiority of the Bible, scanned some of the newly discovered ancient Near Eastern writings, such as creation and flood stories, and claimed that these polytheistic writings were religiously and ethically inferior to biblical monotheism. On the other hand, other ancient material was also being published, such as prayers and hymns that exhibited a highly developed ethical and spiritual awareness. A watershed moment occurred at the dawn of the twentieth century, on the evening of January 13, 1902, when the foremost German Assyriologist at that time, Professor Friedrich Delitzsch, lectured in Berlin before an august audience of representatives of the Royal Academy of Sciences as well as Germany's ruling elite, including Kaiser Wilhelm II.[3] Delitzsch's topic that evening was "Babel und Bibel," that is, "Babylon and the Bible." During the lecture Delitzsch purported to prove that the greatly superior Babylonian civilization had a profound influence on the development of ideas and customs of the Old Testament. Part of what drove Delitzsch to his conclusions was his antisemitism, which prevented him from seeing anything of value in the Hebrew Scriptures.[4] The lecture, and his two subsequent ones in this series, received wide publicity and generated a controversy that swept the country, with reverberations throughout western culture.

It matters little that some of the sensational influences that Delitzsch claimed were eventually disproved; more and more academic scholars adopted Delitzsch's general convictions. The pendulum had begun to swing in the other direction, and there it has stayed. Today a million inscriptions have been discovered in the ancient Near East. Even if most of those on clay tablets have still not been studied, a great many have, as well as inscriptions on tombs, palaces, monuments, papyri, parchment, and stelae. The prevailing sentiment today is that the Jewish Bible's ideas, perspectives, and ethics must not only be viewed as part and parcel of the ancient Near East, but are derived from and are subservient to, or at least no better than, the surrounding civilizations.

Indeed, one scholarly perception is that the ancient Israelites were a small, insignificant, semi-pagan society, and their biblical writings had little, if anything, new to add on either spiritual or moral grounds to our knowledge of other ancient Near Eastern cultures. To the contrary, the old Christian triumphal degradation of the God of the Old Testament as being stern and punishing—as opposed to the moral heights attained by the God of Love of the New Testament—has often been adapted to modern scholarship (never mind the frequent expressions of God's love and kindness in the Jewish Bible). The view of God in the Jewish Bible was now seen as "jealous" and "cruel," commanding the deaths of all who oppose Him (men, women, and children). Think of the flood story, Sodom and Gomorrah, or the command to wipe out the seven Canaanite nations. Thus whatever one finds ethical in the Old Testament is obviated by the immoral behavior of God.

Even when scholars adjudge that some of the Bible's values might actually be ethically superior to those found in polytheistic societies, this evaluation is considered "unfair" to those cultures. After all, the argument goes, once you have only one powerful God, of course that deity will be more moral than the gods who were constantly competing with each other for power and authority. So, in a famous article by Assyriologist Jacob J. Finkelstein published in *Commentary* in 1958 (quite intentionally titled, "Bible and Babel: A Comparative Study of the Hebrew and Babylonian Religious Spirit"), Finkelstein states, polytheism . . . implies the existence of a plurality of superhuman wills. This very condition precludes the absolute omnipotence of any one of these wills. Even if . . . one of these . . . deities . . . is . . . the head of a pantheon, he must at all times be mindful of the purposes of the other deities which are potentially vitiating to his own designs. . . .

If the first thought of the gods, as that of man, must be "to look out for himself" . . . moral and ethical considerations necessarily become secondary.[5]

He then goes on to posit that monotheism inherently tends "to become an ethical religion." Since the god has no real rivals, his will cannot be contested. So the god can be viewed as motivated "by the highest ideals." Furthermore,

he is in a position to lay down a mandate for man's behavior . . . in accordance with these ideals, and to guarantee man's well-being if his will is complied with, an advantage which . . . no polytheistic god could possibly enjoy . . . the gods were not absolutely free; the concept of a "covenant" in a polytheistic society is inherently impossible. . . .

The god of Israel is "ethical" precisely because he is the sole deity.

So, Finkelstein is saying, ancient Near East polytheism should not be condemned or denigrated for failing to achieve certain ethical advancements that appear in the Hebrew Bible, for to compare this polytheism with biblical monotheism is like "despising the elephant because he cannot outrace the horse."[6] It is in the very nature of the polytheistic system that the gods cannot adhere to ethical standards, just as it is in the nature of monotheism that the one god will be ethical.

Yet why couldn't *all* the gods be conceived as ethical? Why must their wills be in conflict? Why couldn't the ancient Near East pantheon have been conceived as a collection of harmonious, complementary wills, where each deity had his or her own role and responsibility and they act in concert to do good for humanity? Why is it impossible for humans to imagine an ethical polytheistic system? After all, conceptions of goodness, justice, peace, and well-being are found throughout the ancient Near East. And if one were to ask how the conquest of one country over another could not be seen as that victorious country's gods overwhelming the gods of the defeated country, one could respond that the gods of the losers were punishing their people for their sins.

Conversely, why must monotheism be ethical and the only God be caringly concerned with humanity? In the fourteenth century BCE, the pharaoh Akhenaten rejected traditional Egyptian polytheism and centered all worship on the Aten (the sun-disk). Akhenaten's short-lived "monotheistic" religion (eradicated some twenty years later) had no morality; evil simply did not exist. His Atenism ignored suffering and was highly elitist.[7] Later Aristotle's impersonal god, the supreme unmovable mover, did not care about humanity. Further, the history of monotheistic religions has provided us with irrefutable evidence that at different times people believed in the one God who was seemingly pleased to have His earthly minions oppress, enslave, torture, and slaughter millions of humans—mind you, also His creations—because the victims either did not believe in Him in the "right" way or did not follow His will "correctly." One need only remember centuries of Christian persecutions of the Jews and Muslim subjugations and wars against anybody who wasn't Muslim, to say nothing of the extreme, joyful brutality of radical Islamists today. Indeed, one can make the case that these perversions supported a satanic view of God, for only a demon would want his followers to cause so much suffering and death.

The Purpose of the Book

This book's premise, then, is that ethical principles did exist in significant idealized understandings of ancient Near Eastern human, if not divine, authority. At the same time, this work challenges the scholarly perception that the Jewish Bible has made, at best, only an inconsequential contribution to the ethical development of ancient Near Eastern values. It is the goal of this book to demonstrate by substantial evidence, derived from various sources (Sumerian, Egyptian, Babylonian, Hittite, Ugaritic, Assyrian, and, of course, biblical), that the Jewish Bible not only changed the course of ethical thought but advanced it far beyond ancient Near Eastern society and religion in key ethical areas. The pendulum has swung too far. It is past time to make a more realistic investigation of the data.

The book will seek to explicate some of the most important ethical innovations of Judaism as first presented in the Tanakh.[8] The goal of the book is neither chauvinistic nor triumphal. It is not an attempt to claim that the Jews are innately morally superior or that the Bible or Judaism is perfect. Indeed, it is an accepted assumption here that the Bible contains some statements that are ethically abhorrent to those who live in the twenty-first century in democracies (although not in terms of the social-cultural norms of biblical times and environment). Rather, what is argued here is that significant portions of the Bible speak in terms of absolute monotheism and that these same portions contain certain specific important ethical advances in contrast to what we know about the ancient Near East. This work is an attempt "to return the crown to its place," to point out that important ethical values and concepts which were the basis of many of the ideals of western civilization are first found in the Jewish Bible. It is hoped that the book will reinvigorate interest in and appreciation for the ethics of the Tanakh among laypeople (whether secular or religious), students, scholars, and clergy.

The Plan of the Book

No one in the world knows when any book of the Torah or the Torah as a whole was written. Instead, many theories abound. Religious traditionalists believe that the Five Books of Moses were written by Moses at the dictation of God on Mount Sinai alone or on Mount Sinai and throughout the desert wanderings. Many modern academic scholars hold that most of the Torah was written during the First Temple period, 1000–586 BCE, to say nothing of oral traditions that may well have preceded the writing down of the material. In recent decades there has been a minimalist tendency among some academic practitioners (located mostly in central Europe) to portray biblical monotheism as totally an outgrowth of the Persian period (late sixth century BCE and on). In other words, they see most of the literature of the Torah, the Prophets, and the Psalms as entirely the product of the first part of the Second Temple period (and some even wish to see Maccabean influence, that is, second century BCE). In the view of many other scholars in North America, Israel (including the present author), and other locales, such late dating is based on poor presumptions, inadequate methodology, inattention to contradictory archaeological and inscriptional evidence, and a blatant disregard for any cogent arguments to the contrary. It is beyond the scope of this book to present a detailed refutation of that position, but for those who might be interested, some relevant bibliography has been provided in the endnotes.

In this work, the general approach will not be to arrive at a particular date when a text was written. What a text says is more important than its date of composition. Again, the endnotes will occasionally refer to different scholarly views on dating the material. The approach that will be taken, based on solid scholarly research together with logical understandings, is that the prophets knew the laws of the Torah and either followed them verbatim or expanded and developed them further (see chapters 3–6).

The book progresses in a purposeful sequence. Each chapter will contain a discussion of relevant ancient Near East literature on a specific topic, followed by an examination of pertinent biblical texts.[9] The first three chapters focus primarily on ideas and laws in the Torah, while the last three delineate prophetic contributions. While that sequence follows the literary order of the Jewish Bible, it also indicates a historical development. Thus chapter 1 compares the creation and flood stories in Mesopotamia and the Torah with a focus on the ethical relationship between divinity and humanity. Chapter 2 delineates four primary understandings in the Torah of God's revelation on Sinai to the Israelites: treaty, law, "kingdom of priests and a holy people," teaching—each in terms of its ancient Near East background and its implications for the ethical relationship between God and the people. Chapter 3 concentrates on how the Torah's treatment of two significant underprivileged societal elements—the resident alien and the poor—is derived from the ethics of the relationship between God and Israel and how it differs from the rest of the ancient Near East. The prophetic innovation of the primacy of morality over ritual is the subject of chapter 4. Chapter 5 illustrates how the prophetic message of repentance exceeds the laws of the Torah and goes far beyond anything imagined in the rest of the ancient Near East. Finally, in chapter 6, the prophetic teaching of redemption enables the people to live with hope for the future despite the tragedies of destruction and exile, a remedy absent in the rest of the ancient Near East. A conclusion sums up the relationship of the specific ethical findings mentioned in this book to the Jewish Bible's unique concept of God.

The word "Bible" in Israel (and for Jews everywhere) refers to the Hebrew Bible, or what Christians refer to as the Old Testament. "Ethics" is used throughout this book as simply referring to principles of behavior that are altruistic, that is, beneficial to others. Morals are beneficial actions on behalf of others. Sometimes, as in common speech, "ethics" and "morals" will be used interchangeably. All dates are given as BCE (Before the Christian, or Common, Era), or CE (the Christian, or Common Era), as is now accepted academic style.

A note on the English translation used here and the translations of "God" and "the Lord": the primary English translation herein was done by a committee of academic experts in the Hebrew Bible over several decades and is known as the NJPS, New Jewish Publication Society translation (*JPS Hebrew-English Tanakh*), which relies predominantly on medieval Hebrew manuscripts. Occasionally I have tweaked the translation on the basis of the work of different scholars and sometimes on my own understanding.

For the sake of variety, I use the terms "Hebrew Bible," "Tanakh," or "Bible" (or the adjective "biblical") when referring to the Jewish Bible. When referring to a Christian scripture, I use "New Testament" or the name of one of its books.

Following long-standing English custom, the NJPS uses the word "God" to translate the Hebrew *Elohim* (an extremely frequent appellation of the God of Israel) and "the Lord" to translate the proper four-letter name of God, Hebrew YHWH, known as the tetragrammaton. The Hebrew root at the basis of the name refers to "being" or "existence." In Hebrew, vowels are not letters but marks or signs that appear beneath, above, or next to a letter. All medieval manuscripts (the first ones that have these signs) use similar marks for the tetragrammaton that appear with the word *Adonai*, meaning "my Lord," indicating that no attempt was made to pronounce YHWH. Indeed, there is considerable evidence that the name was considered too holy to pronounce in the pre-Christian period. Here, too, then, it will be translated as "the Lord." Concerning references to God, it is also important to understand that Hebrew grammatical form does not necessarily indicate meaning. So Hebrew *nashim* means "women" even though the word is in the masculine plural, and *avot* means "fathers" even though it has a feminine plural ending. Therefore, even though the Hebrew *hu* means "he" and is commonly used to indicate God, God is not a sexual being. True, most metaphors in reference to God use masculine images, but feminine images (particularly that of mother) also occur. Thus here, "He" will be used when designating God, capitalized to indicate that God is wholly other and not like any other "he."

On Comparing the Jewish Bible to Ancient Near East Literature

Given the biases and excesses mentioned at the beginning of this introduction (sometimes referred to as "parallelomania"), is comparing or contrasting biblical ideology and ethics to those of the ancient Near East a legitimate enterprise? Is there an acceptable method of comparing literatures?[10] In recent decades, serious scholars have responded to this question. Certain reasonable principles have been enunciated, such as the following:[11]

In comparative studies, differences may be more illuminating than similarities. For example, differing cultural principles are exemplified more in the dissimilarities in the two flood stories compared in chapter 1 than in the commonalities. At the same time, the biblical flood story appears to have modified the Babylonian one.[12]

The interpretation of a feature in a specific culture—whether of a social, political, religious, or literary nature—should always be done with the help of parallels within that culture, before any comparison is made with material from a different culture. For example, law in ancient Near Eastern law collections as opposed to biblical law (see chapter 2).

One should always attempt to understand the historical, social, or literary *development* of a feature within a specific culture before comparing it with the development of the same feature within a different culture. For example, the development of the relationship between ethics and ritual in biblical texts, as opposed to that relationship in other Ancient Near East texts (see chapter 4).

In any comparative study, all the available evidence must be examined. In other words, a phenomenon should be studied within its holistic context—social, religious, political, literary, historical, geographic—if possible. On the other hand, a specific feature or word should not be studied in isolation, that is, out of context. For example, both Babylonian and biblical legal texts mention concern for the poor, but if one does not take note of the elements in the broader literary contexts in which such concern is found, one will fail to understand the significance of that concern in the Jewish Bible as opposed to Hammurabi's collection (see chapter 3).

This study will make use of the above methodological principles in order to arrive at a fair comparison or contrast between biblical material and the rest of the ancient Near East.

Reading Ancient Materials Carefully, Including the Bible

Further, one needs to be aware of using anachronistic terminology or concepts in relationship to the Jewish Bible and the rest of the ancient Near East. In other words, terms that are in use today can rarely be easily translated into the ancient world. What is meant today by "religion" or the ideal of an "egalitarian" society are hardly applicable to the ancient world. That is why, for example, the word "ethics" in this book refers specifically to principles of benevolent behavior, as opposed to general societal values. Biblical Hebrew has no term for "values-principles," but it does have terms for behaving well to others, such as "to be good to," "to show mercy to," and "to have love for." In the course of this book, an effort will be made to explain key terminology and concepts within the ancient contexts.

Additionally, it should be noted that a major difference between ancient Near Eastern texts and the Jewish Bible was the purpose of the literature. The texts of the Jewish Bible were designed to be promulgated to the populace, even if they were originally developed primarily by pious minorities. Those in the ancient Near East were never intended to be propagated to the public at large. Rather, they were always written for a select few, an elite. Only a tiny segment of the ancient world was literate, which is why the Jewish Bible depicts texts read aloud to the public.

It is worthwhile for the careful reader to be aware of the above considerations, and how difficult it may be for him or her to fully comprehend ancient literature, including that of the Jewish Bible. The bottom line is that even accomplished scholars can rarely be completely certain that they have fully understood an ancient text.

Additionally, it should be noted that this work consciously uses the English term "Jewish Bible" to refer to the Tanakh. Using "Jewish Bible" counteracts an academic approach that claims that the Babylonian exile (586–539 BCE) was a watershed in biblical history—that the Israelite religion of the First Temple period (approximately 1000–586 BCE) ended with the Babylonian destruction of Jerusalem and the Davidic monarchy, and that what we know as ancient Judaism began only with the beginning of the Second Temple period under Persia in 539 BCE. The assumption is that, during the exile, groups of Jews redefined monotheism, covenant, and law and created a new theology. The assumption further states that the Torah is the product of this new theology. In other words, the Torah was not written down until the Second Temple period, and that pertains also to most of the prophetic works.

This book bases itself on a different supposition: that the Hebrew Bible is the product of ancient Jewish civilization from the second millennium BCE until the latter part of the first millennium BCE. The contention here is that Judaism, that is, monotheism, the Sinaitic Covenant, the law, the tie of the people to the land (including the establishment of all the rituals connected with the land, such as the holidays, tithes, and providing for the poor from the agricultural produce), the Temple (with its priesthood, sacrifices and their intrinsically Jewish significance), the prophetic messages of repentance and redemption, all originated significantly before the end of the First Temple period. Further, these Jewish memories and texts, ideas and practices, were carried on throughout the exile and the restoration to the land at the beginning of the Second Temple period. It is not a coincidence that the first momentous act of the redeemed community was to rebuild the Temple on the exact site of the previous one in Jerusalem. The returnees from exile sought to reconstitute the ideas, practices, and institutions of the First Temple period. Monotheistic Judaism had not changed; only historical circumstances had. Since the Judaism of First Temple times was the model for

Judaism of the Second Temple period, the Bible that encompassed the times of both Temples should be called the *Jewish* Bible.

The ethics of the Jewish Bible have had, unsurprisingly, an enormous influence on later Jewish thought and law, as well as on Christian thought and the development of modern western civilization, and they still influence Judeo-Christian culture today (but that is a topic for a different book). This book is written with the hope that it will encourage Jews, and non-Jews if they wish, to mine the Hebrew Bible for their ethical thinking. Further, may Christians, Muslims, and members of other civilizations be likewise encouraged to investigate their formative texts, too, for ethics that may benefit all of humanity. If that is our goal, then is there a task more worthy?

1

The Jewish Bible's Unique Understanding of God

The Ethical Relationship of God to the World and Humanity

In modern times, the abundance of unearthed Ancient Near Eastern writings—myths, laws, treaties, temple inscriptions, prayers, wisdom instructions—has provided us with a wealth of information about the gods and their interrelationships with the world and its inhabitants. To be familiar with all of these writings is an impossible task, as much material remains still unread! Nonetheless, certain key universal characteristics about these gods can be confirmed from published discoveries:

- The gods are *natural* beings. In that sense, they are no different than humans. They eat, drink, sleep, fornicate, make war, are born, and even die (or can be killed). They are part and parcel of nature. However, while they are not supernatural, they *are* superhuman in such characteristics as strength, longevity (some can even be resurrected), and other powers.
- While possessed of superhuman powers, the gods are not omnipotent. As natural beings, they are affected by nature. They also are subject to time, magic, divination (trying to ascertain the gods' plans that will affect humans, often in order to circumvent them), and destiny.

- Ethically the gods are capricious. Sometimes they behave justly, and sometimes they don't. Nor do these texts view the gods as ethical paragons. Their attitudes toward humans are notably problematic. On the one hand, Mesopotamian kings see their divine charge as ensuring justice in society. On the other, humans are created to be slaves to the gods and to enable them to rest, as befits their divine royalty.[1]

What emerges is that the least significant difference between polytheism and monotheism is the numerical one.[2] Two of the more pervasive epics—the Babylonian creation saga (*Enuma Elish*), and the flood story in the Gilgamesh epic—will illustrate these characteristics. They will each be compared and contrasted with the relevant Hebrew Bible stories to point out key differences in the latter's perception of God.

It is important to note that while the Babylonian creation epic is a self-contained literary unit (as is the Gilgamesh epic), the biblical creation and flood stories are subunits of a much larger literary creation.[3] Therefore, the observations here will sometimes refer to relevant passages in other portions of the Torah, the larger literary provenance of the biblical creation and flood stories.

The Babylonian Creation Epic

The most famous and prevalent ancient Near Eastern creation epic is known as *Enuma Elish* (Akkadian for "When above").[4] Most scholars date the epic's origins to the First Babylonian Dynasty (1894–1595 BCE), which is considerably earlier than the traditional thirteenth-century BCE date for the giving of the Torah on Mount Sinai.[5] The storyline is as follows:

Before heaven and earth had been created, only the two original divine parents, the male Apsu (the primeval sweetwater ocean) and the female Tiamat (the saltwater ocean) existed. The commingling of their waters brought forth several divine offspring who, in turn, gave birth to others. As typical of teenagers in their exuberance, the clamor of the younger generation of gods disturbs the "great-grandparents," who can't get any sleep. In his rage, Great-grandpa Apsu decides to kill off his younger descendants, who, hearing of his intentions, devise a preemptive strike. Their wisest, Ea, ironically concocts a magical incantation to cause Apsu to sink into a deep sleep, at which point Ea takes his crown and kills him. Ea establishes a palace on top of the slain Apsu and, through the goddess Damkina, gives birth to the future savior (and real hero of the epic), Marduk.

In the meantime, Great-grandma Tiamat, very upset by what has transpired, is incited by the god Kingu to avenge Apsu. She decides to go to war against those responsible for Apsu's death. She gathers her divine and monstrous allies and appoints Kingu as commander. Word comes to Ea of the impending attack, and eventually Marduk is persuaded to lead the younger gods, but he does so only on the condition that he will become the supreme divine authority. His condition is accepted by the assembly of the younger gods, who give him "kingship over the sum of the whole universe."[6] They then give him a test and place a garment before him. At his command, the garment is destroyed. He commands again, and the garment is entirely restored.

Marduk, fully armed, goes out to meet the ostensibly invincible Tiamat. "He let loose the Evil Wind, the rear guard, in her face. Tia-mat opened her mouth to swallow it. She let the Evil Wind in so that she could not close her lips. . . . Her inwards were distended and she opened her mouth wide. He let fly an arrow and pierced her belly. He tore open her entrails and slit her inwards."[7] Having killed her, "He split her into two like a dried fish: One half of her he set up and stretched out as the heavens. He stretched the skin and appointed a watch with the instruction not to let her waters escape."[8] With the other half of Tiamat, Marduk establishes the earth. He takes possession of the tablet of destinies, sets up the stars in constellations to define the twelve-month calendar, fixes the path of the sun, creates the moon, delineates the month into days, and arranges abodes for the gods. Marduk then kills Kingu and out of his blood creates mankind to serve the gods. Finally, he is lavishly praised by the gods. Humans are urged to remember Marduk's fifty names and rejoice in them, so that humanity's land shall be fruitful and it shall go well with them.

Significant commonalities exist between the *Enuma Elish* story and that of the biblical creation story from Gen. 1:1–2:3, both in content and sequence:

- At the beginning, nothing identifiable exists (no heavens and earth in *Enuma Elish*, only chaos in Genesis).

- The first words mention both heaven and earth.
- Water is present as part of the stuff of creation. Apsu and Tiamat are watery beings. Water is mentioned in Gen. 1:2.
- Tiamat and the Hebrew word *tehom* ("deep water" in Gen. 1:2) are probably from the same linguistic root.
- Creation occurs through divine speech (the garment in the Babylonian story; all of creation in the biblical one).
- The creation of the heavens, the firmament to keep the upper waters in place, dry land, the luminaries, and humans all occurs in the same sequence.
- Divine rest follows.

However, the contrasts between the two stories are remarkably revealing:

- While creation occurs through violent, unjustified conflict in *Enuma Elish* (are the noisy activities of youngsters really a good reason to kill them?), the Bible depicts a universe in which creation takes place in complete harmony as God's commands bring cosmic order into being.[9] Not only is there no violence but the biblical ideal (Gen. 1:29–30) is that both animals and humans should be vegetarians.
- The gods are part of nature: they are born, have sex, give birth, and die. They are subject to nature. (Remember how the wind prevents Tiamat from closing her mouth?) The Bible's God is not only supernatural but He alone rules nature.
- The gods are subject to magic. In the Bible, magic can never affect God.
- Humans are created to serve the gods. In the Bible, God creates humans to rule the earth: "*fill the earth and subdue it; rule over the fish of the sea, the birds of the heavens, and all the animals that teem upon the earth*" (Gen 1:28).[10]
- In *Enuma Elish*, humans are made out of the blood of the evil god. In the Bible, the human is made in the image of God (Gen. 1:26–27).
- The constant delineation in Genesis is that creation is "good" (Gen. 1:4, 10, 12, 18, 21) and that the totality is "very good" (1:31). That the word "good" here refers to ethics and not aesthetics ("a good painting," "good-looking," etc.) may be inferred from the

second verse of Genesis. The "wind" (Hebrew, *ruach*) of God "flutters" over the face of the waters.[11] The word "flutters" is used elsewhere in the Torah only of an eagle "fluttering" over its young (Deut. 32:11). Why does the Bible use this rare word to express what the "wind" of God is doing, when other words are commonly used about the movement of the wind ("moves," "blows," "carries")? Apparently the intention in Genesis is to bring to mind a mother bird (the Hebrew verb here is in the feminine), that is, God's spirit is hovering over the stuff of creation like a mother bird over her young.[12] Creation, as it were, is being born, and the goodness of that birth is best understood as ethical. (Ask any mother!)

- God's day of rest at the end of creation is sanctified: *"And God blessed the seventh day and made it holy, because on it God rested from all the work of creation that He had done"* (Gen. 2:3). God's rest explicitly serves as a model in the Ten Commandments for requiring complete rest from work not only of the Israelites but even of their slaves and animals (Exod. 20:8–11).

  - *Remember the Sabbath day to make it holy. You shall work for six days and do all your labor, and the seventh day is the Sabbath of the Lord your God. You shall not do any labor, you, and your son or your daughter, your male servant and your maid servant, and the alien who is within your gates. For in six days the Lord made the heavens and the earth, the sea and all that is in them, and he rested on the seventh day. Therefore, the Lord blessed the Sabbath day and made it holy.*

- In other words, Divine rest in the Bible is in stark contrast to the gods' rest in *Enuma Elish* where the result is the enslavement of humanity to the gods. That enslavement, in turn, is a consequence of the need of the gods for sustenance. As one who is supernatural, the biblical God has no such need. In the words of Psalm 50:10–13, *"For Mine is every animal of the forest, the beasts of a thousand mountains. . . . Were I hungry, I would not tell you, for Mine is the world and all it holds. Do I eat the flesh of bulls, or drink the blood of he-goats?"*

The ethical emphasis in the biblical story, in contrast to the Babylonian, cannot be denied. Three major biblical ethical innovations appear:

a. Humans are blessed by God to be good rulers, not slaves. The implication of the creation of the human in the image of God is to be rulers over the earth! Gen. 1:26 reads, *"And God said, 'Let us make man in our image, in our likeness, and they shall rule over the fish of the sea, and the birds of the heavens, and over the cattle, and over all the earth, and all the teeming things that teem upon the earth.'"* Much ink has been spilled on the question of the specific image of God in which humans are made. Not enough attention, however, has been paid as to how the two halves of the verse fit.[13] It seems logical that the second half of the verse is intrinsically related to the first. That is, the "image of God" here is specifically one of ruler. As God rules over the universe, He gives humanity a fiefdom, the earth. And if humanity is to rule over the earth, then humans must do so in the fashion that God rules over the universe. Since the Bible understands God as a good ruler—indeed, the best possible ruler—then humans also must be good rulers. This viewpoint clarifies the succeeding commandment in verse 29: *"God said, 'Behold, I have given you every seed-bearing plant that is upon the earth, and every tree that has seed-bearing fruit, for food.'"* Why are humans commanded to be vegetarians? Because the ethical purpose of God's nonviolent creation is to lead to a world without bloodshed! Furthermore, humans are supposed to be good rulers over the animals, and a good ruler does not eat his subjects!

b. The "image of God" refers to all men and women equally. Due to the basic biblical understanding of the patriarchal nature of human society, the biblical text does not depict a society in which men and women have equal rights in the legal and socioeconomic systems.[14] At the same time, the equality of the genders in Genesis 1:26–28, in the dialogues between the patriarchs and matriarchs in the Genesis narratives,[15] in the obligation of children to treat their parents equally in the Ten Commandments—*"Honor your father and your mother"* (Exodus

20:12; Deuteronomy 5:16)[16]—and in Leviticus 19:3—*"Each person shall revere his mother and his father,"* and in the view of Proverbs that both parents are seen as equal teachers of the child,[17] all indicate that the Bible did not justify the reality of social imbalance as due to men being innately superior to women. Further, no negative stereotypes are ever attached to women as a whole.[18] The fact that individual women, such as Miriam, Deborah, and Huldah, could be characterized and accepted as "prophetesses" is also evidence that women were not perceived in the Bible as inferior to men. So even if the Jewish Bible itself did not advocate a socioeconomic revolution in women's rights, it created the foundation for such a revolution in the future. In similar fashion, Jefferson's "all men are created equal" in the Declaration of Independence eventually would be understood to encompass all humans.

c. The Divinely established beginning of human rights—the Sabbath rest as the first law of equality in society. The third great ethical implication of this Genesis creation story is God's rest at the end of creation that in the Ten Commandments serves as a model for human behavior. No scholar has succeeded in providing evidence for any weekly or regular day of rest in any other ancient society.[19] The Jewish Bible invented the weekend (which has been adopted, in one form or another, by the vast majority of the world). This concept of the Sabbath rest had a democratizing influence upon society. All were equal for one full day a week (and on certain holidays), and no one could require anybody else to work on that day. Even the king could not ask his lowliest servant to work on that day! The effect of such a desideratum on society cannot be minimized. Here the Bible establishes a weekly rest period as the first labor law: human rights for all members of society, along with the limitation of government.

Truly, as an old observation states, "in the Bible, man was created in the image of God; in Babylon, gods were created in the image of man."[20] More than that, in Babylon humans were perceived as slaves. In the Bible, they are royalty.[21]

The Gilgamesh Epic's Flood Story

The best known and most pervasive Mesopotamian flood story appears in Tablet XI of the Gilgamesh epic.[22] The epic's origins are generally dated to as early as 2000 BCE, and Sumerian versions probably predate that. The main theme of the epic is the hero Gilgamesh's search for immortality. Along his journeys, he hears of a couple, Utnapishtim and his wife, who have been granted immortality by the gods. Most of Tablet XI consists of Utnapishtim's report of how he survived the flood and attained immortality. The main lines of the story follow:

The great gods decide to flood the world (later in the story, blame for the flood is laid on both the goddess Ishtar and the god Enlil). In the Utnapishtim story, no reason is given for the deluge, although near the end of the story there is an allusion to some unstated human sin. However, in another well-known ancient Babylonian flood story, Atrahasis (another name for Utnapishtim), the deluge occurs for almost the same reason that we saw in *Enuma Elish*—the chief god, Enlil, is disturbed by the noise emanating from the increased human population and can't get any sleep (note again the capriciousness of the gods).[23]

The great gods make their decision (to be kept secret from man) in a council attended by the god Ea. Ea repeats this secret to a man who is apparently his favorite, Utnapishtim. That Utnapishtim is a favorite of Ea is a surmise; no reason for Ea's revelation is given in the text. Ea urges Utnapishtim to save himself by building a ship of equal length and width, and upon questioning Ea tells him to hide from the townsfolk what he is doing. Utnapishtim builds the ship as a cube using workmen and pitch, asphalt, and oil. When the ship is completed, Utnapishtim loads it with his silver and gold, his relatives, and whatever he had of "the seed of all living creatures"— the game and beasts of the field.

As it begins to rain, Utnapishtim enters the ship and closes the door. The storm is so strong that "even the gods were terror-stricken at the deluge. They fled and ascended to the heaven of Anu (the sky-god). The gods cowered like dogs." The goddess "Ishtar cried out like a woman in labor . . . [and] lamented . . . 'Because I commanded evil in the assembly of gods . . . how could I command war to destroy my people, for it is I who give birth to these my people!' The . . . gods wept with her." The gods regret their hasty decision.

It rains for six days and nights and then abates on the seventh day. The ship lands on Mount Nisir. On the seventh day after landing, Utnapishtim sends out a dove, which finds no resting place and returns. He then sends out a swallow, and the same thing happens. At last he sends out a raven, which eats and does not return. Utnapishtim then leaves the boat and offers a sacrifice. "The gods smelled the sweet savor. The gods gathered like flies over the sacrificer." Ishtar lifts up the jewels around her neck as a reminder of the flood.

The instigator of the flood, Enlil, joins the gods late. Ishtar says accusingly, "Without reflection, he brought on the deluge and consigned my people to destruction." Enlil becomes angry when he sees that some mortals have escaped. One of the gods tattles on Ea. Ea defends himself by attacking Enlil: "How could you without reflection bring on this deluge? On the sinner lay his sin, on the transgressor lay his transgression." However, the story identifies no particular sinner or sinners, so Ea's after-the-fact ethical principle is only hypothetical. Ea then suggests that Enlil would have done better by bringing a lesser punishment on mankind, such as wild animals or pestilence. Ea further defends himself by prevaricating. He states that he did not reveal the gods' secret to Utnapishtim, but simply showed him a dream. Finally Enlil, having calmed down, makes Utnapishtim and his wife immortal.

The Noah Story

The Noah story (Gen. 6:5–9:17) has both remarkable similarities to and key differences from the Utnapishtim story:

God sees that human selfishness has led to evil and violence, which have saturated and corrupted the earth and its creatures. God therefore regrets his decision to make humanity and decides to destroy it. However, He favors Noah due to the latter's righteousness. God explains His judgment to Noah and tells him to build an ark in the shape of a cube, to use pitch, and to put in a window. He also guarantees His covenant with Noah and instructs him to bring his family into the ark along with pairs of all the animals and birds. Noah faithfully does all that God asks him, and God closes the door of the ark behind him.

It rains for forty days and nights, flooding the entire earth. God remembers Noah, and after the rain stops and the waters recede, the ark lands on Mount Ararat. Noah sends out first a raven and then a dove—twice. The second time it does not return. God commands Noah to leave the ark with his family and all the animals. Noah makes a sacrifice. God *"smells the sweet savor"* and determines never again to *"curse the earth because of man."* He then blesses Noah and his children, telling them to *"be fruitful and multiply and fill the earth"* (like Gen. 1:28), but cautions them that anybody who kills a man must in turn be killed, *"because He made man in the image of God."*[24]

Finally God makes an unconditional covenant with all humans and living beings that never again will a flood destroy all life upon the earth. The eternal sign of remembrance of this covenant is the rainbow, which symbolizes the Divine bow at rest (that is, no longer pointed at the earth).

The many parallels between the two stories, along with the similar sequence of events, leaves little doubt that one story has influenced the other. Again the Babylonian story originates long before the biblical one. However, what are notable here are not the similarities between the stories but the ideological and ethical differences (the Babylonian precedes the biblical):

- The gods wish to destroy all of humankind for a capricious reason (humans are disturbing their rest). God only acts to destroy humanity for a clear ethical reason—when its evil has become so great that violence has polluted the entire earth (Gen. 6:5, 11–13).[25]
- One god disobeys the divine council and saves his favorite. God saves Noah because of his righteousness (Gen. 6:9; 7:1).
- Some of the species of animals are saved by Utnapishtim. All animal species are saved by Noah.
- Utnapishtim closes the door to the ship. God closes the door to the ark.
- The gods, as natural beings, are terrified by the outpouring of nature. One is almost moved to pity the poor little goddies who, like frightened children, run up to the "attic" to escape the rising flood waters. On the other hand, the biblical supernatural Deity

controls all in serenity and is constantly solicitous of the ark's inhabitants (Gen. 6:18; 8:1, 17).

- The gods, not having eaten since the flood began, are starving (they "hover like flies around the sacrificer"). God, anthropomorphically, also "smells the sweet savor," but that only prompts Him to ethical reflection (8:21–22). Unlike Enlil or Ishtar, His behavior is based upon justice. He does not regret His decision to flood the earth.[26] Now that He is starting humanity anew with a righteous man and his family and with the understanding of natural human selfishness, God guarantees that He will never again mete out such an all-encompassing catastrophe. To the contrary, He both establishes a permanent covenant with mankind and blesses humanity's future procreation in the same manner as Genesis 1, with the acquiescence that humanity's selfish nature demands carnivorous behavior and with laws to control that selfishness.[27] Thus God reminds Noah and his family that they are made in the image of God and that the taking of human life must be punished (9:5).

Here, too, as in the creation story, we see key biblical ethical innovations:

- God rules the world with justice: The immorality of the Babylonian gods is sharply contrasted with God's ethical behavior. The Noah story presents us with the ethical innovation of the sole Deity who rules the world in justice and who is a fitting recipient of Abraham's famous challenge and expectation, *Shall not the Judge of all the earth do justice?"* (Gen. 18:25).
- Evil is the result of human behavior, which in turn is the consequence of permitting free rein to human selfishness. Humans, however, have the free will to behave ethically. While ancient Near Eastern civilizations recognized that human behavior could be evil, their deities also could behave amorally and often did so. Further, the idea of demonic evil was common. In the Hebrew Bible, by contrast, the normative view was that human behavior alone was the source of evil, while God's moral essence was only good.[28] Thus for the first time humans were conceived as responsible for their own destiny, despite their innate, selfish character.

This selfishness is prominently displayed in two of the verses in the Noah story, Gen. 6:5,

> *"And God saw that human evil was great upon the earth, and that every formation of the thoughts of his heart was only evil all day long,"*

and 8:21,

> *"for the formation of the heart of man is evil from his youth."*

In the Hebrew Bible, the heart is the seat of both thoughts and emotions. It is important to note that biblical Hebrew contains no purely abstract terms. Every idea, thought, or emotion has practical consequences. Any expression of thought, knowledge, and emotion is related to some sort of action. So "plan" may be a more accurate translation than "thought."[29] If the text had wanted to say that humans are evil, it could have easily done so. However, the text goes out of its way to craft a complex formulation. It is not man who is evil but the "formation of the thoughts of his heart." In other words, people are innately selfish.

This insight into human personality dovetails well with modern understandings of the mind-body dichotomy. A baby is a being totally in need and unable to fend for itself. It cries when it is hungry, tired, hurting, or wet. It cares not nor knows the strains it puts upon those two hulking servants known as parents. The baby, certainly innocently, is completely selfish. As the child grows older and becomes a toddler, for the first time he or she hears the word "no," as the parents try to distinguish for the child the difference between "want" and "need." It may be said that the entire transition of a child into a civilized being is based upon his or her ability to assimilate that differentiation. (Unfortunately, we all know people who think that every want they have must be fulfilled, and they don't care by whom, as long as they are provided with immediate gratification.)

So if humans are basically selfish, then how can they be expected to act with ethical responsibility? The biblical response is that their destiny is dependent solely upon their free will to decide between right and wrong. Free will is a basic assumption of the Bible, for every commandment, every instruction implies that people are free to obey or disobey. The example of Deut. 30:11–19 is instructive:[30]

For this commandment which I enjoin upon you today is not too won-
drous for you, nor beyond reach. It is not in the heavens that you should
say, "Who can go up to the heavens and get it for us, and impart it to
us that we may observe it?" Nor is it beyond the sea that you should
say, "Who among us can cross to the other side. . . ." Rather, the thing
is very close to you, in your mouth and in your heart, to observe it. See
I have set before you this day life and good and death and evil. . . .
choose life in order that you and your offspring shall live.

The Hebrew Bible posits that people have the capability to understand
that obedience to the ethical God is both in their power and in their
own best interest.[31]

- God's permanent, unconditional promise to never again bring such
  worldwide destruction gives humanity hope for the future.[32] The
  Divine covenant with Noah and his descendants (Genesis 9:8–17),
  confirmed for all time by the beautiful appearance of the rainbow,
  relieves humanity of the uncertainty of the preservation of the
  species. Unlike ancient Near Eastern polytheists, the ancient Israelite now knows that whatever catastrophes occur in the future are
  temporary and limited, but life will go on. It is not surprising, then,
  that the innate optimism of this passage will find prophetic usage
  as a model for God's redemption of Israel during the Babylonian
  exile (Isaiah 54:9–10),

  For this is to Me like the waters of Noah: As I swore that the waters
  of Noah would nevermore flood the earth, so I swear that I will
  not be angry with you or rebuke you. For the mountains may
  move and the hills be shaken, but My faithfulness shall never
  move from you, nor My covenant of peace be shaken—said the
  One who has mercy upon you, the Lord.

What Are These Stories Doing in the Bible?

Given the close relationships of the biblical creation and flood stories
to those of Mesopotamia, one must ask, "What is the Bible's purpose in

retelling these stories?" The conclusion seems inescapable that the Bible is trying to "correct" the Mesopotamian accounts of creation and the flood that were circulating (in one version or another) throughout the ancient Near East. Indeed, a fragment of the Gilgamesh epic from the fourteenth century BCE was found near Megiddo in northern Israel.[33] So Genesis is claiming that it was not the amoral gods of nature who were responsible for creation and the flood. Rather, all was the work of the ethical God, creator of the cosmos. Indeed, the unprecedented biblical idea of the one and sole ethical Deity counteracts the possibility of conflicting divine interests, as seen in the Mesopotamian stories.[34] So, for example, the *tehom*, "deep water," of creation is in pointed contrast to a brutally destructive goddess such as Tiamat.[35] The biblical stories are thus designed to refute and replace the polytheistic ones and to shape the moral consciousness of the ancient Israelites.[36]

2

The Revelation at Sinai

Ethical Implications of the God-Israel Relationship

In the Jewish Bible, the most important event in the history of the Israelites was God's revelation at Sinai.[1] Indeed, in all of recorded history, only in the Bible do we have the claim of a god's revelation to an entire people.[2] This revelation is a democratization of divine communication that stands in stark contrast to the revelation claimed in the ancient Near East only by an elite: king, priest, or prophet.[3] The undeniable message is that every single Israelite is significant to God.

The understanding of the relationship between God and Israel which this theophany generates is expressed in essential metaphors. Metaphors (and, to a lesser extent, similes) are the primary ways in which the Bible conveys God's interrelationships with nature, humanity, and Israel. These metaphors are articulated in images based on observable natural and social phenomena, including politics, family, and law. Every image of God produces a counterimage. So when God is called "king" or "father" or "shepherd," there must be a "subject," "child," and "sheep." These images are portrayals not of God but of God's relationships. Thus the God-Israel relationship is depicted variously as that of king-subject, father-children, husband-wife, eagle-nestling, shepherd-sheep, and so on. It is important to note that some of these metaphors are models that reflect the text's actual understanding of the God-Israel relationship.[4]

This chapter will focus on the ethical aspects of four essential metaphors/ understandings of the God-Israel relationship derived from the Sinai experience: covenant, law, "kingdom of priests and a holy nation," and *torah*.

The Sinai Covenant

In the Bible's self-identification, the most dominant understanding of the relationship between God and the Children of Israel is delineated by the covenant at Sinai, elements of which are particularly pervasive in Exodus, Leviticus, and Deuteronomy.

The term "covenant" may, in English, refer to many things: contract, agreement, promise, and the like. However, "covenant" always translates the Hebrew word *brit,* and *brit* primarily means "treaty." That is, the Sinai *brit* is derived from a political idiom. In fact, the biblical description of God's treaty with Israel at Sinai has been shown to have extraordinary similarities with international Hittite suzerain-vassal treaties of the Late Bronze Age (1450–1200 BCE).[5] We will examine these similarities with an eye to comprehending how they affect the ethics of the Sinai *brit*.

Hittite Suzerain-Vassal Treaties

Suzerain-vassal treaties were made by a Hittite emperor with a lesser king and often consisted of the following seven structural elements:

1. Identification of the Treaty-maker—the Hittite emperor states his name and title.
2. Historical Prologue—a description of previous relations between the two parties emphasizing prior beneficial acts done by the great power on behalf of the lesser one. The apparent purpose of the historical prologue was to serve as an explanation for the obligation of the vassal to accept the treaty and its stipulations.
3. Stipulations—the primary demand is for loyalty.
4. List of Witnesses—numerous gods.
5. Blessings and Curses—the gods will reward obedience of the lesser king to the treaty and punish disobedience.
6. Provision for Deposit and Periodic Public Reading—the treaty was deposited in the chief temple of the suzerain, and a copy

was deposited in the temple of the vassal, at the feet of the god (that is, the idol). It was read periodically in public before the king or by him.

7. Ratification—although customs varied, formal ratification was usually accompanied by an animal sacrifice, and some evidence indicates that a ceremonial meal was eaten.

The Sinai Treaty

Both Exodus and Deuteronomy provide us with narratives of the treaty at Sinai. The same elements common to the Hittite suzerain-vassal treaties appear in the Sinaitic one, a key component of which is the Ten Commandments:

1. Identification of the Treaty-maker: *"I am the Lord your God"* (Exod. 20:2; Deut. 5:6, and see 5:2, *"The Lord our God made a treaty with us at Horeb"*—Horeb is another name for Sinai).

2. Historical Prologue: *"Who took you out of the land of Egypt, the house of bondage"* (Exod. 20:2; Deut. 5:6).

3. Stipulations: *"You shall have no other gods besides Me"* (Exod. 20:3–7; Deut. 5:7–11). It should be noted that the rest of the stipulations of the treaty from the Sabbath on comprise the laws of the nation.[6] We will return to the subject of biblical law below.

4. Witnesses: Heaven and earth (Deut. 4:26; 30:19; 31:28)! Deuteronomy also assigns the Song of Moses as a witness (31:19, 21) and *"this book of the Torah"* (31:26). Obviously, in monotheistic texts, the gods cannot act as witnesses.[7]

5. Blessings and Curses: Blessings and curses are listed in Leviticus 26 and Deuteronomy 27:11–28:68 (also 29:17–27).

6. Deposit and Public Reading: The treaty is deposited in the Ark of the Covenant, which is placed in the Sanctuary (Exod. 25:16; 40:21; Deut. 10:1–5; 31:25–26). It is not a coincidence that the Ark is elsewhere called the footstool of God.[8] The treaty is read publicly by Moses (Exod. 24:7), is to be recited once every seven years (Deut. 31:9–13),[9] and is to be read by the king (Deut. 17:18–20). 2 Kings 23:2–3 portrays just such a reading in the days of

Josiah in the seventh century BCE: *"The king went up to the House of the Lord, together with all the men of Judah and all the inhabitants of Jerusalem, and the priests and the prophets—all the people, young and old. And he read to them all the words of the book of the covenant that had been found in the House of the Lord."*[10]

7. Ratification: The people publicly agreed to the treaty (Exod. 19:8; 24:3, 7). Sacrifices are made (Exod. 24:4–8), and a ceremonial meal is eaten (24:9–11).[11]

Ethical Implications

It is undeniable that the Sinai treaty was based upon a structure very much akin to that of the Hittite suzerain-vassal treaties. What is fascinating about this realization is that this is the only time in the ancient world that we have the description of a treaty between a people and its deity.[12]

What are the ethical implications of this unique phenomenon? As the treaty-maker, God is not only the great king but the ultimate monarch with full authority over the entire world.[13] Thus all known treaties pale in comparison.[14] Because in the normal Hittite suzerain-vassal treaty the vassal is always a lesser king,[15] then in the Sinai treaty, the people of Israel are raised to the level of a vassal king. More than that, since the treaty is directed to each member of the people individually, each Israelite has the status of a vassal king.[16] Therefore, the equal status of each adult Israelite, irrespective of social standing,[17] under the Sinai treaty is an important innovation in social ethics.

More than that:

- since the individual Israelite is responsible for each of the stipulations of the treaty, and
- since the stipulations of the treaty encompass all the commandments, that is, the laws of the society, and
- since the actualization of the blessings and curses falls upon the entire nation, that is, reward for obedience to God's commandments or punishment for disobedience, then,
- the future of the entire society is dependent upon the behavior of the individual!

The Sinai treaty thus gives rise to a new ethical concept in society: individual responsibility for the well-being and destiny of the community. As already implied, the treaty model has a good deal in common with that of law.

Divine Law

Mesopotamian Law Collections

Ancient Near Eastern law collections are almost solely concerned with civil or criminal law.[18] The main collections are the Laws of Ur-nammu (2100 BCE), the Laws of Lipit-Ishtar (1930 BCE), the Laws of Eshnunna (1770 BCE), the Laws of Hammurabi (1750 BCE), the Hittite Laws (1650–1180 BCE), and the Middle Assyrian Laws—(1075 BCE).[19] The absence of any Egyptian law collection should be noted. No references to Egyptian laws or mentions of law-giving by a king or official occurs before the tradition of King Bocchoris around 700 BCE. However, since the pharaoh was perceived to be a god, whatever he commanded was effectively law. Further, since every new pharaoh was a new deity, and therefore the equal of the old, he had no need of a legal tradition other than what he himself proclaimed.[20]

Although the ancient Near Eastern law collections cited here may have been primarily royal compilations, the authorities responsible for the administration of civil law were not only the kings but local or provincial courts (tens of thousands of cuneiform tablets document legal agreements and transactions, court cases, and lawsuits). It is noteworthy that religious and ritual regulations do not appear in these legal collections but were gathered in priestly instruction guides, while morality in the form of general admonitions was found in wisdom literature produced by sages.[21]

This is not to say that the ancient Near Eastern law collections were without religious or moral connection. The law collections of Ur-nammu, Lipit-Ishtar, and Hammurabi all have prologues which indicate that these legal inscriptions are evidence that the king fulfilled the responsibility given him by the gods to establish justice in the land. The collections of Lipit-Ishtar and Hammurabi also contain epilogues that call upon deities to punish anybody who erases or defaces these inscriptions.

As an example, we will take the best organized and most complete of these collections, that of Hammurabi. This collection has come down to us in a number of manuscripts and particularly on a famous stela found by archaeologists in the ancient Elamite capital city of Susa and now on exhibit in the Louvre.

The prologue to Hammurabi's collection reads in part:

> At that time, the gods Anu and Enlil, for the enhancement of the well-being of the people, named me by name: Hammurabi . . . to make justice prevail in the land, to abolish the wicked and the evil, to prevent the strong from oppressing the weak . . . who sustains his people in crisis, who secures their foundations in peace. . . .
>
> When the god Marduk commanded me to provide just ways for the people of the land [in order to attain] appropriate behavior, I established truth and justice as the declaration of the land, I enhanced the well-being of the people.

The epilogue concludes:

> These are the just decisions which Hammurabi, the able king, has established and thereby has directed the land along the course of truth and the correct way of life.
>
> . . . In order that the mighty not wrong the weak, to provide just ways for the waif and the widow, I have inscribed my precious pronouncements upon my stela and set it up before the statue of me, the king of justice . . . within the Esagil, the temple . . . in order to render the judgments in the land, to give the verdicts of the land, and to provide just ways for the wronged. . . .
>
> Let any wronged man who has a lawsuit come before the statue of me, the king of justice, and let him have my inscribed stela read aloud to him that he may hear my precious pronouncements and let my stela reveal the lawsuit for him . . . (and may he praise me) saying: "Hammurabi . . . gladdened the heart of the god Marduk, his lord, and he secured the eternal well-being of the people and provided just ways for the land."[22]

It is important to take note of certain details in Hammurabi's prologue and epilogue:

- The king is the author of this stela (written in first person).
- He and no other was chosen by the gods to ensure justice and well-being in society, particularly for the oppressed and disadvantaged, which he achieved.
- The law is the king's law.[23] "My pronouncements" (along with "my verdicts" and "my judgments") are referred to in the epilogue no less than eleven times.
- The law is retrospective and even hidden away in the temple. Only if someone thinks they have been wronged do they seek out the law—at which point, they need a literate priest to read it to them.[24] But if the law is not promulgated to the public, how does the wronged individual even know of its existence? No evidence has turned up for any cultural norm that people would go to temples to consult with priests about civil law collections that might be kept there. Further, none of the legal records found on the tens of thousands of cuneiform tablets mentioned above refers to any of the law collections![25]

Thus the primary purpose of the prologue, laws, and epilogue is the self-justification of Hammurabi before his deities that he has faithfully carried out the moral task assigned to him.

The Biblical Law Collection

In contrast to the Mesopotamian law collections, biblical law has a different framework and raison d'être:

- God is the creator of all the laws of the society.[26] As with Divine commands, laws in the Torah are preceded by "God spoke/said."[27] God is the lawgiver, Moses the law transmitter. As with the treaty metaphor, no other case exists in the ancient world of a god giving its people its law.[28]
- Since God gives *all* the laws of the society, the Bible differs from all ancient Near Eastern collections in that civil and ritual laws are

placed next to each other within the same code. Indeed, it is sometimes difficult to tell them apart. So, for example, in the Ten Commandments, Exodus, 20:3–6 are against idolatry, 7 forbids swearing falsely in God's name (perhaps in a ritual matter, for 13 refers to a false witness in a civil or criminal action which would also have been involved in a false oath), and the Sabbath laws in 8–11 require both sanctifying the Sabbath day and not making anybody else work. Similarly, Exod. 22:19 prohibits sacrificing to another god, while the following verse forbids oppressing a resident alien. Exod. 23:11 requires letting private land lie fallow in the seventh year (seemingly a ritual), while at the same time letting the poor eat of it. Leviticus 19:2 is an introduction commanding the people to be holy in imitation of God, but most of the following laws emphasize ethical obligations. And so on.

- Another unique phenomenon that is a consequence of God giving His law to His people is the *direct address*.[29] All the ancient Near Eastern law collections are written casuistically, that is, as case law: "If/When x occurs, the punishment is y." That is also the case in much of biblical law (for example, Exodus 21:2–23:16). However, some laws are also given by the direct address of God as "I" and the people as "you." This is the case not only in the Ten Commandments but also in such ethical texts as Exodus 22:20–26:

> *You shall not wrong a stranger or oppress him for you were strangers in the land of Egypt. You shall not ill-treat any widow or orphan. If you do mistreat them, I will hear their outcry as soon as they cry out to Me, and My anger will blaze forth and I will put you to the sword. Your own wives shall become widows and your children orphans.*
>
> *If you lend money to My people, to the poor among you, do not act towards them as a creditor; exact no interest from them. If you take your neighbor's garment in pledge, you must return it to him before the sun sets. It is his only clothing, the sole covering of his skin. In what else shall he sleep? Therefore, if he cries out to Me, I will pay heed, for I am compassionate.*

This exceptional style of legal writing reflects not only the fact that the laws are written as part of the stipulations of the treaty but also the intimacy of the caring of God toward His people. So one finds such elements here as motive clauses intended to stir the people's conscience and urge them to fulfill the laws.[30]

- Where King Hammurabi was appointed by the gods to establish justice, in the Bible that becomes the responsibility of each individual (as in the treaty metaphor).
- Whereas Hammurabi's law is retrospective and hidden, biblical law is prospective, prescriptive, and promulgated to the people proactively.[31] Exodus 21:1 declares, *"These are the laws you shall place before them."* This requirement is concretized in Deut. 31:10–13, which requires a public reading every seventh year before the entire people (even small children!) during the Feast of Tabernacles.[32] Think also of the constant refrain in Leviticus and Numbers, *"The Lord spoke to Moses: Speak to the Children of Israel and say to them* (such and such a law).["][33] In other words, each Israelite is required to be knowledgeable of the law.
- The burden of educating the people to the laws is placed not only upon the leadership but also upon the children's parents. This is the thrust of the famous passage in Deuteronomy 6:6–7, *"Take to heart these words which I charge you this day. Teach them to your children and speak of them when you dwell in your house and when you go on your way, when you lie down and when you get up."*[34]

Why? Why is the law so important to the Bible that every Israelite must be familiar with it? The answer is that, in the Bible, the Sinai treaty and Divine law are inextricably intertwined.[35] Thus the stipulations of the treaty equal the laws of the people. That means that the blessings and curses of the treaty are tied to obedience or disobedience of the law. In the ancient Near Eastern law collections, punishment is usually only meted out to the guilty individual (and, in some cases, to family members).[36] However, in the Bible, punishment for disobedience (that is, if too many are disobedient) is meted out not only upon the individual(s) responsible but also upon society as a whole. Further, like typical civil or criminal law in society, in the ancient Near East no benefits accrue for obedience to laws. Not so in the Bible where, in accord with the treaty's blessings, obedience to law is rewarded to the entire society![37] As God is the law-giver, He will also enact the rewards or punishments.

Thus obedience or disobedience to the law in the Jewish Bible (and later Judaism) becomes the determinant of the people's destiny. As such, law in the Jewish Bible takes on a much more important role than law in all other societies. As with the Sinai treaty, for the first time in the ancient world, the individual is responsible for the fate of the community by his or her behavior. In reality, each individual now has a dual responsibility—as an individual and as a member of the nation. The community whom the Bible addresses is now apprised of the extraordinary importance of each individual. So the community must take steps to ensure that its individuals obey the law. Additionally, this concern will be reflected in numerous Divine laws that enjoin the community and its members to care for the vulnerable elements of society. For the first time, the community becomes responsible for the fate of the individual. Thus is born the concept of communal responsibility.

Furthermore, since God is the author of all the laws, then any violation of any law is a sin against God—a new development in the ancient Near East.[38] Not just ritual trespasses but all criminal acts are now religious transgressions, for they contravene the will of God. Since only God gives the law, then each person is held accountable for his or her actions before God.

More than that, God is the source of goodness, as has been illustrated by the Genesis creation story. Indeed, numerous verses affirm that God is good.[39] Therefore, since God is good, His will is good, and human obedience to that will, as expressed in the Divine statutes, is by logical sequence also good and will benefit the compliant.[40] Deuteronomy affirms this concept (6:17–18):

> *Be sure to keep the commandments, decrees, and rules of the Lord your God that He has commanded you. Do what is right and good in the eyes of the Lord so that He will be good to you and you shall come and possess the good land that the Lord promised on oath to your fathers.*[41]

The idea that God's laws represent a higher degree of ethics than is found among the rest of the nations is explicitly recognized in Moses' speech in Deut. 4:5–8:

> *See, I have taught you rules and laws, as the Lord my God has commanded me, for you to abide by in the land that you are about to enter to possess. Keep them and do them because it is your wisdom and discernment in the eyes of the nations who upon hearing of all these rules will say, "Surely, that great nation is a wise and discerning people." For what great nation is there that has a god so close to it as the Lord our God whenever we call upon Him? And what great nation has rules and laws as righteous as all this Torah which I am setting before you this day?*

This goodness of God is directly correlated to another ethical advancement—the value of human life.

The Value of Individual Human Life

Concerning the value of the individual human life, ancient Near Eastern civil and criminal law collections allow for the following punishments: the death penalty for certain crimes against property, the ransom of the guilty person for killing another human, and vicarious punishment— substituting another human for the guilty person who causes death or commits adultery. All of these cases are contradicted by biblical law.[42]

The Death Penalty for Crimes against Property

In Babylonian and Assyrian law, the death penalty may be given for crimes against property.

ATTEMPTED ROBBERIES

Eshnunna, laws 12–13

> A man who is seized in the field of a commoner among the sheaves at midday shall weigh and deliver 10 shekels of silver; he who is seized at night among the sheaves shall die, he will not live.[43]

> A man who is seized in the house of the commoner, within the house, at midday shall weigh and deliver 10 shekels of silver; he who is seized at night within the house shall die, he will not live.

Hammurabi, law 21

> If a man breaks into a house, they shall kill him and hang him in front of that very breach.

All three laws above have an interesting parallel in Exodus 22:1–2:

> *If the thief is seized while tunneling* (that is, under a wall for house-breaking), *and he is beaten to death, there is no bloodguilt upon him* (the householder). *If the sun has risen upon him, there is bloodguilt upon him.* He (the thief) *must make payment* (and is not subject to death). *If he cannot, then he is to be sold for his theft* (but he is still not subject to death).

Note that in Eshnunna, the key factor for enacting the death penalty is an attempted robbery at night, while in Hammurabi it is home invasion. In the Bible, the only way in which the thief may be killed is by the homeowner acting in self-defense—on the assumption that the night thief who breaks into someone's home is prepared to kill that person in order to achieve his goal. (Presumably a thief who comes in the daytime into a person's home expects to find the home empty and the occupants out working in the fields.) Unlike the Babylonian laws, the Bible provides no death penalty for the thief.

THEFT

In Hammurabi, numerous laws decree the death penalty for theft of property. Law 6 relates that anybody stealing valuables or receiving stolen goods "belonging to a god or the palace" receives the death penalty. Law 7 states that any person who purchases an object, an animal, or a slave without witnesses or a contract, or accepts stolen goods for safekeeping, receives the death penalty. Law 8 states that a man who steals an ox, sheep, donkey, or pig can make restitution (at ten or thirty times the value, depending on the status of the owner), but if he does not have the resources to do so, he is to be executed. This is in contrast to Exod. 22:2 above, where the thief has to pay off his debt as a slave. However, law 22 claims the death penalty for any robber. Laws 9, 10, and 11 relate cases in which lost property appears in another man's possession or is falsely attested to. If proper witnesses and/or the seller's proof cannot be produced, then the guilty party is executed. Law 25 declares that anyone stealing something from a house on fire (while ostensibly helping to put out the fire) shall be cast into the fire. The Middle-Assyrian Laws (A3) punish the wife who steals something from her husband's house while he is ill or has died (presumably before the estate has been turned over to his male heirs), as well as anybody who has received those goods, with death.

In the Torah, all laws about theft of property require compensation by property:[44]

Exodus 21:37

> When a man steals an ox or a sheep, and slaughters it or sells it, he shall pay five oxen for the ox and four sheep for the sheep.[45]

Exodus 22:3, 6 (compare Lev. 5:20–26 and Num. 5:5–10)

> But if what he stole—whether ox or ass or sheep—is found alive in his possession, he shall pay double.
> When a man gives money or goods to another for safekeeping, and they are stolen from the man's house—if the thief is caught, he shall pay double.

It should be noted that, in the Torah, all cases of civil property damage require property compensation.[46]

RANSOM FOR HOMICIDE

In all ancient Near Eastern societies, homicide was a particularly heinous crime. Although the murderer was legally liable for the death penalty, payment of ransom was often an option. The operating principle in aggravated murder (as with premeditation or gross negligence) was that the victim's family had the choice to demand execution or ransom.[47] As Edict 49 of the Hittite king Telipinu states:

> And a case of murder is as follows: Whoever commits murder, whatever the heir himself of the murdered man says [will be done]. If he says, "Let him die," he shall die; but if he says, "Let him make compensation," he shall make compensation. The king shall have no role in the decision.

Biblical law allows no possibility of ransom in such cases:

> Exod. 21:12 (compare 13)
> *"He who fatally strikes a man shall be put to death."*

> Num. 35:31
> *"You may not accept a ransom for the life of a murderer who deserves the death penalty; he must be put to death."*

VICARIOUS PUNISHMENTS

Vicarious punishments are common in ancient Near Eastern law. In Hammurabi's collection, in laws 116 and 230 a guilty man's son suffers the death penalty for the killing of someone else's son (also, Hittite Law 44a), and in law 210 a daughter is executed for the killing of a woman. In the Middle Assyrian laws (A55), if a man rapes the daughter of another, the rapist's wife is given over to be raped. In the first four Hittite laws, a guilty person has to compensate for the killing of another with one or more people (perhaps, to be slaves).[48]

In biblical law, only the individual is culpable.[49] Vicarious punishment is explicitly repudiated by Deut. 24:16 (and Exod. 21:31):[50]

> *Parents shall not be put to death for children, nor children be put to death for parents. A person shall be put to death only for his own crime.*

Ethical Conclusions

Alone in the ancient Near East, in biblical law, human life and property are not commensurable. No way exists to legally equate them or to measure one against the other. The standard in biblical law is that human life cannot be substituted for vicariously or ransomed. No economic value can be applied to human life. Only the person who is guilty can be executed. By the same token, no civil property damage or theft can be compensated for by a human life. Property must be compensated by property, and life by the life of the guilty person.[51]

What lies behind these diametrically opposed perceptions of human value? As we have seen, *Enuma Elish*, the Babylonian creation epic that was recited annually, has a very explicit understanding of human value.[52] This epic explains that the purpose of the creation of humans was to be the gods' slaves, thereby enabling the gods to rest from the drudgery of serving themselves. The humans fill the gods' needs for food, drink, and shelter by providing sacrifices, libations, and temples. In other words, the humans have a utilitarian purpose. They are created not for their own sake but as a means to an end, a tool to be used by the gods for their own relaxation. It is not too great a jump to go from the view of all humans as the gods' slaves to that of a single human life as having limited value.

In light of *Enuma Elish*, the perspective of both the biblical creation story and the flood story presents a revolution in evaluating human life. As already mentioned, Gen. 1:26–28 reveals a totally novel, majestic view of humans—made in the Divine image and given the world to rule. In God's address to Noah and his children at the end of the flood story, Gen. 9:6 imparts a new legal repercussion of being created in God's image:

Whoever sheds the blood of man, by man shall his blood be shed, for in the image of God did He make man.

This uniqueness of human life gives it a supreme value. It cannot be equated with any object or any amount of property or money. Human life becomes invaluable. The extraordinary value of human life results, to be sure, in a paradox. Human life can only be compensated by that which is of equal value—another human life. Yet that, too, is justice. Bothered by the possibility (however remote) that a person, the image of God, will be executed mistakenly, ancient Rabbinic law will create legal hurdles that will make it almost impossible to enact the death penalty. However, at no point is property compensation considered an alternative, for human life has sacred value.

"Kingdom of Priests and a Holy Nation"

The first appearance of the biblical concept of the holiness of the Israelite people occurs in Exodus 19,[53] in a passage which depicts the first words of God's revelation at Sinai (verses 3–6),[54]

> (3) *The Lord called to him* [Moses] *from the mountain, saying, "Thus shall you say to the house of Jacob and declare to the children of Israel:* (4) *'You have seen what I did to the Egyptians, how I bore you on eagles' wings and brought you to Me.* (5) *Now then, if you will obey Me faithfully and keep My covenant, you shall be My treasured possession among all the peoples, for all the earth is Mine.* (6) *And you shall be to Me a kingdom of priests and a holy nation.' These are the words you shall speak to the children of Israel."*

The idea of an entire nation described as a priesthood or as holy is without precedent in the ancient Near East. Indeed, the idea of a whole people selected as the chosen of its god is without precedent in the ancient Near East.[55] Within the context of the previous verses, it is apparent that the people's acquisition of the characteristics of holiness and priesthood is conditional upon their keeping the terms of the Sinai treaty (5). For something to become holy, it needs to be dedicated for that purpose and separated from the profane. Thus the people are challenged to attain a level of holiness not known among the nations so that they will become God's "treasured possession." Indeed, the primary meaning of "holy" in the Jewish Bible is "separated," "belonging to," or "designated for," almost always in the context of ritual and relating to God's awesome divinity.[56]

"Kingdom of priests" is evidently to be understood here like "kingdom of Israel" in 1 Samuel 24:20. In other words, "priests" delineates the ruled, not the rulers. Who then is the king of the kingdom? It can only be the Deity. The implication is that the Israelites are analogous to the priesthood of a nation.

Priests of ancient Near Eastern societies had (somewhat simplistically)[57] two primary functions: (a) to be the personal servants of the deity in the sphere of holiness, that is, the temple—the palace of the god—and presumably (b) to inform the people what sacrifices to bring. As servants of the god, the priests had to keep the temple purified (clean), give sacrifices and libations (in polytheism, the god's food and drink), keep the "house" well lit and perfumed (by means of candelabras and incense), and generally supervise all aspects of the deity's "estate." Since the priests worked in the sphere of holiness, they had to maintain a higher degree of sanctification than the rest of the people. Therefore, they were subject to special purity laws and behavior. The biblical evidence clearly affirms that the Israelite priest had a much greater function than ancient Near Eastern priests in instructing the people: Israelite priests were responsible for teaching the people God's laws.[58]

In context, "kingdom of priests" implies that the people of Israel are to have the status of priests vis-à-vis the rest of the world, just as they are to be *"My treasured possession among all the peoples"* (5). As God is the lord and creator of the entire earth, then all the nations, in a sense, make up only one people, of whom Israel is chosen to be the priesthood.[59] Thus all the Israelites are to be God's personal servants.[60] In this image, the stipulations of the treaty and the laws of the society become the restrictions upon the priesthood.[61] A further implication may be that Israel is to teach the rest of the nations, perhaps by example, how God wants them to behave.

The idea of Israel's holiness is reiterated and expanded upon in Leviticus,[62] in which the ethical dimension is specifically emphasized. Following the introductory declaration in verse 2, *"You shall be holy, for I, the Lord your God, am holy,"* Leviticus 19 enumerates more than sixty positive ("Do") and negative ("Don't do") commandments/laws, approximately two-thirds of which belong to (or are associated with) the ethical sphere,[63] while the rest belong to the ritual domain. Herein one finds a wide range of moral requirements—on providing food for the poor and stranger, not lying or acting deceitfully, not defrauding or holding back wages, not exploiting the helpless or slandering, not rendering unfair judgment or cheating in business, not standing idly by while your fellow is in danger, and others. Most of these are written in the direct address style that we witnessed in the Ten Commandments.[64] One of the effects of this style is to raise moral statements to legal status.

More than that, in some views[65] the Jewish Bible reaches its ethical pinnacle in this chapter due to two complementary laws:

"You shall not take revenge or nurse a grudge against members of your people, but you shall love your neighbor as yourself. I am the Lord" (verse 18), and *"When an alien resides with you in your land, you shall not oppress him,* [rather] *the alien residing with you shall be to you as a citizen among you, and you shall love him as yourself, for you were aliens in the land of Egypt. I am the Lord your God."* (33–34)

A literal translation of the phrase here "you shall love . . . as yourself" would require something like "you shall have love for . . ." The phrase means "to behave with love toward" or "to treat/act lovingly." The words "as yourself" (in Hebrew, only one word) is a call to have empathy. Just as you love the good for yourself, love the good for your fellow/the alien.[66]

Moral-legal obligations to help others (who are not first-degree family members), such as those listed in Leviticus 19, have no parallel in the ancient Near Eastern law collections. Nowhere does one find a law such as those just cited.

When you reap the harvest of your land, you shall not reap all the way to the edges of your field, or gather the gleanings of your harvest. You shall not pick your vineyard bare, or gather the fallen fruit of your vineyard. You shall leave them for the poor and the alien. (Lev. 19:9–10)

or

Do not stand idly by the blood of your fellow. (Lev. 19:16)

According to ancient Near Eastern law, one was only obligated not to do wrong.[67] Only in the Bible did the law necessitate helping other members of society, whether one's fellow or the disadvantaged.

Leviticus 19 also brings to light another ethical innovation. Whereas in some non-legal ancient Near Eastern literature, such as Mesopotamian litanies and a late (third century BCE) Egyptian temple inscription,[68] cultic and ethical violations appear side by side, only in the Jewish Bible is ethical behavior presented as part of the requirements for holiness.[69] This idea, similar to the "image of God" of Genesis 1 and 9, represents an emulation of Divinity—*imitatio dei*, *"You shall be holy for I, the Lord your God, am holy"*—an ideal that did not occur at all elsewhere in the ancient Near East. Obviously the people's obedience to the ethical obligations of holiness is not a precise imitation of Divine ethical behavior, for God does not engage in business, revere parents, and so forth. Rather, if Israel strives for holiness by behaving ethically, they shall be separated from the nations as God is separated from His world. So by following God's rules, the people cannot become God, but they can become Godly.[70]

Torah *and the Parent-Child Relationship*

The noun *torah* means "instruction" or "teaching." Its importance is illustrated by the fact that it occurs 220 times in the Jewish Bible, 208 times in the singular.[71] More than 95 percent of these occurrences refer either directly or indirectly to the instructions of God originating at Sinai. As such, the term may refer to the instruction concerning a particular ritual (for example, *"This is the instruction of the burnt offering,"* Lev. 6:2), as a summary of a complex of previously stated rituals (*"This is the instruction of the burnt offering, the meal offering, the sin offering,"* Lev. 7:37), the ultimate priestly function to teach the Torah of God concerning any civil or criminal matter (Deut. 17: 8–11), and the composite literary elements of the book of Deuteronomy itself (speeches, laws, blessings, and curses).[72] By the time of Ezra, Nehemiah, and Chronicles (fifth century BCE), *torah* may sometimes refer to the Pentateuch (the Five Books of Moses) as a whole.[73]

Although *torah* already appears in Gen. 26:5 (in the plural) in reference to Abraham's behavior, and in Exodus before the Israelites leave Egypt (12:49; 13:9—the Passover; 16:4, 28—the Sabbath), it refers to the commandments and laws of God given at Sinai in Exod. 24:12,[74] throughout Leviticus, and in the first part of Numbers.[75] *Torah* parallels *brit* (the Sinaitic treaty) in Hosea (*"they have transgressed My brit and rebelled against My torah,"* 8:1) and Psalms (*"They did not keep God's brit and they refused to follow His torah,"* 78:10), and in Jeremiah it is the Sinaitic instructions of the future treaty (*"For this is the brit that I will establish with the House of Israel. . . . I will put My torah within them and write it upon their heart,"* 31:33).[76]

Where does this ubiquitous understanding of *torah* as Divine teaching or instruction originate? Just as treaty, law, and holiness/priesthood are derived from human institutions, what is the human foundation from which *torah* was transposed to the God-Israel relationship? To answer this question, we have to seek out those biblical texts which provide evidence of a nontheological understanding of the term. Only a few such texts exist, and they are focused in the book of Proverbs.[77]

Aside from the possible use of *torah* in the normal biblical sense of God's teaching,[78] Proverbs expresses *torah* as coming from one of two sources, the sage (once) and parents (eight times). Representative examples include the following:[79]

Sage

> *The torah of a wise man is a source of life* (13:14).[80]

Parents

> *My son, heed the discipline of your father,*
> *And do not forsake the torah of your mother* (1:8)

> *My son, do not forget my torah,*
> *But let your mind retain my commandments* (3:1)

> *Sons, heed the discipline of a father . . .*
> *For I give you a good lesson,*
> *Do not forsake my torah* (4:1–2)

> *My son, keep your father's commandment,*
> *And do not forsake your mother's torah* (6:20)

As is clear from the above, most of the occurrences of *torah* in Proverbs refers to the teaching or instruction of both father and mother, which the wise child will heed and keep. It is probable then that the parents' *torah* is the source of the metaphor for God's *torah*.[81] This idea gains greater credence when we consider that, since no school system existed in ancient Israel,[82] how else was instruction of children going to take place?

At the same time, we cannot ignore that the sage was also known as a teacher, as is attested to not only in Prov. 13:14 but in wisdom literature elsewhere in the ancient Near East. So could not the sage's instruction have been the human basis for the metaphor of God's *torah*? It is noteworthy, therefore, that the sage-student connection in the ancient Near East was itself portrayed as the relationship of a father to a son and is often biologically true![83] That being the case, it seems, then, that no reason exists to deny that the usage of *torah* in the God-Israel relationship signifies metaphorically parental instruction to the child.

The idea of the deity as parent is already present in Mesopotamian culture.

The Deity as Parent—The Mesopotamian Background

The Mesopotamian pantheon, at the highest, most powerful level, consisted of the ruling cosmic deities. At a lower level was the personal god of the individual. The idea of the personal god in third millennium BCE Mesopotamia, who would intercede on behalf of the individual with the cosmic (ruler) god, eventually gave rise in the second millennium BCE to the image of the parent god. This personal, parent god of the individual, at that time, would sometimes be identified with one of the cosmic gods. This god was understood as parent in four aspects: (a) the physical-father as creator of the child; mother as giving birth to it; (b) the provider-father as providing for the family's needs; (c) the protector and intercessor (with higher powers); (d) the requirements of children to honor and obey the parents.[84]

It is possible that the concept of the god as father gave rise to the idea that the king was the son of the god, and this was passed on generationally (so that the king's son was also the son of the god) and sideways (the king's sister was the daughter of the god).[85] Nonetheless, this understanding of the parent god was never wholly transmuted from the realm of the individual person to the nation. Mesopotamian nations were still dominated by their obeisance to the deities as slaves to the master-rulers. Only in Israel would the concept of the parent god be transformed from the personal to the national realm.[86]

God as the Nation's Parent—The Biblical View

Similarly to Mesopotamia, the Bible presents the metaphoric idea of the king as the son of God, in reference to the Davidic line.[87] However, the new idea of *God as father of the nation* makes its first explicit appearance in the narrative of Moses' election to leader. In fact, the first thing that Moses is instructed to tell Pharaoh is *"Israel is My firstborn son"* (Exod. 4:22),[88] which becomes the raison d'être for the tenth plague— the destruction of Egypt's firstborn. *"I have said to you, 'Let My son go that he may worship Me,' but you have refused to let him go. Therefore, I will slay your firstborn son"* (23). It is also a universalistic statement. In other words, all nations are "children" of God.[89] However, Israel, as the appointed firstborn, has superior status.[90] Thus for Egypt to attempt to destroy Israel is a revolt against God's authority.[91]

Deuteronomy also depicts this concept: *"You are children to the Lord your God"* (14:1); *"Do you thus requite the Lord. . . . Is He not your father"* (32:6);[92] *"You neglected the Rock that begot you"* (32:18).[93] Additionally, Deuteronomy describes this relationship as a simile in 1:31, *"and in the wilderness, where you saw how the Lord your God carried you, as a man carries his son"*[94] (8:5), *"as a man disciplines his son, so does the Lord your God discipline you,"* and 32:11 (as a father eagle), *"Like an eagle who rouses his nestlings, hovering over his eaglets."* It is important to point out that Deuteronomy 32 (the Song of Moses) speaks of the Israelites as children in two ways—as ungrateful and rebellious, *"Children with no loyalty in them"* (20),[95] and as those whom God loves and saved from the desert (10–11).

This double-sided depiction in Deuteronomy 32 carries on into prophecy where the portrayal of God and Israel as parent and child appears in one of two modes—(a) as rebuke of ungrateful, rebellious children, and (b) as beloved children whom God will redeem. A few examples will suffice.

Hosea (mid-eighth century BCE) reproaches the Northern kingdom of Israel (often named "Ephraim," the chief son of Joseph) over their idolatry. However, as the passage continues, God's love overcomes His anger and results in restoration:

> *When Israel was a youth, I loved him, and from Egypt I called to My son* . . . [but] *they sacrificed to Baals. They burned incense to idols. But I had pampered Ephraim* . . . *yet they did not know that I had healed them.* . . . *I drew them with cords of love.* . . . *No!* . . . *They refuse to repent.* Hosea 11:1–5 [similarly, *"he is an unwise son"*—13:13].

> *How can I give you up, Ephraim, surrender you, Israel?* . . . *My heart is overturned within Me, My tenderness is stirred up.*[96] *I will not act upon my wrath. I will not turn to destroy Ephraim.* . . . *The children will come trembling from the West. They shall flutter from Egypt like sparrows, from the land of Assyria like doves, and I will settle them in their homes.* (Hosea 11:8–11)[97]

The theme of rebuke of the wayward child is also found in Isaiah (late eighth century BCE): *"Oh, rebellious children!* . . . *Making plans not derived from Me* . . . *for they are a defiant people, deceitful children, children who refused to heed the torah of the Lord."* (Isa. 30:1, 9)[98] Note how in verse 9, Isaiah explicitly mentions the people as children who don't pay attention to God's torah.

Jeremiah (late seventh to early sixth century BCE) continues the theme of faithless children who reject God. Indeed, in chapter 3, he is influenced by Hosea 11:8.[99]

> (a) *And I said, "How shall I place you among the sons?" I will give you a desirable land—the fairest heritage of all the nations. And I said, "Call me 'my Father' and never turn away from Me." Yet* . . . *you have betrayed me, O House of Israel!* (Jer. 3:19–20)[100]

However, also like Hosea, Jeremiah 31[101] (in a prophecy of comfort directed to the Assyrian exiles of the Northern kingdom) predicts God's parental redemption of the people. In verses 7–9, God turns to Jacob the father of the people and promises to restore the repentant children to their land because He is the ultimate father:

Sing of happiness to Jacob. . . . Behold, I am bringing them in from the Northland and gathering them from the ends of the earth. . . . They shall come with weeping and with supplications I will guide them. . . . For I am Father to Israel, and Ephraim is My firstborn!

God then turns to Rachel, the beloved wife of Jacob and mother of Joseph (and thus grandmother of Ephraim):

Rachel is crying over her children. . . . Restrain your voice from weeping and your eyes from tears. . . . Is not Ephraim My dear son, a boy that is dandled? . . . Therefore, My womb is moved for him, I will surely have mercy upon him—says the Lord. (15–16, 20)

Here, in a poetic tour de force, God assures Rachel that He will redeem His son, the people, because He is the ultimate mother![102]

Other prophecies of redemption that emphasize the God/parent to Israel/child relationship are found in the second part of the book of Isaiah (chapters 40–66) and belong to an anonymous prophet (second half of the sixth century BCE). They are directed to those who were exiled by Babylonia (596–586 BCE) from Judah, the Southern kingdom:

I will say to the North, "Give back," and to the South, "Do not withhold! Bring My sons from afar, and my daughters from the end of the earth." (Isa. 43:6)

As a mother comforts her son, so I will comfort you; you shall find comfort in Jerusalem. (66:13)

This theme reappears in the last of the prophets, Malachi (early fifth century BCE):

And on that day that I am preparing, said the Lord of Hosts, they shall be My treasured possession; I will be compassionate towards them as a man is compassionate to his son who ministers to him.[103] And you shall come to see the difference between the righteous and the wicked, between him who has served God and him who has not served Him. (3:17–18)

The reference in Mal. 3:17 to the people as God's "treasured possession" deliberately points back to the same term in the statement of God at Sinai in Exod. 19:6. So, too, the model of the parent-child relationship continues straight through to the end of prophecy.

Ethical Conclusions on *Torah* and the Parent-Child Relationship

The above survey of relevant texts concerning both the significance of *torah* and the usages of the parent-child model to understand the God-Israel relationship now allows us to draw inferences concerning the biblical perception of the Sinai experience.

The stipulations of the treaty, the laws of the people, and the restrictions upon the priesthood, are now seen also as God's parental teaching to His children. However, the implications of the first three metaphors for the future of the people may very well be disastrous, for if the people are sufficiently disobedient of God, then their bond to their Deity could be permanently sundered. The curses of Leviticus 26 and Deuteronomy 28, if fully materialized, could very well result in the destruction of the people—the end of the Divine experiment, so to speak, with the Israelites.

Here is where the understanding of the God-Israel relationship as that of a parent teaching his or her child makes a major contribution. Yes, a treaty can be broken, laws can be transgressed, and holiness can be profaned. Any one of those actions can lead to tragic consequences. However, when a child is punished for disobeying the parent, such punishment is inevitably seen as temporary, with the purpose being to correct the child and to restore the proper relationship to the parent. Even though the law in Deut. 21:18–21 allows for the killing of the "wayward and rebellious son," this is a case so extreme that the rabbis of antiquity saw it as only a threat that was never enacted. The normal understanding of severe punishment to a child was corporal, *"He who spares the rod hates his son"* (Prov. 13:24), but endangering him was forbidden, *"Discipline your son, for there is hope, but do not desire to kill him"* (Prov. 19:18). That is why the very prophets quoted above who portray God's anger at His rebellious son—the people—still depict, after an impermanent punishment, God's redemption of that child.

The parent-child model, then, means that the nation can view whatever negative fate befalls them as a passing penalty for misbehavior. The people can live with the security that they have a two-way personal, intimate, eternal relationship with their God, who is also the Master of the universe. Thus, for the first time, a nation is given an expectation of permanence. Hope for the future becomes a fixture in their religious belief. This hope is indeed an ethical advancement, for it enables the people to live, even under the worst conditions, with the constant anticipation of a better tomorrow.

Each of the four metaphors of the Sinai revelation, then, results in the fusing together of the transcendent and the personal in the understanding of the one God's relationship to His people—and effects ethical change in conceptions of both society and religion.

3

Providing for the Disadvantaged

The Stranger, the Poor, the Widow, and the Orphan (with a Note on Slavery)

Social justice in ancient Near East societies was not identified with equality, nor was it identical with the elimination of poverty as such, since it was accepted that large sections of the population would constantly exist at subsistence level. Social justice was perceived rather as protecting the weaker levels of society from being wrongly deprived of their due: the legal, property, and economic rights to which their place within the social hierarchy entitled them.[1] Then or now, any government or society concerned with social justice needs to address the condition of its economically and socially disadvantaged elements. Such attention to this need should minimally result in a system for alleviating this condition and enabling the disadvantaged to attain enough practical support to continue to coexist with the more privileged members of society. A related question concerns the social standing of the disadvantaged: are they perceived as inferiors or as equals, and what are the parameters of this perception?

This chapter will survey the Jewish Bible's consideration of the disadvantaged by focusing on the poor, the widow, the orphan, and the stranger. It will be conclusively shown that in each category the Bible, in ethical terms, far outstrips the literature of the surrounding ancient

Near East societies. Here we will begin our analysis with the non-Israelite underprivileged element of society, the stranger.

The Stranger in the Ancient Near East

It would be hard to find a more problematic issue in human cultures than the perception of and position accorded to the stranger—the classic outsider. The stranger is the person who doesn't look like you, or doesn't act or dress like you, or doesn't speak like you, or doesn't think or believe like you, or doesn't come from the same society as you, or any combination of the above. Thus the stranger might be from a different race, religion, nation, ethnicity, sexual preference, or even gender and educational background. In defining the other, a group will determine what it is not.[2] The result has often been the sad historical fact that the stranger has been adjudged negatively, as an imagined fearful threat, and therefore the group has developed means to exclude or restrict the stranger. This xenophobia has had the ultimate consequence of horrific massacres, such as the genocidal wars against the Jews and Tutsis, as well as the rampant discrimination in the past century against blacks in the United States and South Africa, and the ongoing abuse of women in most Muslim countries. Unfortunately, the list of horrors engendered by xenophobia is too long to mention in their entirety here.[3]

It behooves us, then, to examine how the stranger was looked upon in ancient Near Eastern literature and that of the Jewish Bible. It should be noted that we will not examine how individual foreign nations were perceived in either ancient Near Eastern texts or the Jewish Bible, as those relationships might be determined by the particular history of the subject society with a specific nation. Rather, the focus will be on strangers as a general group or as unidentified individuals.

Although ancient Near East law collections have prologues and epilogues that speak of the self-professed duty of the king to ensure that the weak are not oppressed by the mighty (see chapter 2), none of them mention the stranger or alien in this context (while the widow and orphan are mentioned). In fact, the only Mesopotamian law that mentions the stranger is Eshnunna #41 (no later than 1760 BCE), which states, "If a stranger (perhaps, a resident alien) . . . wishes to sell his beer, the tapster (the person responsible for trading beer) shall sell the beer for him at the current rate."[4] The law seems to indicate that the stranger is not to be discriminated against in the selling price of his beer.

Additionally, one legal statement about the stranger, or foreigner, may occur in a Hittite text relating to conquered territories, "Instructions to Commanders of Border Garrisons," #39: "A foreigner who [has been] settled on the land you must supply with winter food stores, seed, cattle, [and] sheep, rennet [and] wool."[5] It is important to note that these instructions only involve conquered territories outside of the proper Land of the Hittites, while the Torah will speak of the treatment of the stranger within the Israelite tribal lands.

One final text from the ancient Near East comes from the Egyptian "Instruction of Amenemope," usually dated to the thirteenth century BCE.[6] In chapter 28, Amenemope says, "Do not refuse your oil jar to a stranger." Although ancient Near East wisdom literature written by sages sometimes advocates ethical behavior to the disadvantaged, this is the only such text that has been discovered so far that instructs one to treat the stranger in a kindly manner.[7]

It seems that the first time outside of the Torah that the stranger appears in ancient law as a group (and with significant details, to boot) is the case of the metics (aliens) of Athens.[8] In the fifth and fourth centuries BCE, three classes of people lived in Athens: the citizens, the metics, and the slaves. In order to be a citizen, both parents had to be citizens. Only citizens could own land, so the metics primarily turned to trades and commerce. They were free of Greek parentage or not and dwelled in Athens and Attica. Their legal status is known from fourth-century BCE texts. Laws concerning the metics included the following:

- Upon entering Athens, foreigners had to register by a certain time or they could be sold as slaves.
- Metics had to pay a tax upon their persons or could be sold as slaves.
- Metics had to pay for the right to trade in the marketplace, in addition to those taxes which citizens had to pay.
- A metic had to find a patron who could represent him in court or be sold into slavery.
- Metics had no political rights.

In short, the metics were second-class citizens with more responsibilities and none of the privileges of the average citizen.

Only Eshnunna indicates that the stranger had, at least in the sale of beer, the normal rights of any citizen. Among the Hittites, in conquered lands, he was granted certain privileges under careful observation. One Egyptian sage advocates that he be given some charity. Athenian law, however, makes him a second-class citizen in danger of being sold into slavery should he make one misstep. Otherwise, the lack of the inclusion of the stranger in any other law collections in the ancient Near East (including the introductions and epilogues) leads to the conclusion that the stranger was a legally unprotected element of society.[9]

The Resident Alien (ger) in the Jewish Bible

As opposed to the paucity of appearances in ancient Near East legal or wisdom material, the classical Hebrew noun for stranger, *ger,* occurs ninety-two times in the Jewish Bible, approximately two-thirds of which are in the Torah.[10] The verbal form actually means "sojourn" or "reside."[11] *Ger,* then, is more closely defined as "resident alien."[12] To be more explicit, the *ger* is an alien who dwells in the land, that is, in the midst of the dominant society. He or she has no familial or tribal affiliation among that society.[13] Whether this alien is a foreign refugee from conquest, famine, or brutal treatment or a native whose land and people have been conquered by the dominant society is beside the point. In all cases, she or he is a member of a class that is both alien and defenseless. In our treatment here, the *ger* is always understood in the text to refer to a resident alien.

It is important to realize that the Hebrew Bible differentiates between the stranger as resident alien and the "foreigner" (Hebrew, *nokhri*). This foreigner is, at best, a temporary visitor to the land, probably either a mercenary or a trader, but he is connected to his homeland and plans to return to it.[14]

Another term, *zar,* often appears in English translations as "stranger," but that definition is imprecise. *Zar* usually has negative connotations. It is sometimes used in terms of dangerous foreign gods.[15] Concerning the cult, it refers to that which does not belong or unauthorized persons.[16] In prophetic literature it often means "enemy, destroyer."[17] In other texts, it may simply represent an "outsider."[18]

One might think, then, that the term *ger* will always refer to a non-Israelite. Both poignantly and surprisingly, this is not the case![19] It is not an accident that the first place in the Torah in which the *ger* is mentioned is in reference to the future people of Israel when God announces to Abraham that *"your seed will be strangers* (that is, residing aliens) *in a land not theirs"* (Gen. 15:13). This recognition that the entire people will have been resident aliens in Egypt will serve as a significant motivating force for the Torah's law.

The next mention is by Abraham himself to the Hittites when he wishes to buy a burial place for his wife Sarah: *"I am a resident alien among you"* (Gen. 23:4). As a resident alien, Abraham must obtain the right to buy land, which is granted to him at a steep price: 400 silver shekels (15–16), for which he does acquire a good-sized plot, a field with its trees and burial cave (17–20).

The third mention refers to Moses who, upon naming his son *gershom* (that is, "a stranger/alien there"), states the line that was famously translated in the King James Bible as *"I have been a stranger in a strange land"* (Exod. 2:22, repeated in 18:3). In this verse, the word for "stranger" is *ger* and the word for "strange" is *nokhri*, that is, "foreign," meaning, *"I have been a resident alien in a foreign land."* (The King James translation is more poetic.)

Even more so, from God's perspective, the Israelites are resident aliens on their own land, *"for the land is Mine, for you are but resident aliens with Me"* (Lev. 25:23; similarly, Ps. 39:13; 119:19 below). In other words, the earth is the Lord's and all humans are but tenants who dwell there upon the graciousness of the owner.

As we turn to examine biblical law concerning the non-Israelite resident, the importance of the self-identification of the Israelites as having themselves been resident aliens cannot be overstated, for it creates empathy to the strangers in their midst.

The Non-Israelite Ger in the Torah's Law

It cannot be overemphasized that in the Jewish Bible, each of the Torah's laws has unique importance, since they were all God-given and determinants of national destiny (chapter 2). However, given the Hebrew

Bible's ancient Near Eastern provenance, it is startling that the legal portions of the Torah contain more than fifty references to the resident stranger—almost all positive. These fall into several categories:

General Admonitions: Do Not Harm the Stranger

Do not afflict or oppress the stranger, for you were strangers in the land of Egypt (Exod. 22:20; compare with Deut. 23:8).[20]

Do not oppress the stranger, for you know the soul of the stranger, for you were strangers in the land of Egypt (Exod. 23:9). The previous verses 6–8 indicate that the context is fairness in a court, as is stated in Deut.1:16, *I charged your judges . . . judge righteously between any man and his brother* (that is, fellow Israelite) *or his* (*his* indicates responsibility) *stranger.*

When a stranger lives with you in your land, do not afflict him. As one of your citizens, the stranger who lives with you shall be to you, and you shall love him as yourself, for you were strangers in the land of Egypt. I am the Lord your God (Lev. 19:33–34). On loving the stranger, see also Deut. 10:19 below.

You shall not subvert the justice (that is, the legal rights) *due the stranger and orphan* (Deut. 24:17). Most of verses 12–22 are concerned with the rights of the poor, widow, orphan, and stranger.

Cursed is he who subverts the justice due to the stranger, orphan, and widow (Deut. 27:19). This verse is part of a series of twelve curses that are to be pronounced in a public ceremony once the Israelites have entered into the Promised Land. One curse is against idolatry, six are against moral crimes, four are against sexual crimes, and the final one is against general failure to uphold the Torah. It is noteworthy that the majority of the specific crimes mentioned are ethical.

Even though each law is understood as being of supreme importance, the existence of motivational statements attached to a specific law lays even greater stress on the necessity of obedience. Of particular significance, then, is the fact that most of the above laws contain a motive clause that emphasizes the empathy that the Israelites should have with the aliens in their midst, since the Israelites themselves were aliens (or in the case of Deut. 24:18 and 22, slaves) in Egypt. Nowhere else in the ancient world does any kind of similar motivational statement appear. This focus on empathy receives an astonishing boost by the requirement to love the stranger as oneself. As indicated in chapter 2 above, this obligation in Leviticus 19 demands that the Israelite must treat the resident alien as he himself seeks to be treated (also Deut. 10:19, *"You, too, must love the stranger, for you were strangers in the land of Egypt,"* and see below). The attitude of empathy now elevates the stranger to a level of equality.

Specific Laws of Social Justice

Several statements in the Torah demand that specific acts of social justice be performed on behalf of the resident alien.

PROMPT PAYMENT TO THE POOR ALIEN LABORER

> *You shall not abuse a poor and destitute laborer, either from your brethren or from your stranger in your land in your gates. You must pay his wages on that very same day* [that it is due] *... for he is poor and urgently depends upon it, else he will cry against you to the Lord, and you will incur sin.* (Deut. 24:14–15).

Two motivations occur here for the prompt payment of the poor Israelite or alien laborer—the implication that one should immediately fulfill one's agreement to pay the desperately poor worker (whether he be Israelite or alien) and to avoid God's punishment. In the ancient world, this would have been an extraordinary idea—that a member of the citizenry would receive divine punishment for not promptly fulfilling an agreement with an alien worker.

PROVISION OF FOOD AND CLOTHING

> "[God] *loves the stranger to give him food and clothing. You, too, must love the stranger, for you were strangers in the land of Egypt.* (Deut. 10:18–19)

Verses 18–19 are placed after a discourse on God's own ethical behavior (17 and 18) and the stated purpose of His commandments to benefit the Israelites (13). These verses imply an additional motivation to the idea of empathy—a requirement to imitate God. As God provides food and clothing to the resident alien, so must the Israelite. Again, nowhere in the ancient world is such a divine concern for the alien evinced.

SHARING THE HARVEST

When you reap the harvest of your land, you shall not reap all the way to the edges of your field, or gather the gleanings of your harvest. You shall not pick your vineyard bare, or gather the fallen fruit of your vineyard. Leave them for the poor and the stranger. I am the Lord your God. (Lev. 19:9–10; similarly, Lev. 23:22)

Note that Leviticus unites the poor and the stranger, since the assumption of the text is that the stranger is generally destitute.

When you reap the harvest in your field and forget a sheaf in the field, do not turn back to get it. It shall be for the stranger, the orphan, and the widow, in order that the Lord your God may bless you in all that you do. When you beat your olive trees, do not go over them again—it shall be for the stranger, the orphan, and the widow. When you gather the grapes of your vineyard, do not pick it over again. It shall be for the stranger, the orphan, the widow. Remember that you were a slave in the land of Egypt [and the Lord your God redeemed you from there— these words in verse 18 carry over to verse 22], therefore I command you to do this thing. (Deut. 24:19–22)

In these verses, in comparison to Leviticus, Deuteronomy replaces "the poor" with "the widow" and "the orphan" (who undoubtedly are poor, else why would they need to glean the leftovers of the harvest?) and also adds the olive harvest. The obligation to remember the slavery in Egypt and God's redemption of the people is a motivational comment to reflect both empathy and a way of imitating God. Just as God redeemed Israel from slavery, the people must act kindly toward the destitute elements of society (the widow, orphan, and stranger).[21]

THE THIRD-YEAR TITHE

Every third year, you shall bring out the full tithe of your yield in that year, but place it within your gates [that is, of your city]. Then, the Levite, who has no hereditary portion as you have, and the stranger, the orphan, and the widow who are within your gates can come, eat and be satisfied, so that the Lord your God will bless you in all that you do (Deut. 14:28–29).

Deut. 26:12–13 is the declaration made by the Israelite upon fulfilling this commandment.[22] It may very well be that the natural growth of the Sabbatical year is similarly available to the resident alien, just as to the other members of society. See Lev. 25:6, where the word "resident" may also stand for resident alien.[23]

ENJOYMENT OF FEASTS

You shall take some of every first fruit of the soil . . . put it in a basket and go to the place where the Lord your God shall choose to have His name dwell there (that is, the sanctuary) *. . . and you shall enjoy, together with the Levite and the stranger in your midst, all the bounty which the Lord your God has given you and your household.* (Deut. 26:2, 11)

Similarly, the stranger joins in the celebrations of the Feast of Weeks (Shavuot) and the Feast of Booths (Sukkot) (Deut. 16:11, 14).

The Passover laws are exceptional. The resident alien is still enjoined (Exod. 12:19–20), just like the Israelite, to cleanse his home of leavened bread and eat matzah (unleavened bread). However, since only the Israelites in Egypt experienced the original eating of the Paschal lamb, no one else is included in that annual feast. Nonetheless, the stranger has the option of joining the Israelite community for the Paschal lamb, if he chooses to undergo circumcision (Exod. 12:48–49; Num. 9:14)—the sign of the covenant between God and the Israelites (Genesis 17).[24] Indeed, male circumcision may have been the only way that the stranger could have become a full member of the Israelite people prior to Second Temple times.

CESSATION OF WORK ON HOLY DAYS

On the weekly Sabbath (Exod. 20:10; 23:12; Deut. 5:14) and on the Day of Atonement (Yom Kippur, Lev. 16:29), the stranger is included along with all other members of society in refraining from work. That the motivation is ethical is made explicit in Exod. 23:12, *"so that your bond-man and stranger may be refreshed."*

Indeed, the resident alien is treated so well that Lev. 25:35 states that the impoverished Israelite must be treated as the stranger, at least in that he should not be charged any interest (36–37).[25]

Although none of the above laws specifically mention providing the stranger with shelter, that may be implied by the oft-repeated refrain *"the stranger . . . among you"* (Deut. 16:11; 26:11), *"within your gates"* (Exod. 20:10; Deut. 5:14; 14:21, 29; 16:14; 24:14; 31:12), *"within your camps"* (Deut. 29:10; and see the discussion on Job 31:32 below).

Laws of Parity with the Israelites

The following laws illustrate the Torah's system of equality between the Israelites and the resident aliens in terms of civil law and certain cultic prohibitions.[26] While the stranger is equal to the Israelite in observance of civil law, he or she is only liable to certain cultic prohibitions. In the area of ritual, the *ger* is liable for the negative commandments, but not the positive ones. The issue here is that trespass of civil and/or cultic prohibitions causes pollution of the land and the sanctuary. Anybody who resides in the Lord's land can make it or the sanctuary impure. However, neglecting to do the positive, performative commandments is a sin of omission, not commission. Although such sins by the Israelites can have dire consequences, they do not result in pollution, and the stranger (as a nonmember of the covenanted community) is not obligated to them.

DIETARY LAWS

As in the case of the requirement to eat matzah on Passover, other biblical dietary laws applying to the Israelite also apply to the resident alien. The prohibition against eating blood was combined with the requirement to pour out the blood of permitted animals or birds and cover it with dust. Covering the blood with dust is a form of burial, thus showing respect for animal life, as all life is created by God (Lev. 17:10–13).

If one has eaten of an animal which has died naturally or been killed by another animal, then he must wash his clothes and bathe in water, and he is deemed unclean until evening, at which point he is purified. If he does not follow these instructions, he incurs guilt (Lev. 17:15–16), which in the priestly requirements calls for a purification offering for unintentional violations (as opposed to "being cut off" for intentional ones).[27] However, Deut. 14:21 enjoins the Israelite to give that which has died a natural death to the resident alien. The resident alien is then permitted to eat it or to sell it to a foreigner. Deuteronomy understands that only the people of Israel are subject to the constraints of purity and finds a way here to extend further charity to the resident alien. The difference between Deuteronomy and Leviticus here may be due to Deuteronomy's emphasis that eating of that which dies naturally is simply unbecoming to a holy nation, while Leviticus applies the purity laws to all who reside in that land.[28]

SACRIFICES

The stranger follows the same procedures as Israelites for both voluntary sacrifices and sacrifices required to atone for a wrong (Lev. 17: 8–9; 22:18; Num. 19:10).[29] Numbers 15:14–16 is representative,

> *When a stranger has taken up residence among you, or who is in your midst for generations, and he would present an offering by fire of pleasing odor to the Lord, he shall do as you do. For the congregation there shall be one law for you and for the resident stranger. It shall be a law for all time throughout your generations. You and the stranger shall be alike before the Lord. One torah and one law shall be for you and for the stranger who resides among you.*

CRIMES

The same crimes and punishments apply to both the resident alien and the citizen, in other words, the resident alien is obligated to obey the Torah's criminal law.[30] This is explicitly stated in terms of violent crimes against a person or animal (Lev. 24:17–22), blaspheming the Lord's name (Lev. 24:16; Num. 15:30), pagan worship (Lev. 20:1–2), and sexual crimes (Lev. 18:26 in reference to verses 6–25). In terms of inadvertent crimes of both the community and individual, the same procedures pertain (Num. 15:22–29; concerning the accidental homicide, see Num. 35:15 and Josh. 20:9 below).

It should be noted that the phrase *"there shall be one law for you and the stranger"* (or, *"like the citizen, the stranger"*—Exod. 12:47–48; Lev. 24:16, 22; Num. 9:14; 15:15, 29–30) only relates to the case or parameters given in context.[31]

PARTICIPATING IN THE COVENANT CEREMONY

Deut. 29:10 includes the stranger in the covenant ceremony that Moses leads in the land of Moab (28:69) before the Israelites will enter into Canaan. Chapter 31:12–13 seems to apply all laws of Deuteronomy also to the resident aliens and their children. However, the strangers involved may be those who have already been incorporated as members of the people, since they are understood as having been with the people in the desert wanderings, or the laws involved may be the civil laws and certain cultic prohibitions.[32]

Exceptions

In contrast to all the legal material cited above, two laws indicate that the resident alien was not always on a par with the Israelite.[33]

Leviticus 25:47 depicts a situation in which the stranger has so prospered that an impoverished Israelite has been sold to him.[34] Verses 48–55 take pains to stress the significance of redeeming the impoverished Israelite as soon as possible, even before the normal time of remission of debt servitude. Response to the idea that a resident alien should have an Israelite slave, even temporarily, is unquestionably negative. The law, however, does permit it, just as it posits what was probably a fairly rare occurrence—that a resident alien would be able to attain enough wealth to have Israelite slaves, even temporarily. In actuality, this law is ambiguous when it comes to parity, for although the law's attitude is not to achieve parity between the Israelite and the alien, the *ger* is on a level of parity with those Israelites of means who have Israelite slaves.

The situation in Lev. 25:45–46 is a more serious detriment to the stranger. These verses permit Israelites (assumedly of sufficient means) to buy resident aliens as slaves in perpetuity:

You may also buy them from among the children of aliens resident among you, or from their families that are among you whom they gave birth to in your land. These shall become your property. You may keep them as a possession for your children after you to inherit them for all time. Such you may treat as slaves.[35]

On the one hand, this text seems to contradict all the benefits that the Torah has afforded the stranger. The moral problem in these texts comes about due to competing values—the desire to treat the resident alien well and the right to the possession of the land by the Israelites. In this instance, the latter trumps the former. Since only the Israelites have right of ownership of the land, Israelite slaves must be released by the jubilee year in order to exercise those rights. However, the *ger* has no such rights and, therefore, does not need to be released.[36]

On the other, it is probable that such instances, like the situation of the prosperous stranger, were atypical. Note also that the Israelite *buys* the slave from the resident alien population. This is not enslavement through captivity. It is servitude brought on by the resident alien's debts or simply to enable one to acquire the necessities of existence during extended severe economic times (such as drought and famine). Although the text does not state that one cannot treat such a slave harshly, a number of the laws mentioned above, including the Sabbath rest and festival celebrations, make it clear that the resident alien slave was still to be treated as a member of his or her master's household.[37] Further, one may expect that the *ger* slave was still treated with care, for the right to buy a stranger as a slave does not obviate the injunctions to do him no harm (see the "general admonitions" listed above) or the command to love the *ger*.

The Inconvenient Case of the Seven Canaanite Nations

A deeply troubling ethical issue is the laws in Deuteronomy requiring the annihilation of the seven Canaanite nations upon the Israelites' invasion of the Land:

When the Lord your God brings you to the land that you are about to enter and possess, and He dislodges many nations before you—the Hittites, Girgashites, Amorites, Canaanites, Perizzites, Hivites, and Jebusites, seven

nations more numerous and mightier than you—and the Lord your God
delivers them to you and you defeat them, you must surely proscribe them.
Do not make a treaty with them and do not spare them. (Deut. 7:1–2)[38]

Proscription (Hebrew, *cherem*), in the context of people, denotes total destruction.[39] Clearly the purpose of this extreme interdiction is to prevent the Israelites from adopting any Canaanite polytheism (Deut. 7:3–4, 10, 25–26) so that God won't destroy them (as in the law of Deut. 13:13–18, which dooms to destruction the Israelite town that has turned polytheistic).

To the modern sensibility, these laws are indeed odious. That the Moabites (against the Israelites), Celts, Gauls, Teutons, and Romans engaged in this practice of eradicating whole populations is irrelevant.[40] Obviously, two wrongs do not make a right. Even more so, in light of all the positive laws pertaining to the resident alien in Deuteronomy, these commands seem doubly incongruous. How can the same book that preaches God's love for the resident alien and demands that the Israelite behave likewise (10:18–19) here require the obliteration of the Canaanite peoples?

Before we attempt to answer this question, certain textual inconsistencies must be pointed out, as Deuteronomy 7 leaves some wiggle room. Verse 1 predicts, *"When God . . . dislodges"* the seven nations. The word for "dislodges" only appears seven times in the Hebrew Bible: twice in this chapter (also in verse 22); twice in terms of removing shoes (Exod. 3:5; Josh. 5:15); once of an ax head being dislodged (Deut. 19:5); once for olives dislodged from olive trees (Deut. 28:40); and once for Judahites expelled from the town of Elath (2 Kings 16:7). This last instance is instructive, for it may well signify that here God is going to chase out the seven nations, with the implication that only those who are left should be proscribed. Furthermore, verse 22 seems to allow for the "dislodging" of these nations to take place over an indeterminate length of time: *"The Lord your God will dislodge these nations before you little by little, you will not be able to put an end to them quickly, lest the wild beasts would multiply to your harm."*

At this point, it is essential that we turn to Exodus 23 to understand what is going on in Deuteronomy 7:

I will send forth My terror before you . . . and I will send out the hornets ahead of you, and it shall drive out before you the Hivites, the Canaanites, and the Hittites. I will not drive them out in a single year, lest the land become desolate and the wild beasts multiply to your harm. I will drive them out before you little by little, until you have increased and possessed the land. (Exod. 23:27–30)

Evidently Deuteronomy 7 has expanded upon Exodus 23 (note that even the "hornet" appears in Deut. 7:20).[41] God's promise in Exodus is only to chase out the Canaanite people, without any mention of extermination. Deuteronomy 7 builds upon that promise but apparently adds the idea of proscribing those who are not driven out, yet not immediately.

Now, with the qualification that not *all* the Canaanites are required to be executed, let us repeat our question. How can Deuteronomy depict Moses as even commanding that all remaining Canaanites must be killed? Two primary answers have been given: (a) by Rabbinic interpreters, and (b) by modern academic scholars:

(a) From the first centuries of the Christian era, the early rabbis have refused to see these commands as unconditional genocide. In their view, even before entering the Promised Land, Joshua announced that those who wanted to leave or surrender would be allowed to do so. In medieval times, Maimonides, the great Jewish philosopher and codifier, further explicated that the Canaanites could save themselves by submitting to forced labor and by accepting certain universal commandments applicable to non-Jews (including the ban against polytheism). Additionally, he stated that the Israelites were permitted to besiege the Canaanite cities only on three sides, leaving the fourth side open so that the inhabitants could escape.[42] The Rabbinic rejection of the idea that Deuteronomy commands the utter destruction of the Canaanite nations is probably due to the incompatibility of such a ruthless decree with other ancient Jewish values: the Jewish legal principle that evildoers cannot be punished if they have not been forewarned both that their behavior is illegal and the specific punishment involved; the idea of repentance; and the prophetic prediction that polytheists will one day discard their false deities.[43]

(b) Modern academic biblical scholars and archaeologists are in agreement that most of Deuteronomy was written during the monarchy (1000–

586 BCE), with the largest group believing that it comes from the later period (eighth and seventh centuries). Further, the overwhelming majority of these scholars, as well as historians of the period, are convinced that no such genocide ever took place. Thus they view the proscription of the Canaanite population as theoretical and idealized. At the most, only a few towns were eradicated, and various accounts in Joshua, Judges, and Kings reveal that a great many Canaanites were subjected to forced labor. So why did Deuteronomy include this demand of annihilation? These scholars opine that since at the time Deuteronomy was written no recognizable polytheistic Canaanites were left in the land, then the author of Deuteronomy must have concluded that the indigenous population had been eliminated in the Israelite invasion. He must have concluded further that this was due to proscription commands from God, who would not tolerate idolatry in the land and so wrote these commands into the text.[44] Why do these laws opt for killing off the population rather than expulsion? Probably because the author of Deuteronomy "knew" (that is, had knowledge passed down to him) about past instances where the entire population of a city had been destroyed.

It is interesting that, although the Rabbinic and academic approaches are vastly different, they arrive at the same conclusion: genocidal destruction of the Canaanite population never occurred. The question, however, still remains: how could Deuteronomy treat the resident alien so positively and the Canaanites so negatively? The answer seems to come down to the twin issues of polytheism and idolatry. Immoral Canaanite polytheism, replete with such abhorrent practices as child sacrifice (Deut. 12:31), was the antithesis of Israelite ethical monotheism.[45] A Canaanite who cleaved to polytheism could not live among the Israelites. On the other hand, a Canaanite who gave up polytheism and its idolatrous rites was accepted as a resident alien.

The Resident Alien in the Prophets and the Writings

Not surprisingly, most of the incidences of *ger* in the Prophets and Writings follow Torah themes:

That God perceives the Israelites as resident aliens on their own land (Lev. 25:23) is reflected by the Psalmist, "*I am an alien, resident with you, like all my forbears"* (Ps. 39:13, echoed in David's prayer in 1 Chron. 29:15). Similarly, *"I am a resident alien upon the land"* (Ps. 119:19).

The warning in Exod. 22:20 and Lev. 19:33 not to "afflict" (the root *y-n-h*) the stranger is repeated by the prophet Jeremiah (22:3), *"the stranger, orphan, and widow do not afflict."*

The particular language used in Deut. 24:14 of not "abusing" the hired laborer who is a resident alien (the word *ashok*) is echoed by the prophets in Jer. 7:6; Ezek. 22:7, 29; Zech. 7:10.[46]

Just as the *ger* is clustered together with the orphan and widow in Exodus and Deuteronomy,[47] so he is in Jer. 7:6; 22:3; Ezek. 22:7; Mal. 3:5; Pss. 94:6; 146:9. While in these passages Jeremiah is warning against harming the stranger, widow, and orphan, Ezekiel, Malachi, and the verse in Psalm 94 are accusations of harm already done. Psalm 146:9, *"God watches over the stranger; He encourages the orphan and widow"* is particularly reminiscent of God's care in Deut. 10:18.

Similarly, as the *ger* appears with the poor in Leviticus and Deuteronomy, so he does in Ezek. 22:29.[48] Ezekiel's indictment is *"the people . . . have abused the stranger without* [recourse to] *justice,"* which harkens back to the context of subversion of justice in Exod. 23:9.

In a comparable context to Ezekiel, Zech. 7:10 is the only verse that brings together the *ger* with the widow, orphan, and poor, *"Do not abuse the widow, orphan, stranger, and poor"* (probably a conflation of the usages in Exodus, Leviticus, and Deuteronomy).

The inference of providing shelter in the refrain *"your stranger . . . within your gates"* in passages in Exodus and Deuteronomy is mentioned explicitly by Job. In defending his actions before God, Job (31:32) proclaims, *"No stranger slept* [the night] *in the open; I opened my doors to the visitor."*[49]

Concerning the accidental homicide, the command in Num. 35:15 to supply cities of refuge for both the resident aliens and the Israelites is fulfilled in Josh. 20:9.

Joshua 8:33–35 includes the participation of the *"stranger who accompanied them"* in the ceremony at Mount Gerizim and Mount Ebal that is the fulfillment of the commands in Deut. 11:26–32; 27:1–26.[50]

Ezekiel 14:7–8 mentions the resident alien along with the Israelite in the context of forbidding idolatry: *"If any man of the House of Israel, or*

*the stranger who resides in Israel, breaks away from Me and turns his
thoughts upon his fetishes . . . I will set My face against that man . . . and
I will cut him off from the midst of My people.*" These verses seem to rely
on Lev. 20:2–6, "*Any man among the Children of Israel, or among the
stranger who resides in Israel, who gives any of his offspring to the
Molech . . . I will set my face against that man . . . and will cut him off . . .
from among his people.*"[51]

God's care for the resident alien seems to be reflected in the book of
Ruth, even though the term *ger* is not mentioned.[52] Boaz's magnani-
mous acts of kindness to Ruth (in Ruth 2) appear to be built upon the
commandments enabling the stranger to glean from the harvest in Lev.
19:9–10; 23:22, and Deut. 24:19. Ruth is a Moabite woman, the widow of
an Israelite who left Bethlehem during a famine and came to Moab with
his mother and brother. There the two brothers married Moabite women
and then died. Ruth attaches herself to her mother-in-law, Naomi, and
returns with her to Bethlehem at the beginning of the barley harvest.
Since Naomi is destitute, Ruth goes to glean behind the reapers in a field
that just happens to be that of Boaz, a relative of Naomi. Such "coincidences" are often recognized as due to God's hand at work.[53]

Not only does Boaz permit her to glean in his field, but he even
instructs his workers to leave her extra sheaves. Even though Ruth is
not an Israelite, and therefore the laws of the poor and widow do not
apply to her, she is a stranger, and those laws do apply, as assumed by
Ruth 2:2–7. Note that she is introduced to Boaz as a Moabite lass (verse
6), and she herself wonders why Boaz has been so kind to her when she
is a foreigner (verse 10). Eventually Boaz marries her (chapter 4), and
they become the great-grandparents of King David. It is quite possible
that, prior to Second Temple times, the offspring of female aliens who
married Israelites would be counted among the nation's members.

The law allowing enslavement of the resident alien in Lev. 25:44–46
is exemplified by passages in 1 Kings as interpreted by 1 and 2 Chronicles. (Chronicles was most probably written approximately two centuries after the final editing of Kings.)[54] In 1 Kings 5:29–30, Solomon's
70,000 porters and 80,000 quarriers, along with 3,300 supervisors, are
unidentified. However, 1 Kings 9:20–21 states that Solomon made the
remnants of the descendants of the Amorites, Hittites, Perizzites, Hivi-

tes, and Jebusites into a workforce for his building projects *"until this day,"* that is, probably sometime before the destruction of Jerusalem by the Babylonians in 586 BCE.[55] In 1 Chronicles 22:2 David orders the gathering of the *"gerim in the Land of Israel"* to become hewers/quarriers of stones for the building of the Temple. Following this, in 2 Chron. 2:16–17, Solomon numbers these resident aliens and finds 153,600 of whom he makes 70,000 porters and 80,000 quarriers of stone, with 3,600 supervisors (see also 2 Chron. 8:7–8).[56] Chronicles, then, identifies the remnants of the Canaanite peoples as resident aliens forced into working on building projects on behalf of the Davidic monarchy.

Relating to the strangers participating in the Passover feast in Num. 9:14, 2 Chron. 30:25 mentions *gerim* from both Israel (the northern kingdom) and Judah as joining in the celebration of Hezekiah's Passover, which is delayed to the second month due to priestly impurity (2–3, 13, but see also 18–20). However, it is conceivable that the strangers mentioned here are already included in the membership of the people due to religious conversion (that is, male circumcision). Another biblical text that mentions the *ger* in this post–First Temple context of religious conversion is Isa. 14:1–2, dated to the early Second Temple period (compare Isa. 56:3).[57]

Most interesting is the statement in Ezekiel's depiction of the future division of the land in the time of redemption that *"the gerim who reside among you, who have given birth to children among you,"* are given land within the tribes among whom they reside (47:22–23)—something that the Torah nowhere considers.[58] Ezekiel's proclamation may be alluding to the reality that, by the time of the Babylonian exile, the strangers had become assimilated within the Israelite people through the intermarriage of their children with the Israelites.[59]

It is noteworthy that the first translation of the Hebrew Bible, written in the third century BCE in Greek (known as the Septuagint), translates *ger* almost exclusively by the word for "proselyte"—evidence that, by that time, *ger* usually referred to someone who had undergone religious conversion to Judaism.[60]

Clearly the vast majority of the references to the resident alien in the Prophets and the Writings are influenced by the Torah's laws and narratives.

The Stranger as Resident Alien: Conclusion

Although the actual historical process is by no means unambiguous,[61] it appears that the Bible's own understanding of the chronological development of the concept of the "stranger," that is, the resident alien, incorporates the following stages:

1. The patriarchal families were resident aliens in the land of Canaan vis-à-vis the local inhabitants. During that period, they were prosperous "strangers," that is, their social status was high.

2. The Israelites in Egypt were resident aliens in the land. Indeed, it was Pharaoh's paranoia about their potential to turn into an enemy that resulted in their enslavement (Exod. 1:9–14). They then became the lowest level of society and were abused.

3. Upon entering the Promised Land, the Israelite tribes now included those aliens who had accompanied them through the desert wanderings (Exod. 12:38; Numbers 11:4).

4. Once the Israelites had established their hegemony over Canaan, the remnants of the native peoples they had conquered (along with those from the surrounding nations who immigrated there) became the strangers in the land, most of whom were poor. It was particularly to these strangers during that epoch (the age of the Judges and that of the monarchy) that the laws of the Torah applied concerning the resident aliens, of which more than 90 percent either benefited them or required parity with the Israelite.

5. By the Babylonian exile and the Persian period, the resident alien begins to be acknowledged as having assimilated into the Israelite people either through circumcision or the children resulting from intermarriage.

6. By the Hellenistic period, the word *ger* has come to mean proselyte. The emphasis has switched from acceptance as a member of the people to religious conversion.

It is clear from the Torah's laws, as well as the Prophets and the Writings, that the stranger was a member of the disadvantaged elements of society. He is grouped with the widow, orphan, and the poor.[62] Particularly characteristic is the stranger's lack of right to be a landholder.[63]

Nonetheless, despite the fact that the stranger is *not* a member of the people of Israel, she or he is entitled, by Divine fiat, to all the benefits given the poor, widow, and orphan. Beyond that, the resident alien is singled out to ensure that no harm befalls him or her, that he or she receives food and clothing, and that his or her rights of justice are protected.[64] Special emphasis is placed on the stranger's parity with the Israelite in both civil law and negative cultic commandments.

In order that the Israelite should fully comprehend the significance of treating the stranger well, exceptional motivational clauses (that is, logical reasons) are introduced:

- Appeal to empathy through remembrance of the past in which you were in a similar inferior social situation—*for you were strangers in the land of Egypt* (Exod. 22:20).
- Appeal to empathy, since your identity was affected in a similar fashion due to your similar precarious experience—*for you know the soul of the stranger* (Exod. 23:9).
- Appeal to the ultimate moral authority, God, who commands the law—*I am the Lord your God* (Lev. 19:34).
- Appeal to humanitarian impulse—*You shall not abuse a poor and destitute laborer, either from your brethren or from your stranger in your land in your gates. You must pay his wages on that very same day* [that it is due]*. . . for he is poor and urgently depends upon it* (Deut. 24:14–15).
- Threat of punishment—*"else he will cry against you to the Lord, and you will incur sin"* (Deut. 24:15); *"Cursed is he who subverts the justice due to the stranger, orphan, and widow"* (Deut. 27:19).
- Imitation of God's ethics—*"[God] loves the stranger . . . so you must love the stranger"* (Deut. 10:18). The very idea of imitating the deity's ethics is a wholly biblical innovation.[65] A further motivation may be present here. Verse 17 emphasizes God's supremacy in transcendence and ethical character, *"For the Lord your God is the God of gods, and the Lord of lords . . . who shows no favor and takes no bribe."* Perhaps one can find here a corollary to the God of creation.

God loves the strangers, for they are part of the humanity that He, as the supreme ethical Being, created in His own image (as discussed in chapter 1).

- In order to receive reward—*"so that the Lord your God will bless you in all that you do"* (Deut. 14:29).[66] Thus the Torah creates an understanding of, and an attitude toward, the stranger who resides among the people that is unique in the ancient world.[67] From a legal nonentity with little or no rights, who lives in constant danger of losing his or her freedom, the resident alien has been transformed into a divinely, legally protected member of society with both wide-ranging benefits and significant parity with the average citizen. More than that, the Israelites are threatened with the Divine devastation of Egypt if they abuse their own innocent resident aliens. The take-home lesson is obvious, "Do not mistreat your resident aliens, or else what happened to Egypt will happen to you."

Although absolute equality would have to await the advent of modern democratic ideals (which have yet to be fully implemented even in most democracies), the motivational content attached to the Torah's laws served to eliminate any shred of xenophobia.[68] Would that our modern societies only duplicate this ethical achievement of the Torah!

A Note on Slavery

In any study of the disadvantaged elements of Israelite society, slavery must be included. No matter how caring the owner, slavery is a dehumanizing institution, if only for the fact that the slave has no choice but to obey his or her master. Thus the acceptance of slavery in the Torah is morally problematic, to say the least.[69] One cannot point to the Bible's view of slavery, therefore, as a comprehensive ethical advancement over ancient Near East practice. Nonetheless, certain striking ethical divergences exist between Torah law and the ancient Near East. One of these is the question of what is to be done with the escaped slave.

All ancient Near East laws require returning runaway slaves, sometimes on pain of death. A few examples will suffice (other laws include

Ur-nammu #17, Lipit-Ishtar #12–13, Eshnunna #49–51, Hammurabi #15, 17, 18, 20, Hittite #22–23):

> Laws of Hammurabi #16—"If a man should harbor a fugitive slave or slave woman, of either the palace or of a commoner, in his house and not bring him out at the herald's proclamation, that householder shall be killed."
>
> #19—"If he should detain that slave in his own house and afterward the slave is discovered in his possession, that man shall be killed."
>
> Hittite Law #24—"If a male or female slave runs away, he/she at whose hearth his or her owner finds him/her shall pay one month's wages: 12 shekels of silver for a man, 6 shekels of silver for a woman." (A later revision substitutes one year's wages: 100 shekels of silver for a man, 50 shekels of silver for a woman.)

It should be noted that none of these laws contemplate the possibility that the person who has taken the fugitive slave frees him or her!

This same rule applies to international treaties, for example:

> Alalakh, Treaty #2—"If a fugitive slave, whether male or female, flees from my country to yours, you must seize and return him" (lines 22–23).[70]

In truly revolutionary contrast, in the Torah an escaped slave may not be returned to his or her owner, must be freed, and may not be illtreated. *"You shall not turn over to his masters a slave who seeks refuge with you from his masters. He shall live with you, in your midst, in any place that he chooses in one of your settlements, wherever he pleases. You must not afflict him"* (Deut. 23:16–17). It is not a coincidence that these verses would later be prominently used by abolitionists in fighting slavery in America in the nineteenth century.[71]

More than that, this law has within it the potential of the abolishment of slavery, for all the slave in Israel has to do to become free is to run away! Thus the implication of the law is that slavery becomes an issue of freedom of choice.[72] That may not have been the intention of the law, but the implication is there nonetheless.

A second major difference between the Torah and ancient Near East law collections concerns injury done to a slave. The ancient Near East law collections view injury done to a slave as a felony against the slave owner, not the slave himself or herself (Hammurabi #199, 213, 214, 217, 223, 231; Hittite #8, 12, 14, 16, 18).[73] For example:

Hammurabi #199—"If he [a citizen] should blind the eye of a citizen's slave or break the bone of a citizen's slave, he shall weigh and deliver one-half of his value" in silver.

Hittite #8—"If anyone blinds a male or female slave or knocks out his tooth, he shall pay 10 shekels of silver."

Again, the Torah, in stark contrast, states in Exod. 21:26–27, "*When a man strikes the eye of his slave, male or female, and destroys it, he shall let him go free on account of his eye. If he knocks out the tooth of his slave, he shall let him go free on account of his tooth.*" Once more, the Torah has not only promulgated a radical law but has created a reversal of ancient Near East law. Whereas injury to the slave in ancient Near East law gave no consideration to the slave and all consideration to the owner, the Torah creates the opposite. Now absolutely no consideration is given to the slave owner, while all consideration is given to the slave. *A slave cannot be treated with impunity by his owner. Once injured, he or she is given freedom.*[74]

Finally, *the slave rests on the weekly Sabbath* (in the Ten Commandments: Exod. 20:10, and its revision in Deut. 5:14). Similarly, the slave participates in the celebrations of the Feast of Weeks (Shavuot) and the Feast of Booths (Sukkot) (Deut. 16:11, 14). He and she undoubtedly enjoy the first fruits, since they are members of the household—"*all the bounty which the Lord your God has given you and your household*" (Deut. 26:11). Again, no such statement exists elsewhere in the ancient Near East.

It is vital to note the explicit ethical statements in Exod. 23:12, "*so that the son of your maidservant* [that is, the lowest member of your household] *may be refreshed,*" and at the end of Deut. 5:14, "*so that your male and female slave may rest as yourself.*" The latter statement in the Ten Commandments is tied to the new explanation of the Sabbath in verse 15, "*Remember that you were a slave in the land of Egypt and the Lord your God freed you from there with a mighty hand and an outstretched arm. Therefore, the Lord your God has commanded you to observe the Sabbath day.*" Here the motivation for the rest prescribed for the slave is the empathy required of the individual Israelite slave owner, derived from the Exodus experience. More than that, the term *"as yourself"* in verse 14 is reminiscent of the identical term in Lev. 19:34 concerning the stranger: *"you shall love him as yourself, for you were strangers in the land of Egypt."* Amazingly then, one day each week the slave is equal to the master.[75]

Thus the biblical laws providing freedom for the escaped or injured slave, and rest on the Sabbath, forever positively transform the status of the slave in society.

The Poor, the Widow, and the Orphan

Fifty years ago, Charles Fensham's famous academic article, "Widow, Orphan, and the Poor in Ancient Near Eastern Legal and Wisdom Literature," argued that "the basic conception in all the literature discussed is that the protection of the weak is the will of the god."[76] The author further stated, "This is one of the most important ethical doctrines of the Old Testament, but definitely not unique in comparison with conceptions in neighboring cultures."[77] Finally, the author concluded:

> The attitude taken against widow, orphan, and poor is to be looked at from a legal background. These people had no rights, no legal personalities, or in some cases possibly restricted rights. They were almost outlaws. Anyone could oppress them without danger that legal connections might endanger his position. . . . Therefore, it was necessary to sanction their protection by direct command of the god and to make it the virtue of kings. . . . In the history of the ancient Near East the compulsion was felt to protect these people. . . . In the Israelite community this policy was extended through the encouragement of the high ethical religion of Yahweh to become a definite part of their religion, later to be inherited by Christians and Moslems.[78]

At no point does Fensham mention the fact that *only* in the Jewish Bible is the concern for the poor, widow, and orphan translated into law, along with its specific periodic obligations, as we shall see below.

Note: As many of the texts concerning the poor, the widow, and the orphan have already been dealt with in the section on the stranger/res-

ident alien, this section will focus on other aspects and texts, while
lightly referring to the others. Since the references to the widow and
orphan in both the ancient Near East and Israel usually refer to impoverished widows and orphans (with the exception of actual ancient Near
East laws, see below), they are subsumed together here under the general designation of poverty. Further, the poor in the literature cited below
refer to members of the dominant society (and not resident aliens).

First, we will briefly survey the relevant ancient Near East literature.

Poverty in Ancient Near East Literature

Egypt

Before it came under Greek Ptolemaic rule, Egypt's extraordinary civilization lasted some 2,700 years, with its first dynasty founded in approximately 3000 BCE.[79] Its many inscriptions, monuments, pictorial depictions,
and papyri provide a wealth of information about Egyptian society and
religion. As noted in chapter 2, no ancient Egyptian law collection exists.[80]

Throughout much of the Egyptian kingdoms, idealized biographies
and protestations of innocence (before dying) were written which attested
that the authors took care of the poor: "I did that which men praise and
with which the gods are pleased. I gave bread to the hungry and satisfied those who have nothing" (ca. sixteenth and fifteenth centuries BCE);[81]
"I gave bread to the hungry, water to the thirsty, clothing to the naked"
(ca. twenty-first century BCE);[82] "I spoke for the widow on the day of
justice" (2700–2200 BCE); "I gave to the beggar [poor], I nourished the
orphan" (Amenemhet I, ca. twenty-first century BCE); "there was no
widow whom I oppressed" (Sesostris I, ca. twenty-first century BCE); "I
was a father to the poor, one who cared for the widows" (Mentuwoser,
twenty-first century BCE).[83]

Numerous declarations of innocence appear in the Book of the Dead
(sixteenth and fifteenth centuries BCE), in which the deceased addresses
each of the forty-two divine justices: "I have not done violence to a poor
man. . . . I have given bread to the hungry, water to the thirsty, clothing
to the naked, and a ferry-boat to him who was marooned . . . so rescue
me, you; protect me, you."[84] These set phrases (and others) only applied

to the upper class in the Old Kingdom (2700–2160 BCE). In a democratization of the netherworld by the Middle Kingdom (end of the third millennium BCE), the common man is recognized as having some duty of beneficence to those more needy than himself. These declarations alone seem to have some magical effect—to clear away sin even if pronounced by someone who led an immoral life. However, that the deceased aligns himself with these ethical statements implies an acceptance of these standards as willed by the gods.[85]

Governing these statements was a philosophy of reward and punishment. Good acts brought good fortune; evil acts brought misfortune. In the early period, Egyptian ethics saw the connection between an act and its consequences as a natural occurrence that took place without any divine intervention. By the late period, the connection between an act and its consequences was seen as being divinely mediated. In later Egyptian thought, misfortune came to be seen as evidence of wrongdoing, while good fortune was proof of virtue. Reward and punishment in the afterlife could function as a theodicy (justification of divine behavior) to explain how an evil man could prosper in this life despite the gods' wishes. The soul of the dead would appear before a tribunal of the gods. It could be found so wicked that it would be immediately extinguished or so virtuous that it was raised to the position of a god in union with the god Osiris.[86]

Grave inscriptions which state that the deceased "fed the hungry, watered the thirsty, and clothed the naked" afterwards request that the visitor to the grave offer bread and beer for the soul of the deceased, as the deceased is seen as in poverty and need, with an emphasis on hunger and thirst. So funerary offerings of food and water were necessary to sustain the dead and were often placed at his tomb site. The listing of beneficent acts was designed to motivate the readers to do corresponding acts of kindness for him, that is, he is "owed" these acts as recompense for his own similar behavior. This listing, then, is induced not so much by altruism as by the wish to maintain one's own existence.[87]

The purpose of Egyptian wisdom instructions was to teach the son that to be a successful ruler he must learn the behaviors in accord with the right ordering of society, the principles of *maat* (truth/justice/right order) that correspond to the divine order.[88] Examples of instructions to care for the underprivileged include "Do justice that you may live long upon the earth. Calm the weeper, do not oppress the widow, do not oust a man from his father's property" (Merikare, twenty-first century BCE).

> Be not greedy for the property of a poor man, nor hunger for his bread. . . . Be not greedy after a cubit of land, nor encroach upon the boundaries of a widow. . . . Do not recognize a widow if you catch her in the fields [perhaps implying that the widow has some permission to glean in those fields], nor fail to be indulgent to her reply. Do not neglect a stranger [with] your oil-jar. . . . God desires respect for the poor more than the honoring of the exalted. (Amenemope, thirteenth century BCE)[89]

Examples of hymns and petitions or prayers that portray both gods and officials as concerned for the disadvantaged are "free from partiality, justifying the just . . . servant of the poor, father of the fatherless, . . . protector of the weak, . . . husband of the widow, shelter of the orphan" (of Intef, the royal herald, sixteenth to fourteenth century BCE); "Because you are the father of the fatherless, the husband of the widow . . . the apron of him that is motherless . . . one who destroys falsehood and brings justice into being" (Protest of the Eloquent Peasant, twentieth through eighteenth centuries BCE); "he who hears the prayer, who comes at the voice of the poor and distressed . . . you are Amon . . . who comes at the voice of the poor man" (to the god Amon-Re, eighteenth to sixteenth century BCE); "Do [not] widows say, 'Our husband are you' and little ones, 'our father and mother'? . . . the poor worship your face" (Hymns to the Gods as a Single God, ca. 1300 BCE).[90]

In sum, in the Egyptian worldview one owes loyalty and obedience to one's superior and kindness to one's inferior. The beneficence given to the inferior is reciprocated by loyalty and obedience.[91] According to their textual prominence, the Egyptian who wishes to live a virtuous life must display these characteristics: respect and love for parents and solicitude for siblings and offspring; honesty and truthfulness in all circumstances; justice and fairness to all (the special concern of the public official); kindness and benevolence to all; loyalty and devotion (to one's superiors and gods); diligence and competence; and moderation, including modesty, calm, and peacefulness.[92] Of course, one must temper these moral attitudes with the realization that they did not apply to the lives of slaves.[93]

Mesopotamia

In ancient Mesopotamian literature, concern for the disadvantaged was not as prominent as it was in Egyptian. Only infrequent mentions of the widow and orphan occur.[94]

Reminiscent of the prologues and epilogues to certain law collections, references to the underprivileged are found in building inscriptions that were buried from view and meant to address the gods or future kings, including the reform of Urukagina of Lagash (twenty-fourth century BCE), as opposed to what happened previously, "the one in charge of the food supplies did not dare enter the garden of the indigent mother" to take the fruit, and "if the son of a poor man laid out a fish pond, the influential man did not dare take away its fish. . . . Urukagina made a compact with Ningirsu that a man of power must not commit an injustice against an orphan or widow"; of Sennacherib (Assyria, eighth century BCE) "Guardian of the right, lover of justice . . . who comes to the aid of the needy"; Sargon II (also Assyria, eighth century BCE) claims he was elected by the gods "to maintain justice and right, to give guidance to those who are not strong, not to injure the weak."[95] Such ideas are also mentioned in hymns, petitions, and incantations.[96] Similarly to Egypt, Akkadian wisdom literature (eighth century BCE) states that the wise should honor and clothe, "The one begging for alms. . . . This is pleasing unto the god Shamash, he rewards it with good."[97]

Of primary interest, particularly in contrast to the Jewish Bible, are references to the disadvantaged in ancient Near East law collections. The prologue of the Ur-nammu (king of Ur) collection (ca. 2100 BCE) states, "I did not deliver the orphan to the wealthy man; I did not deliver the widow to the mighty man; I did not deliver the man of one shekel to the man of one mina [that is, 60 shekels]." Similarly, the epilogue of the Hammurabi law collection (ca. 1750 BCE) declares his aim as "that the strong might not oppress the weak, that justice might be dealt the orphan [and] the widow, . . . to give justice to the oppressed." Corresponding language appears also in the prologue. [98] As is evident, the divine commission obliges the king to protect the weak from harm by the wealthier or more powerful. However, unlike Egypt, there is no mention of the king's responsibility to provide beneficence to the underprivileged.[99]

In the laws themselves, numerous statutes mention the widow (less so, the orphan) in the context of her late husband's estate. Two laws are concerned specifically with the status of the widow who has no living adult male relative to support her. The Middle Assyrian laws (ca. 1076 BCE, A 33) state, "If her husband and her father-in-law are both dead and she has no son, she becomes a widow, she may go where she wishes." A woman whose husband has been captured and who has no father-in-law must wait two years before she may remarry. During these two years, the state is obligated to provide her support, at least to the value of her husband's estate, if she is in need (A 45). All the other laws deal with property disposition to the widow or orphans.[100] These inheritance laws have several purposes: (a) to provide for the systematic transfer of property after the death of its owner and the succession of real property to the male children; (b) to support the widow for the rest of her life or until she remarries; (c) to maintain any minor children until they reach majority. Only three resources are subject to dispersal: the bride-price, the dowry, and the husband's/father's estate.[101]

No laws discuss what happens to those who do not have such resources. No mention is made of any payments for necessities from the king's treasury. Similarly, no laws exist on behalf of anyone else who is indigent. The needs of the poor are simply outside the purview of both law and government. As Leon Epsztein concludes, "The principle of the protection of the widows, orphans and the poor [that] appears in different prologues of the Mesopotamian laws . . . is presented as a prescription without any legal sanction and consequently the chances of its application in actual life would seem to have been very limited."[102]

Ugarit

Ugarit was a city on the Mediterranean coast of modern Syria that had its heyday between 1400 and 1200 BCE. Hundreds of clay tablets were discovered there upon which were written fascinating polytheistic epics that cast light upon Canaanite mythology. Even more fascinating is that the language, called now Ugaritic, is as close to biblical Hebrew as Portuguese is to Spanish. Two texts refer to beneficence to the disadvantaged: in the Aqhat legend, the king, Daniel, is depicted "sitting at the . . . city-gate. . . . He judged the cause of the widow, made decisions regarding the orphan"; in the Kirta epic, the king is condemned by his son who says that he does not deserve to reign because "You judge not the cause of the widow, nor adjudicate the case of the oppressed, drive not out them that prey on the poor, feed not the orphan before you, the widow behind your back."[103] This latter reference is particularly reminiscent of the Egyptian kindness to the widow and orphan and may indicate Egyptian influence.

Poverty in the Torah's Laws

It is important to realize that a variety of terms are used to indicate poverty in the Hebrew Bible.[104] The most common noun (or adjective) for a poor person in the Hebrew Bible is *ani*. Another noun of the same root (*ayin-nun-heh*) means "misery," which is how the word for "poor" originates. In other words, the connotations are of someone who is ill-treated, afflicted, humbled, or oppressed. Some other terms used are *evyon* (often translated as "needy"), *dal* ("weak"), and *rash* ("in want"). Additionally, certain phrases indicate impoverishment, such as "his hand cannot reach/attain" (Lev. 5:7–13). The result is that poverty is referred to hundreds of times in the Jewish Bible. Since a comprehensive examination is beyond the scope of this book, in this section we will look at the biblical connections to the *condition* of poverty, irrespective of its particular terminology.

As indicated earlier, most occurrences of "widow" and "orphan" presume penury. The husband/father was the protector and breadwinner of the family, and without him subsistence was precarious.

The legal categories concerning poverty have parallels with and differences from those of the stranger. The divergences are due to the fact that the poor, widow, and orphan are themselves full members of the people of Israel. With the exception of the few instances of inheritance laws, the laws of the Torah concerning the poor have no parallel in ancient Near East law.

General Admonitions: Do No Harm; Do Not Subvert Justice

"You shall not mistreat (the root *ayin-nun-heh*, see above) *any widow or orphan. If you do mistreat him, I will heed his outcry as soon as he cries out to Me, and My anger shall blaze forth; I will kill you by the sword and your wives will be widows and your children orphans"* (Exod. 22:21–23). As with the general admonition concerning the ger, here, too, the law is accentuated by a motive clause. Note the tit-for-tat correspondence between the lack of mercy by the Israelite to the victim and God's punishment of the criminal. Deut. 10:18 adds that it is God Himself who upholds the cause of the orphan and widow.

"You shall not subvert the rights of the needy in his dispute" (Exod. 23:6). The necessity of ensuring strict justice for each disputant, by not favoring one side over the other, is reinforced by verse 3, *"You shall not show deference to a poor man in his dispute."* The requirement for fairness in judgment is reiterated in Lev. 19:15, *"You shall not render an unfair judgment. Do not favor the poor or show deference to the rich. In righteousness you shall judge your kinsman."*[105] Similarly, *"Do not subvert the rights of the stranger or fatherless"* (Deut. 24:17), and *"Cursed be he who subverts the rights of the stranger, fatherless, and widow"* (Deut. 27:19). The fact that the rights of the underprivileged are included in the twelve curses to be pronounced upon entry into the Promised Land is indicative of their abnormal importance.

Specific Laws of Social Justice

Numerous laws in the Torah seek to ensure that the poor are treated justly and provided with basic needs.

PROMPT PAYMENT TO THE POOR LABORER

Deut. 24:14–15 (including the stranger—see above). The law is reiterated at the end of Lev. 19:13, *"The wages of a laborer shall not remain with you until morning."* Day laborers were frequently poor and needed immediate payment.

FREE LOANS AND RETURN OF CLOTHING AS PLEDGE BY NIGHTFALL

If you lend money to My people—to the poor among you—do not act towards them as a creditor; you must not exact interest from him. If you take your neighbor's garment from him in default of debt, you must return it to him before the sun sets, for it is his only clothing, the sole covering for his skin. In what [else] *shall he sleep? Therefore, if he cries out to Me, I will pay heed, for I am compassionate.* (Exod. 22:24–26)

On the heels of verses 21–23, these verses give a specific example of how one is not to abuse the poor. In ancient Israel, people would only borrow money if they were in dire straits, as inability to pay back could entail debt slavery. The law concerning the pledge is replicated in Deut. 24:12–13, with the additional exclusion of taking a widow's garment in default of debt (17). Perhaps this exclusion is illustrative of the law's greater sensitivity to the widow's needs and dignity.[106]

Deuteronomy 15:7–11 particularly encourages the giving of free loans.

Should there be a needy person, one of your kinsman in any of your settlements in the land which the Lord your God is giving you, do not make your heart callous and shut your hand against your needy kinsman. Rather, you must open your hand to him and surely lend him sufficient for whatever he needs. Beware lest you harbor the base thought, "the seventh year, the year of remission, is approaching," so that you are mean to your needy kinsman and you give him nothing, and he will cry out to the Lord against you, and you will incur sin. Give to him readily and have no regrets when you do so, for in return the Lord your God will bless you in all your efforts and all your undertakings. For there will never cease to be needy ones in your land, which is why I command you, "Open your hand to the poor and needy kinsman in your land."

The reason that the Israelite may be reluctant to loan to the needy as the seventh year approaches is that the loan might end up as a gift, because the needy will not have enough time to either pay it back or work it off before the sabbatical year and the consequent remission of debts at that time. The text attempts to assure the lender that any loss will be more than made up for by God's bounty (similarly on the third year tithe, Deut. 14:29).[107]

The law here against lending on interest is expanded upon in Lev. 25:35–37:

> *If your kinsman becomes impoverished, and comes under your author-*
> *ity . . . do not exact from him advanced or accrued interest* (interest
> deducted in advance or taken at the time of repayment), *but you shall*
> *fear your God and let your kinsman live with you* (that is, provide him
> with the means of subsistence, since he is your kinsman and that is
> what God wants of you). *Do not lend him your money at advance*
> *interest, or give him your food at accrued interest.*

Deuteronomy 23:20–21 adds that no interest may be taken on anything
else besides money and food (except to the foreigner, which may be a
reference to international trade), and includes a motive clause, *"so that*
the Lord your God may bless you in all your undertakings in the land that
you are entering to possess."

The law of Deut. 15:7–11 actually contradicts verses 4–6:

> *For there shall be no needy among you, for the Lord your God will bless*
> *you in the land that the Lord your God is giving you as a hereditary*
> *portion, if only you heed the Lord your God and take care to keep all*
> *these commandments that I command you this day. For the Lord your*
> *God will bless you as He has told you.*

How can verse 7 state, *"Should there be a needy person"* when verse 4
says, *"For there shall be no needy among you"*? The answer is that the
promise of verses 4–6 is conditional: if the people fully obey God's commandments, then He will so bless the land's produce that there will be
plenty of food for everybody, that is, no one will be needy. Verses 7–11,
on the other hand, indicate Deuteronomy's concession to reality. Disobedience will mean that the land's fertility will not be blessed by God,
resulting in poverty. Nonetheless, those who take care of the poor will,
in turn, be taken care of by the Lord.

PROVISION OF FOOD

Along with the stranger, the poor are included in the laws of the harvest
gleanings and the third year tithe. Concerning the gleanings, Lev. 19:10–
11 and 23:22 mention the poor, while Deut. 24:19–21 refers to the orphan
and widow. The third year tithe in Deut. 14:28–29 (and the farmer's affir-

mation in 26:12–13) also specifies the widow and orphan (as well as the Levite). The substitution of widow and orphan in Deuteronomy for the poor in Leviticus may be due to the perception in the former that the poor man can always be granted a loan and then can work off his debt, while the widow and orphan cannot. Thus, additional provision is made for the widow and orphan to obtain food.[108]

Additionally, the poor are provided for by the Exodus laws of the sabbatical year: *"In the seventh year you shall let it* [your land] *rest and lie fallow. Let the needy among your people eat of it. . . . You shall do the same with your vineyard and olive groves"* (Exod. 23:11).[109]

As the book of Ruth illustrates (Ruth 2:17), the gleanings at harvest time could, at least theoretically, provide food for a lengthy period of time. Thus following the above laws may have enabled the poor to gather enough food to survive.

REDEMPTION OF THE PROPERTY OF THE POOR

The poor have a prominent place in the laws of Leviticus 25, which deal with the sabbatical and jubilee (fiftieth) years, as well as difficult circumstances in which the impoverished Israelite finds himself. Earlier, we referred to the free loan law in verses 35–37. Verses 25–28 apply to the destitute Israelite who has had to sell off his land. *"If your kinsman becomes impoverished and sells part of his holding, his nearest redeemer* (the closest relative who has the means to redeem the property) *shall come and redeem what his kinsman has sold"* (25). The text then describes a situation in which the destitute Israelite gains enough funds to redeem the land himself. However, *"If he lacks sufficient means to recover it* [the land], *what he sold shall remain with the purchaser until the jubilee; in the jubilee year it shall be released, and he shall return to his holding"* (28). The extraordinary institution of the jubilee year (like the sabbatical year, not known elsewhere in the ancient Near East) is designed to restore all property to the original family landowners (verses 10, 13–17), for the land is ultimately owned by God and cannot be sold in perpetuity (23).[110] The jubilee law was obviously intended to prevent a permanent economic imbalance in the social fabric due to the acquisition of large tracts of land by wealthy landowners.

THE ISRAELITE POOR SOLD INTO SLAVERY

Leviticus 25 also legislates two instances of the impoverished Israelite sold into slavery—when sold to another Israelite (39–43, 46) and when sold to a prosperous resident alien (47–55). The condition of the latter reflects the former. In both cases, the Israelite must be treated beneficially as a resident alien and must be released no later than the jubilee year, whereupon he returns to his family and ancestral holding. Similar laws, but without identifying the Israelite slave as impoverished, appear in Exod. 21:1–11 and Deut. 15:12–18, where the maximum term of servitude is six years. In the Hammurabi Laws #117, the term for debt slavery is listed as three years, although if the debtor provides a slave to work out the debt, the term can be longer (#118).

Both laws contain motive clauses: *"For they are My slaves whom I freed from the land of Egypt; they may not be sold as slaves are sold* (that is, forever). *You shall not rule over them ruthlessly; you shall fear your God"* (Levi. 25:42–43).[111] These motive clauses reminding the Israelites that God freed them from slavery not only serve to negate the possibility of holding an Israelite slave permanently but also forbid mistreating him because the word "ruthlessly" is the very term used in Exod. 1:13–14 to describe the harsh labor imposed upon the Israelites by the Egyptians.

The law on the sale of an Israelite to a resident alien further emphasizes that, since the Israelites belong to God, it is not becoming that an Israelite be a slave to a non-Israelite. Therefore, everything should be done to redeem him quickly (48–49).

ENJOYMENT OF FEASTS

The widow and orphan must be included in rejoicing along with the stranger and the slave during the holidays of the Feast of Weeks and Tabernacles (Deut. 16:11, 14). The motivational statement of verse 12 is of particular importance: *"You shall remember that you were a slave in Egypt—take care to observe these laws."* The fact that "you" in verse 12 is in the singular is a cogent pointer to each Israelite to bear in mind that he was a slave, that is, that each Israelite was a member of the weakest, poorest, most downtrodden segment of society.[112] As such, the Israelite must always be conscious that, just as God cared about him, he must care about the deprived members of society.

MORAL AND RITUAL LAW, POSITIVE AND NEGATIVE COMMANDMENTS

Since the poor, widow, and orphan are all Israelites, they are obligated to the same laws as the rest of the people. However, sacrificial law takes their poverty into cognizance and significantly readjusts the purification offering (for sin) to substitute two turtledoves or pigeons for a sheep or goat, and if that is still too costly, the individual may bring a cereal offering equivalent to the value of a day's bread (Lev. 5:7–13). Similar laws concern the indigent woman who gives birth (12:6–8), the poor person who is leprous and brings a reparation offering (14: 21–32), and the penurious vower (27:8). These cultic allowances for poverty, though, are not unusual in the ancient world.[113]

INHERITANCE LAWS

In resemblance to the Mesopotamian laws mentioned above, inheritance laws protected the rights of widows and orphans: inheritance of the firstborn son (Deut. 21:15–17); levirate marriage, where the brother of the deceased husband, who leaves no son, marries the widow (Deut. 25:5–10). Further, a widow or divorcee is a free agent to impose a vow upon herself without being checked by a father or husband (Num. 30:10).

The levirate marriage law has affinities to the legal case of the daughters of Zelophehad, whose father died leaving neither son nor brother (Num. 27:1–11; 36:1–12);[114] the story in Genesis 38 in which Judah refused to give his daughter-in-law Tamar to his youngest son after the older two sons had died; Ezekiel's prophecy that priests may marry the widows of other priests (Ezek. 44:22); and the marriage of the widow Ruth to Boaz, a kinsman of her husband (Ruth 3:1–4:17).

In sum, the Torah's laws differ from those of the ancient Near East by not only demanding justice and protection for the poor but also requiring that the poor be provided with free loans (even if they will not be repaid), several means of obtaining food, options for redemption from debt slavery, and restoration of property in the jubilee year. Particularly, the laws of free loans and the right of the poor to glean after the harvesters will eventually evolve into the *requirement* in later Jewish law to give the poor money. Given the Torah's ethical stance on the poor, it is no coincidence that the term for this giving will be the Hebrew *tzedakah—*

the biblical word for "righteousness." This evolution will already be seen in certain biblical texts outside the Torah (below).

Poverty in the Torah's Laws Reflected in the Rest of the Jewish Bible

Terms for poverty, including references to widows and orphans, appear some 250 times in the Hebrew Bible outside of the Torah's laws, including about 75 times in prophecy—far more material than this work can cover. Unquestionably, then, poverty is a major subject in the Jewish Bible, with many ramifications, such as allegories about poor people used as object lessons in 2 Samuel: the poor man's ewe lamb in relation to Uriah (12:1–7); the widow's son in relation to Absalom (14:4–21); the prophets Elijah and Elisha each help feed a poor widow and her progeny;[115] the psalmist claims poverty and affliction and pleads to God for forgiveness and/or deliverance;[116] the wicked oppress the poor,[117] but God saves them;[118] even the entire people are referred to as poor.[119]

Further, many biblical passages reiterate the Mesopotamian theme of the protection of the poor, weak, widow, and orphan from the strong and wealthy,[120] as well as the additional Egyptian emphasis on feeding the hungry and clothing the naked.[121] Again, in parallel to the appearance of this theme in ancient Near East hymns/petitions and wisdom literature, it is no coincidence that many biblical occurrences are found in the hymns/petitions of Psalms and the wisdom books of Proverbs and Job.

This brief section, then, will focus primarily on examples of the influence of the Torah's legislation on later texts.

As above, concerning the stranger, the use of specific language in the prophets copies the general admonitions in the Torah:

The prohibitions not to *"subvert the right"* of the needy (Exod. 23:6) and the orphan (and stranger, Deut. 24:17, along with the curse of one who subverts the right of the widow, orphan, and stranger in 27:19) reverberates in Amos (usually dated to 775–750 BCE) 5:11–12, *"because*

*you levy a straw tax on the poor and exact a grain tax from him . . .
and you subvert* [the right] *of the needy in the gate"* (courts of justice
sat at the gate of the city). Similarly, Isaiah (740–700 BCE) 10:2 discusses the negative effect of the decrees of wicked authorities, *"to
subvert the case of the weak and to rob the rights of the poor of My
people, so that widows may be their booty, and they will despoil orphans."*
Likewise, Malachi (early fifth century BCE) 3:5 depicts God's anger
against those who subvert the rights of the widow and orphan.[122]

The particular language used in Deut. 24:14 of not to *"abuse"* (*ashok*)
the poor and needy hired laborer (whether Israelite or stranger) is echoed
by the prophets in Jeremiah (620–580 BCE) 7:6, "[If] *you do not abuse
the stranger, orphan, and widow"* and Zechariah (525–500 BCE) 7:10, *"Do
not abuse the widow, orphan, stranger, and poor."* In Amos 4:1, greedy
wealthy wives *"abuse the weak and crush the needy."*[123]

Apparently the close proximity of the prohibition not to *"afflict"* the
stranger in Exod. 22:20 with that of not to *"mistreat"* the widow and
orphan in verses 21–22 (the words in Hebrew are also close in sound)
influenced later prophetic texts: *"Do not afflict the stranger, orphan, and
widow"* (Jer. 22:3); *"They abused the stranger . . . they afflicted the orphan
and widow," "They afflicted the poor and needy and they abused the
stranger"* (Ezekiel [ca. 600–570 BCE] 22:7, 29).

Specific Torah legislation concerning the poor is reflected in a passage in Amos. In a prophecy against the northern kingdom of Israel,
the prophet predicts destruction due to moral crimes, *"because they
have sold . . . the needy for a pair of sandals. [Those] who [even] desire
the dust on the head of the poor, and thrust the humble off the road.*[124] . . .
*Upon garments seized for default of debt, they stretch themselves out beside
every altar"* (2:6–8).[125] Amos here draws upon Exod. 22:25, *"If you take
your neighbor's clothing in default of debt, you must return it to him by
sunset"* (similarly, Deut. 24:17, *"Do not take a widow's garment in default
of debt"*). The idea of stretching themselves out beside altars on top of
garments taken from the poor adds insult to injury (whether or not
these altars are those of God). Nowhere else in the ancient Near East is
there a reference to the taking of garments in default of debt.

Two Historical Accounts

Jeremiah 34:8–22 and Nehemiah 5:1–13 provide us with two historical accounts of social upheaval that reflect the Torah's laws concerning the poor, particularly concerning the sabbatical and jubilee years.[126]

JEREMIAH 34:8–22

In this famous passage, at the time when the Babylonian siege of Jerusalem (588–87 BCE) had been temporarily lifted, King Zedekiah of Judah makes a covenant with the people of Jerusalem *"to proclaim liberty to them,"* that is, a complete release of all their Hebrew slaves (verses 8–9). The phrase "to proclaim liberty" hearkens back to Lev. 25:10 concerning the jubilee year—*"you shall proclaim liberty throughout the land to all its inhabitants."*[127] Perhaps Zedekiah hoped that, by effecting the release of all the Hebrew slaves, God would bless the people and save the city from the Babylonians. As it says in Deut. 15:6, if the people heed God's commands, *"the Lord your God will bless you as He has promised you . . . you will rule over many nations and they shall not rule over you."*

Initially the Jerusalemites obey the covenant and release their slaves. However, in a short while they recapture those who were set free and force them back into slavery (10–11). This heinous behavior prompts Jeremiah to prophesy (12–14):

> *Thus says the Lord, the God of Israel: "I made a covenant with your fathers when I brought them out of the land of Egypt, the house of bondage, saying, "In the seventh year each of you must let go any fellow Hebrew who may be sold to you; when he has served you six years, you must set him free."*

In these verses, Jeremiah paraphrases Deut. 15:1, 12–15, 18 concerning the requirement in the sabbatical year laws to let debt slaves go free (and see also Lev. 25: 39–43, 46 above). Now Jeremiah 34:15–17 draws on the laws of the jubilee year in Leviticus 25 in pronouncing God's judgment:

> *Recently, you . . . did that which was right in My eyes . . . to proclaim liberty each man to his fellow . . . but now you have profaned My name; each man has brought back his male and female slaves whom*

you set free, and you have forced them back to be your male and female
slaves [again]. *Therefore, thus says the Lord: you would not obey Me*
to proclaim liberty each person to his kinsman and countryman, then
I proclaim liberty, declares the Lord, to the sword, and the pestilence,
and the famine, and I will make you a horror to all the kingdoms of
the earth.

Jeremiah then culminates the prophecy with the promise of the destruction of Jerusalem and the rest of Judah by the Babylonians and the death of all those who violated the covenant (34:18–22).

NEHEMIAH 5:1–13

In contrast to the failed attempt at slave release in Jeremiah 34, some 150 years later an extraordinary event without parallel in the ancient world takes place in Nehemiah 5 (perhaps 438–437 BCE). Persia now rules the Middle East. Cyrus the Great had allowed the return of the Jews to the Land of Israel in 539–538 BCE, after he had conquered Babylon. By 515 BCE, the Temple in Jerusalem had been rebuilt, although on a much more humble scale than had existed under the Davidic monarchy. By the middle of the fifth century BCE, the Jewish population of Judah was in dire economic straits, and the walls of Jerusalem—destroyed by Babylon—were still in ruins. Nehemiah, a Jew, is cupbearer (possibly indicative of high office, in similarity to the cupbearer of Pharaoh in Genesis 40) to the Persian king, Artaxerxes I (465–424 BCE). Devastated by the sad news of the state of Judah and Jerusalem, Nehemiah requests to go on a mission to Judah to rebuild Jerusalem. Not only does the king grant him official permission, but he makes Nehemiah governor of Judah. Nehemiah journeys to Jerusalem and begins rebuilding the walls.

It is at this time that Nehemiah 5 opens with the outcry of the impoverished Judeans, heard by Nehemiah (5:1–5). The common people lack food, have pawned their property to their wealthier coreligionists, and because they have had to pay the royal tax, their children are being taken into debt slavery. Not only are the common folk impoverished but they have no way to redeem their debts. At this moment of crisis, Nehemiah calls a plenary assembly to win popular support and thereby to force the creditors to take immediate action on behalf of their poor brethren.[128] He calls upon them to stop their unethical behavior, to forego all that is still owed, and to return all property taken in default of the debts. Amazingly they do so (6–13)! One highly impressed modern scholar says that in the ancient world, this incident is

> the most complete paradigm of what is meant by social justice as distinct from righteousness or the call to upright living. . . . Social justice is clearly a form of justice involving different classes of society and not between individuals. In this case, . . . the lower classes apparently had a recognized right of complaint . . . to the ruler . . . the upper classes voluntarily, and without any sanction, yielded justice and restored the possessions of the poor. The appeal of the poor had been made on the basis of the equality of those different classes. (Nehemiah 5:5)
>
> This single incident differs from all others in the ancient and medieval worlds. While our knowledge about the reforms of . . . [others] is extensive, there is not the slightest indication that the lower classes enjoyed a recognized right to demand social justice, and certainly, in almost all cases, the upper classes refused to concede voluntarily any rights to the oppressed.[129]

To understand the Torah's influence, it is worthwhile pointing out the connections between Nehemiah 5 and the laws of Leviticus 25:[130]

- The motivational statement in Neh. 5:9, *"What you are doing is not right. You ought to act in a God-fearing way."* Lev. 25:43, *"You shall not rule over him ruthlessly, but you shall fear your God."*[131]
- Restitution of property, as required in the jubilee year, with the verb "to return" (Neh. 5:11–12; Lev. 25:25–28, 41).
- Prohibition of treating fellow Israelites like slaves (Neh. 5:8; Lev. 25:39, 46).
- Prohibition against taking interest (Neh. 5:11; Lev. 25:36).

Even if one were to challenge the historical accuracy of both Jeremiah 34 and Nehemiah 5, it is indisputable that the authors of both accounts were influenced by the Torah's legislation on behalf of the poor.

Conclusions on the Concern for the Poor in the Jewish Bible

The desire to protect the poor and weak from exploitation by the strong and wealthy is pervasive in ancient Near East literature, and the particular ethic of sustaining the impoverished is a characteristic of Egyptian literature. Additionally these virtues were seen to be a concern of the gods and were initially directed at the monarchs and their officials. In Egyptian society, eventually such behavior was seen as meritorious by all who had the means. Failure to care for the needy would make the individual liable to be punished by the gods.

The Jewish Bible, while echoing similar concerns as the surrounding cultures, moves this state of affairs to a more advanced ethical level. For the first time, the obligation of each member of the society to care for and sustain the poor is enshrined in law.[132] More than that, new laws are created on behalf of the poor that are unattested by any kind of societal behavior elsewhere: free loans, tithes, harvest gleanings, the return of property at the jubilee, regular cancellation of debts, regular release from slavery, the Sabbath rest, and partaking in festival celebrations.[133]

Of particular significance are the laws providing food for the poor, including the needy resident alien. The ancient world was constantly under the threat of drought, food shortages, and famine, where subsistence living was often, if not generally, the norm.[134] In such a world, the Jewish Bible is the first text to legislate food supplies for the poor. The advantage of these laws for the needy cannot be overestimated. While other societies only attempted to deal with food shortages and famine when crises occurred, the Torah's regulations afforded continual relief to the destitute.

Even these ethical progressions do not tell the whole story. One must always remember the biblical claim that its laws are not only given by God but are themselves the stipulations of the Sinai treaty. Thus not only will the people as individuals be rewarded or punished conditional upon their obedience or disobedience, but the future of the entire society is decided thereby. Therefore, as seen in the verses cited above, Deuteronomy promises God's blessings on the entire society for generosity to the poor. At the same time, the verses of the prophets cited above—

Amos, Isaiah, Jeremiah, Ezekiel, Malachi—all appear within prophecies that decree destruction due to the abuse of the rights of the needy. The idea that the destiny of a society is determined by how its members behave toward the needy is a biblical invention, and it prefigures the modern, ethical conceptions of government, ranging from democracy to socialism, to create societies in which the needs of the impoverished will be met.[135]

4

The Primacy of Morality over Ritual
A Prophetic Innovation

Chapter 3, concerning the poor, widow, and orphan, affirmed that ethical ideals existed in ancient Near Eastern law collections, wisdom literature, and other writings. Specifically, in Mesopotamia, the king was understood to be legally obligated by the gods to ensure that the weak were not oppressed by the strong, and in Egypt, superiors were socially enjoined to feed the hungry, give water to the thirsty, and clothe the naked. Chapter 2 noted that, in Mesopotamia, civil and criminal law formed a different category from cultic requirements and under a different administration. Similarly, in Egypt, legal adjudications (such as lawsuits based upon accusations of harm, whether involving property or person) took place outside of the jurisdiction of the priesthood. In contrast, we saw how the Torah's law codes encompassed and even interwove both ethics and ritual, while introducing detailed ethical laws in a variety of social areas.

Throughout the ancient Near East, including Israel, the cult was of major concern to the maintenance of religion and, therefore, to the preservation of society. Indeed, nowhere in the ancient Near East could society be conceived of in nonreligious terms that are commonplace today, such as "secular" or "atheistic."[1] Each society had, at its base, a concept of the divine and of the attendant human obligation to worship and sacrifice to the divine.

Given the focus of ethics in this book, we need to ask, "Does a connection exist between ethics and cult in ancient Near East writings, including the Jewish Bible? If so, what is the nature of that linkage?" We will begin our discussion by briefly defining the terms "cult," "ritual," and "symbol."

- A cult is a system of religious worship that is usually emphasized by its rituals.
- A ritual is "a complex performance of symbolic acts, characterized by its formality, order, and sequence, which tends to take place in specific situations and has as one of its goals the regulation of the social order."[2] Note that ritual is a common activity of a particular society or culture, not just a religion. A woman may be said to have a ritual of setting her alarm clock before going to sleep, or brushing her teeth upon rising, etc.
- A symbol may refer to any object, activity, movement, relation, event, gesture, spatial unit, or temporal unit that serves as a vehicle for a concept or conveys a socially meaningful message. The symbolics of ritual derive their meaning from the cultural system within which human beings live their lives.[3] The singing of "God Bless America" at the end of the first half of the seventh inning at some professional baseball games in the United States is a ritual fraught with obvious symbolic meaning. Prayers at set occasions and sacrifices in the ancient world are two types of palpably symbolic rituals.

At this point, it is worthwhile to touch on the purposes of sacrifices in the ancient Near East, since sacrifice was the most pervasive ritual of the cult. Scholars of primitive, ancient, and comparative religions have identified six possible primary motivations:

- To provide food for the deities;
- To inculcate the life force of the sacrificed animal;
- To bring about union with the god;

- As a gift, to persuade the deity to respond with aid;
- As a substitute for human victims of aggression;
- To assuage feelings of guilt caused by the killing of the animal by devoting the victim to the god.[4]

The above list, however, is not exhaustive. Other researchers have pointed to added incentives for sacrifices, from magic (that is, compelling the deity to do one's will) to showing respect, to giving thanks. While thanksgiving would certainly apply to Israel, in the above list, only the notions of a gift or assuaging feelings of guilt would relate to the concept of sacrifice in the Jewish Bible. In particular, the aid mentioned in the category of a gift would include everything from receiving God's blessing to the forgiveness of sin and removal of impurity.

A crucial difference between ancient Near Eastern cultures and Israel (touched on in chapter 1) is that the temple in the ancient Near East, that is, the house of the deity, was primarily for the benefit of the god as he or she was provided with food, drink, and a dwelling place. In the Jewish Bible, however, God's supernatural character means that He has no natural needs. In Israel, then, the temple is for the benefit of the people. Accordingly, the entire significance to God of a sacrificial "gift" was symbolic.[5]

Ethics in Cultic Contexts in the Ancient Near East

The idea that the gods desire both ethical human behavior and appropriate ritual appears in some texts such as Mesopotamian hymns and litanies and in late (third century BCE) Egyptian temple inscriptions:

A. "Hymn to Enlil" (Sumerian). The god Enlil establishes his seat in the temple of Nippur due to both moral and ritual characteristics of the city:

enmity, oppression, envy, (brute) force, libelous speech, arrogance, violation of agreement . . . (all these) evils the city does not tolerate. Nippur . . . whose "hand" the wicked and evil cannot escape, the city endowed with truth, where righteousness (and) justice are perpetuated. . . .

Of the rituals, so precious, of the festivals overflowing with rich fat (and) milk, . . . every day a festival, at the break of dawn a grand harvest (feast), the house of Enlil is a mountain of overflow, where beggar, scavenger, and idler are tabu . . . its Abzu-lustration priests are well suited for rites, . . . fit for the holy prayers.[6]

Note that the first paragraph speaks only of ethical issues and the second of ritual ones.

B. *Shurpu* Litany (Akkadian; perhaps as early as the second millennium BCE), Tablet II. The litany lists the ritual and ethical sins of a certain individual,

(who is . . .) sick, in danger (of death), distraught, troubled, who has eaten what is taboo to his god, who has eaten what is taboo to his goddess, who said "no" for "yes," who said "yes" for "no," who . . . despised his goddess, . . . spoke evil things, . . . has oppressed the weak woman, . . . who estranged friend from friend, who did not release a captive, . . . his sins are against his god, his crimes are against his goddess, . . . he despised his parents, . . . gave with small (measure) and received with big (measure) . . . he took money that was not due to him, . . . he set up an untrue boundary, . . . he entered his neighbor's house, had intercourse with his neighbor's wife, shed his neighbor's blood, . . . did not clothe a young man when he was naked, . . . altogether he speaks untrue words.[7]

In this litany, most of the concerns are ethical, but ritual is present in the references to eating "what is taboo" to the deity.

C. "The Offering of Truth," Temple of Horus at Edfu (Egyptian, Ptolmaic Period, third century BCE), speech of Seshat. The goddess of writing, Seshat, lists good and evil actions, both ethical and ritual, which make a person either acceptable or unacceptable to the god in his house:

I have come unto thee . . . that I may set down in writing before thee the doer of good and the doer of evil, to wit: he who initiates wrongfully [perhaps, in the sacred writings]; he who enters when unclean; he who speaks falsehood in thy house; he who knows right from wrong; he who is pure; he who is upright and walks in righteousness; . . . he who loves thine attendants exceedingly; he who receives bribes; . . . he who covets the property of thy temple; . . . I write down for the doer of good in thy city; I reject the character of the evil-doer . . . the sinner perishes everlastingly.[8]

Here the words "initiates," "unclean," and "pure" and the reference to loving the "attendants" of the god all speak of ritual matters, while speaking falsehood, being upright and righteous, receiving bribes, and coveting the temple's property are ethical topics.

Consequently, the three sources cited above—hymn, litany, and temple inscription—all are evidence of religious texts in which ethical behavior appears side-by-side with ritual action. They also indicate that the god desires both ethics and proper ritual. Further, source C, even though it is written long after the Torah and the Prophets, nonetheless implies that the presence of the unscrupulous individual in the temple is abhorrent to the gods. Although that implication may suggest that the sinner's sacrifice is also to be rejected, that thought is never transparently expressed in writing in the ancient Near East.[9]

The one text that comes closest to that idea appears in Egypt (approx. twenty-first century BCE) in wisdom literature. "The Instructions of Merikare" are spoken by an old (unnamed) king to his son, Merikare. Here is found a call to please the sun-god "by being upright, by doing justice . . . the loaf of the upright is preferred to the ox of the evildoer."[10] The ethical lesson here has no resemblance to any other extra-biblical text in the ancient Near East. At the same time, it does not totally negate the sacrifice of the wicked. Rather, by the very fact that it is a comparison, it only indicates that the large, expensive offering of the evildoer is of lesser value to the god than the small, inexpensive offering of the righteous. Although the offering of the righteous is preferred, the gift of the wicked is not rejected.

Lastly, one prophetic text contains both ritual and ethics. Some 140 prophecies,[11] that is, divine messages transmitted by one person to another (usually a monarch), have been found throughout the ancient Near East, although most come from excavations at only two cities—Old Babylonian Mari (eighteenth century BCE), on the Euphrates River, and from Assyrian Nineveh (seventh century BCE), on the Tigris. Only two of these prophecies, both from the prophet Nur-Sin to the king of Mari, Zimri-Lim, contain ethical content (they also have stylistic similarities).[12]

The first prophecy is the one that speaks of both ritual and ethics. It begins with a complaint from the god Adad about the failure to provide a certain ritual offering and a particular estate (presumably to be added to the temple's properties). The prophecy then quotes the god:

> Am I not Adad . . . who raised him (the king) in my lap, and restored him to his ancestral throne? . . . Now since I restored him to his ancestral throne, I may take away the estate from his patrimony as well. Should he not deliver (the estate), I . . . can take away what I have given. But if, on the contrary, he fulfills my desire, I shall give him throne upon throne, house upon house, territory upon territory, city upon city. I shall give the land from the rising of the sun to its setting.

Later in the text, Nur-Sin quotes another prophet:

> A prophet of Adad, lord of Aleppo, . . . spoke . . . as follows: . . . 'Am I not Adad, lord of Aleppo, who raised you in my lap and restored you to your ancestral throne? I do not demand anything from you. When a wronged man or woman cries out to you, be there and judge their case. This only have I demanded from you. If you . . . heed my word, I will give you the land from the rising of the sun to its setting.

This prophecy reveals that the god can punish the king for either a ritual or ethical crime and can reward him for fulfillment of his ritual or ethical desire. It is noteworthy that the god's ethical demand, to provide justice, is similar to that made of the king in Mesopotamia in legal and royal contexts (as seen in chapters 2 and 3).

To answer the questions posed at the beginning of this chapter: in cultic settings in the ancient Near East, evidence exists that the gods were displeased by immoral people who entered the sanctuary. A late Egyptian text (source C) may imply that the sacrifice of the wicked was abhorrent to the gods, but that idea is never unambiguously enunciated. A late third millennium BCE Egyptian wisdom text, "The Instructions of Merikare," does proclaim that the god favors an offering based not upon its objective value but upon the ethical behavior of the offerer. Nonetheless, the sacrifice of the malefactor is not rejected. Finally, a prophetic text affirms that the king's obedience or disobedience to a god's ritual or ethical desire will result in reward or punishment, respectively.

Ethics and Ritual in the Jewish Bible

The Torah

What of the Jewish Bible? As we have seen in chapter 2, the Torah's law codes list ethical and cultic requirements next to each other. Further, it is not possible to infer from the Torah's legislation whether ethics or ritual has greater value. The only ways to tell the relative importance of a specific law in the Torah are if a harsher punishment or a greater reward is attached to it. For example, the death penalty is mandatory for both severe ethical (murder, Num. 35:16–21) and ritual violations (working on the Sabbath, Exod. 31:14–15). Conversely, in Deuteronomy, the assurance of long life is attached specifically to three ethical laws:

- honoring one's parents—in the Ten Commandments (5:16)[13]
- taking young birds from a nest only after chasing away the mother bird:

  > *If, along the road, you chance upon a bird's nest, in any tree or on the ground, with . . . the mother sitting over the fledglings or eggs, do not take the mother along with her young. Send the mother away, and take only the young, in order that you may fare well and have a long life.* (22:6–7)

- honest weights and measures:

  > *You shall not have in your pouch alternate weights, larger and*

> *smaller. You shall not have in your house alternate measures,*
> *larger and smaller. You must have completely honest weights; you*
> *must have completely honest measures—in order that you will*
> *long endure on the soil that the Lord your God is giving you, for*
> *all those who do such dishonest things are an abomination to the*
> *Lord your God.* (25:13–15)

At the same time, long life is also promised for obedience to all the commandments, including the ritual acts of tying God's words on one's hand and forehead and writing them on the doorposts of one's house (11:18–21). Similarly, one may not ingest the blood of an animal *"in order that it may go well with you and your descendants after you, for you will be doing what is right in the sight of the Lord"* (12:23–25). This seemingly ritual injunction is actually derived from an ethical ideal: blood is the tangible symbol of the life that God has given all birds, land animals, and humans. Accordingly, eschewing the ingestion of blood shows reverence for God-given life.[14]

However, at the end of the section in Deuteronomy in which the blood prohibition appears, along with a series of laws about sacrifices and food (12:8–27), is a concluding verse emphasizing the reward for obedience to those ritual enactments: *"Be careful to heed all these commandments that I enjoin upon you in order that it will go well with you and your descendants after you forever, for you will do what is good and right in the sight of the Lord your God"* (12:28). Thus, whether by severity of punishment or magnitude of reward, one cannot determine from the Torah's laws the relative importance of ethics and ritual.

Nonetheless, two factors may indicate that a greater significance is found in the Torah for ethical acts as opposed to ritual ones. First, the multiplicity of motivational statements exhorting the Israelites to care for the stranger, poor, widow and orphan (chapter 3) has no ritual equivalence. Second, the twelve curses that the Israelite tribes, upon entering the Promised Land, are to proclaim on Mount Ebal and Mount Gerizim (Deuteronomy 27) may be instructive: the first curse is against idolatry; the second through the fifth are moral crimes (insulting parents; theft by moving a landmark; misdirecting a blind person; subverting the rights of the stranger, orphan, and widow); the sixth through ninth are sexual crimes (with one's stepmother, an animal, one's sister, and one's mother-in-law); the tenth and eleventh are against murder and taking a bribe to kill an innocent (perhaps referring to accepting a bribe as a judge or witness); the twelfth is against anyone who does not uphold the Torah's instructions. Where is there a curse against one who violates the Sabbath, the holidays, the sancta? The absence of any ritual crime at this crucial moment may minimize the importance of the ritual act as opposed to the moral.

Even if the possibility exists that the Torah, on some level, values morality more than ritual, all doubt will only be removed by the prophets.

Psalms

Both in poetic style and cultic content, the Book of Psalms has some similarity to the literature of hymn, litany, and temple inscription found in the ancient Near East. Two examples from Psalms are particularly instructive of a development in ethical contemplation:

> Psalm 15
>
> *A psalm of David. Lord, who may sojourn in Your tent, who may dwell on Your holy mountain? He who lives without blame, who does what is right, and in his heart acknowledges the truth; who has no slander upon his tongue; who has never done harm to his fellow, or borne reproach for [his acts toward] his neighbor; for whom a contemptible man is abhorrent, but who honors those who fear the Lord; who stands by his oath even to his hurt; who has never lent money at interest, or accepted a bribe against the innocent. The man who acts thus will never be shaken.*

> Psalm 24: 3–5
>
> *Who may ascend the mountain of the Lord? Who may stand in His holy place? He who has clean hands and a pure heart, who has not taken a false oath by My life or sworn deceitfully. He shall carry away a blessing from the Lord, a just reward from God, his deliverer.*[15]

Both of these psalms exemplify ethical progressions beyond the ancient Near Eastern material cited above. Here, no combination of ethical and ritual deeds enables a man to stand before the Lord in the House of God in Israel. One who wishes to enter the Temple precincts must be solely of high moral character—proven through his ethical behavior. To achieve the goal of entrance to the sanctuary, no previous ritual action is significant. If it were, it would have been delineated.

Proverbs

What of the statement in the Egyptian wisdom "Instructions of Merikare"—"the loaf of the upright is preferred to the ox of the evildoer"? Does the Jewish Bible have something similar? Here, too, when we compare apples with apples, that is, the Bible's wisdom literature with Egypt's, an ethical uniqueness is perceived.[16] Three examples from the book of Proverbs will suffice:

> Proverbs 15:8
>
> *The sacrifice of the wicked is an abomination to the Lord, but the prayer of the upright pleases Him.*[17]

> Proverbs 21:3
>
> *To do what is right and just is more desired by the Lord than sacrifice.*[18]

> Proverbs 21:27
>
> *The sacrifice of the wicked man is an abomination, the more so as he offers it in depravity.*

Unlike "Merikare," these verses in Proverbs do not indicate that the expensive sacrifice of the wrongdoer is less preferable than the minor offering of the upright. Rather, the sacrifice of the wicked is anathema to God. Proverbs 15:8 emphasizes that even the prayer of the decent person is acceptable, without the necessity of an offering. The lesson of 21:27 is that the evildoer's sacrifice is unacceptable not because he offers it, but because he offers it with an ulterior motive (such as "buying" God's aid), as opposed to the sincerity of repentance.[19] Proverbs 21:3 goes one step further: ritual is not as desirable to God as is righteousness and justice. This verse presents the kind of literary comparison found in "Merikare," but here it is not between two rituals offered by moral polar opposites, but between ethical and ritual conduct. Again, the Jewish Bible takes an ethical step beyond the ancient Near East. The message here is clear: "God wants ethical behavior more than He wants ritual." Israel's prophets will become the greatest promulgators of this revolutionary concept—the primacy of morality over ritual.

The Prophets

This section will focus on prophetic texts during the First Temple period until the Babylonian exile of 587–586 BCE.

1 SAMUEL 15

According to the Jewish Bible's own internal chronology, the first prophetic text that explicitly contrasts ritual unfavorably to something else appears in 1 Samuel 15. Saul, the first Israelite king, has been ordered by God, by way of the prophet Samuel, to utterly wipe out the Amalekites and all their animals as punishment for their attack on the Israelites in the desert (verses 1–3). Saul and the people carry out the command only in part, sparing the Amalekite king, Agag, and taking the best of the flocks and cattle, presumably as booty (7–9). God's reaction is to inform Samuel that Saul is no longer worthy to be king (10–11). When Samuel confronts Saul, the latter proclaims his innocence and claims that the people only took of the animals to sacrifice them to God (15, 20–21). At this juncture, Samuel says (22–23),

> *Does the Lord delight in burnt offerings and sacrifices as much as in obedience to the Lord's voice? Surely, obedience is better than sacrifice, compliance than the fat of rams. For rebellion is like the sin of divination, and defiance like the iniquity of teraphim* (a type of idol). *Because you rejected the Lord's word, He has rejected you as king.*

The obvious message is that submission to God's precise demand is a superior means of showing one's fealty than are sacrifices. Just as obviously, these verses decree no outright negation of ritual, as the book itself attests in earlier passages.[20] Indeed, in 1 Sam. 2:28, a *"man of God"* (verse 27) affirms that God has assigned sacrifices to the Israelites: *"I assigned to your father's house all offerings by fire of the Children of Israel."* In chapter 7, Samuel himself sacrifices a lamb to God before all the people at Mizpah as part of his beseeching the Lord to save them from the Philistines, which He does at the very moment of the Philistine attack (5–10). In chapter 11, Samuel inaugurates the monarchy with the people at Gilgal, accompanied by sacrifices (verses 14–15). Evidently, then, Samuel's pronouncement in the above-quoted passage does not condemn sacrifice per se but only when it is offered by someone who thinks that it will be a trade-off for his own disobedience. Samuel compares such an act to idolatry, for it was inconceivable in polytheism that a god would totally reject a sacrifice, especially since one of the purposes of such sacrifices was to persuade the god to accept the sacrificer, no matter how the latter had behaved. As shall be seen, this message of Samuel is critical for understanding the passages of later prophets who unambiguously contrast ethics and ritual. 1 Samuel 15:22–23 consequently serves as a precursor and precedent for the passages that follow.

The "classical" or "literary" prophets are those whose words and deeds are captured in the books known as the "Latter Prophets."[21] The first of these—in chronological order,[22] Amos, Hosea, Isaiah and Micah—all flourished in the eighth century BCE. They scrutinize their people's conduct at a time when the Torah's laws and treaty requirements were already well known.[23] What do they see? Are the people adhering to the Torah or not? Or are they following only some of the commandments and not others? Where do ethics and ritual fit in, according to God's will?

AMOS

In historical sequence, the first prophetic text that speaks of both ethics and ritual is found in Amos, who prophesied about 775–750 BCE:[24]

I hate, I despise your festivals; I take no delight[25] in your solemn assemblies. Even if you offer me burnt offerings and your meal offerings, I will not accept them. And the gift offerings of your fatlings I will not look upon favorably. Remove from Me the din of your hymns! And to the melody of your lutes I will not listen. But let justice roll on like water, and righteousness like an ever-flowing stream. Did you offer me sacrifices and meal offerings those forty years in the wilderness, O house of Israel? (5:21–25)[26]

This last verse has a parallel in Jer. 7:22–23,

for when I freed your fathers from the land of Egypt, I did not speak with them or command them concerning burnt offerings or sacrifice. But this is what I commanded them: Do My bidding, that I may be your God and you may be My people; walk only in the way that I enjoin upon you, that it may go well with you.

These verses in Amos and Jeremiah have confused many scholars who thought that both prophets were unaware of the Torah's statements that the Israelites offered sacrifices in the desert wanderings. However, these verses use terminology that only refers to the voluntary offerings of individuals, as opposed to the mandatory communal sacrifices offered at scheduled times.[27] Voluntary sacrifices were neither desired by God in the desert (Jeremiah) nor offered by the people at that time (Amos). Therefore, neither Amos nor Jeremiah rejects the cult in total. The prophets are using the circumstances in the desert to highlight the travesty that, in the prophet's day, the same people who are acting unjustly are the ones bringing the voluntary offerings.

To put 5:21–25 in context, Amos frequently rebukes the people for numerous moral crimes,

Because they have sold for silver the innocent, and the needy for a hidden gain. They who trample the heads of the poor into the dust of the ground, and thrust the humble off the road. A man and his father cohabit with the same young woman, thereby profaning My holy name. Upon garments seized in distraint they stretch themselves out beside every altar, and the wine of the fined they drink in the House of their God. (2:6–8)

Ergo, the wine they drink was bought with money that the affluent received through fines exacted from the poor![28]

Look at the manifold outrages within her (Samaria) and the oppression in her midst! For they are incapable of doing what is right . . . those who store treasures of violence and rapine in their fortresses. (3:9–10)

The prophet understands that the riches of the upper class are derived from, and therefore equated to, brutal exploitation of the underprivileged.

Hear this word, cows (rich women) *of Bashan . . . who oppress the poor, crush the destitute, who say to their husbands, "Bring, and let us drink!"* (4:1)

The wives of the wealthy are complicit in the oppression wrought by their husbands. All they care about is their luxurious lifestyle and not how it was attained.[29]

They who turn justice into wormwood and hurl righteousness to the ground. (5:7)

They hate the arbiter in the gate (in the court) *and the one who pleads honestly they loathe. Therefore, because you levy a straw tax on the poor and exact a grain tax from him . . . you persecutors of the innocent, takers of bribes, who subvert the cause of the needy in the gate. . . . Seek good and not evil that you may live. . . . Hate evil and love good! And set up justice in the gate!* (5:10–15)

These two passages in Amos 5 emphasize the corruption of the judges who are accessories in the subjugation of poor.

Hear this, you who trample upon the needy, exterminating the poor of the land, saying, "When will the new moon be over, so that we may sell corn; and the Sabbath, so that we may open the grain[-bins]"—making the ephah small and the shekel large, and distorting with false scales, buying the poor for silver, the needy for a prerequisite—"that we may sell the chaff of the wheat." (8:4–6)

In the passage just cited, Amos mentions the new moon and the Sabbath. Both the beginning of the month and the weekly Sabbath were prominent religious festivals frequently mentioned throughout the Jewish Bible.[30] It is noteworthy that the passage implies that the prohibition of commerce on the new moon and Sabbath is appropriate. Indeed, it is not the people's observance of the new moon and Sabbath that is reprehensible; it is their craving to violate the constraints of those holy days.[31] The grain merchants are impatient for the day to end so that they can once again resort to cheating the underprivileged by using false measures and scales and even selling chaff as wheat!

The above passages on the moral crimes of the northern kingdom of Israel focus on the abuse of the needy and poor (Amos 2:6–8; 4:1; 5:10–15; 8:4–6), corrupting justice in the courts (5:7, 10–15), sexual crimes (2:7), and perverting sanctuaries and holy days (2:8; 8:6). The perversion of the sanctuary is pronounced particularly in 4:4–5,

> *Come to Bethel and transgress! To Gilgal, transgress even more! Bring your sacrifices on the morn! Your tithes on the third day! Burn a thank—offering of leavened bread! And proclaim freewill offerings aloud! For you love that, O Israelites—declares my Lord God.*

Bethel and Gilgal were two northern cultic centers of great antiquity. Amos is here mocking the people's actions. They think that they are gaining God's approval by coming to these venerable sanctuaries and multiplying sacrifices, bringing them every morning, and tithes (which are to be brought at the most once a year) "every three days." Furthermore, they are shouting out their voluntary offerings, boasting rather than humility. Actually, their sacrifices are no more than attempts to bribe God. Hence God sees these offerings as purposeful, rebellious sins.

In sum, the Lord wants right, not rite.[32] As one scholar put it, "God requires devotion, not devotions. Sacrifice and prayer cannot serve as substitutes for justice."[33] Under such immoral conditions, it is futile to worship at the sanctuaries.[34] The result will be that God will destroy the ancient shrines, even the royal temple at Bethel, along with the palaces of those who have oppressed the poor and needy.[35] Blight and mildew will come upon the land, along with drought, locusts, and the plagues of Egypt—all reminiscent of the treaty curses of Deuteronomy 28.[36] At the end, the people shall be exiled.[37] Destruction and exile are the ultimate punishment for disobedience to God's treaty and laws in the Torah. Amos's innovation is to proclaim that the determining factor is Israel's transgression of the Torah's moral laws.

HOSEA

Hosea prophesied to the northern kingdom of Israel from about 760 to 735 BCE.[38] He castigates the people for their idolatry, their illegitimate worship of God, their disobedience to the Sinai Treaty and the Torah, their seeking political help from foreign nations, and their immorality. On the topic of the relationship between ethics and ritual, the most quoted verse is 6:6, *"for I* [the Lord] *desire goodness,*[39] *not sacrifice, and knowledge of God more than burnt offerings."* "Knowledge of God" is an idiom that Hosea uses to refer to the moral behavior that God wants from the Israelite:[40]

> . . . *I* [the Lord] *will betroth you to Me with* [the bride-price of][41] *righteousness and justice, and with goodness and mercy, and I will betroth you to Me with faithfulness and you will know the Lord.* (2:21–22).

> *Hear the word of the Lord, O Children of Israel, for the Lord has an indictment against the inhabitants of the land, because there is no honesty, and no goodness, and no knowledge of God in the land. Malicious curses, perjury, murder, theft, and adultery are rife; bloodshed prompts yet more bloodshed.* (4:1–2)[42]

In the first instance, "knowing the Lord" is an outcome of "righteousness and justice . . . goodness and mercy." In the second, when there is no such "knowledge," gross immorality prevails.

Undeniably, Hosea 6:6 proclaims that God wants morality and not sacrifices. However, does this verse make a stand against all ritual,[43] or only that offered by immoral people? Three passages in the book will help us determine an answer:

> *For the Children of Israel shall go a long time without king and without officials, without sacrifice and without cult pillars. . . . Afterward, the Children of Israel will turn back and will seek the Lord their God and David their king—and they will thrill over the Lord and over His bounty in the days to come.* (3:4–5)

This passage predicts a time when the Israelites will either be exiled or under the rule of foreigners. They won't have their own king, government, or cult. However, after they repent, they will be given their true king once again from the line of David. If they get their king back, why not the cult? It is easy to conceive of a time that the "bounty" they receive will generate thanksgiving offerings.

> *When he already had altars so as to sin, Ephraim multiplied altars so as to sin.*[44] *Though I write for him the principal requirements of My Torah, they are considered as those of an alien [god]. In his (Ephraim's) frequent sacrifices, it is but flesh for them to eat. The Lord has not accepted them. Now He will remember their iniquity, and will punish their sins.* (8:11–13)

> *For their evil deeds, I will drive them out of My House.* (9:15)

In both of these passages, it is evident that the cult itself is not intrinsically evil but that the people's conduct is. In the first passage they offer many sacrifices only so that they can eat more meat. The second one affirms that it is not God's temple that is worthless but the people's wicked behavior. It can then be concluded that Hosea, like Amos, does not see the cult as integrally flawed. Rather, the people's immorality makes their offerings unacceptable.

ISAIAH

Isaiah the son of Amoz prophesied to the southern kingdom of Judah from about 740 to 700 BCE.[45] Isaiah's key verses on the relationship of ritual to ethics appear at the beginning of the book:[46]

> *Hear the word of the Lord, you rulers of Sodom! Give heed to the torah of our God, you people of Gomorrah! "What are your many sacrifices to Me?" says the Lord. "I have had enough of burnt offerings of rams, and the suet of fatted animals; I take no pleasure in the blood of bulls, or of lambs and goats. When you come to appear in My presence, who has asked this of you (literally, "of your hand," that is, the bringing of offerings), this trampling of My precincts? Bring no more useless offerings; incense disgusts Me. New moon, Sabbath, holy convocation—I cannot stand iniquity combined with solemn assembly. I hate your new*

moons and festivals, they have become a burden to Me. I am tired of putting up with them. When you stretch out your hands in prayer, I will hide My eyes from you. Even though you keep on praying, I will not be listening; you have blood all over your hands. Wash yourselves, make yourselves clean; remove the evil you are doing from My sight. Stop doing evil. Learn to do good. Seek after justice. Rescue the oppressed. Defend the rights of the orphan. Plead the widow's cause. (1:10–17)

One could have thought that this passage is a wholesale repudiation of the cult—until the words, *"I cannot stand iniquity combined with solemn assembly."* Unmistakably, Isaiah here condemns the rituals because they are offered by people engaged in immoral activities. That the issue is not sacrifices and offerings in and by themselves is made obvious by the continuation: *"Even though you keep on praying, I will not be listening."* Why? Because *"you have blood all over your hands."* Even prayer is unacceptable in an immoral climate. What must the people do in order to attain the ritual purity necessary for proper offerings? *"Wash yourselves. . . . Stop doing evil. Learn to do good. Seek after justice. Rescue the oppressed."* Spiritual cleanliness will be produced by ethical behavior.

Further proof that Isaiah does not intend to disavow the cult appears at the beginning of chapter 2, in the prophet's famous vision of the future:

In the days to come, the Mount of the Lord's House shall stand firm above the mountains . . . and many peoples shall go and say: "Come let us go up to the Mount of the Lord, to the House of the God of Jacob, that He may instruct us in His ways, and that we may walk in His paths." . . . Thus He will judge among the nations . . . and they shall beat their swords into plowshares and their spears into pruning hooks. Nation shall not take up sword against nation, and they shall never again learn to make war. (2:2–4)

The existence of the great Temple of Jerusalem at the end of days is evidence that Isaiah sees the sacrificial rituals as continuing, for the Temple is the primary symbol of the cult. Indeed, affirmation of the future cult appears in what is an apparent interpretation on this passage in chapter 56 (from the anonymous prophet of over 150 years later whose words are appended to the Book of Isaiah),

As for the foreigners who attach themselves to the Lord . . . all who keep
the Sabbath and who hold fast to My covenant, I will bring them to My
sacred mount and will make them happy in My House of prayer. Their
burnt offerings and sacrifices shall be welcome on My altar; for My
House shall be called a House of prayer for all peoples. (56:6–7) [47]

Isaiah 2:2–4, then, confirms that the problem has not been with the
cult itself but with the context of the people's immoral acts. When ethics
is pervasive, signified by a time of peace and harmony, ritual has a substantial role.

MICAH

Micah of Moreshet[48] prophesied to the people of the kingdom of Judah
during the last quarter of the eighth century BCE.[49] These verses from
chapter 6 comprise the one, famous passage in his book on the relationship between ethics and ritual,

With what shall I approach the Lord, [with what] *shall I bow to God*
on high?
Shall I approach Him with burnt offerings, with calves a year old?
Will the Lord be pleased with thousands of rams, with myriads of
streams of oil?
Shall I give my first-born for my rebellious[50] transgression, the fruit
of my body for the sin of my soul?
He has told you, O man, what is good, and what the Lord requires of
you: only do justice, and [act with] *love of kindness, and walk*
modestly with your God. (6:6–8) [51]

In this passage, Micah, in seeming innocence, begins by asking what
God wants of the worshipper. However, it is quickly apparent that the
sacrificial content is escalated to an absurd degree—from the normal
"burnt offerings" of year-old calves to the exaggerated "thousands of
rams" (only affordable by a king in a one-time ceremony)[52] and "myriads of streams of oil" to the most heinous kind of sacrifice, that of a
child (condemned in the Torah and Prophets).[53] It emerges, then, that
these are not real questions, but rhetorical ones! The response of the

prophet is solely based upon ethics. Note that "what is good" equals "what the Lord requires of you"—practicing justice and love of kindness (as demanded in Hosea, above), and to "walk modestly with your God," that is, the opposite of arrogance.[54]

If taken out of context, it appears that Micah leaves no place for ritual. Elsewhere, however, Micah emphasizes the people's immorality.[55] Indeed, Micah is the first prophet to predict the destruction of the Temple and Jerusalem due to the people's moral crimes.[56] Nonetheless, that Micah does not denigrate ritual per se is obvious from the fact that he includes in chapter 4, verses 1–3, in almost identical language, the same prophecy found in Isaiah 2:2–4 of the future establishment of the House of God in Jerusalem (the question of who borrowed from whom, or whether both prophets borrowed from a different source, may be impossible to ascertain).[57] Just as Isaiah saw a future for the cult, so did Micah—within the context of a peaceful, just society.

JEREMIAH

Jeremiah the son of Hilkiah of a priestly family from Anatoth (a few miles northeast of Jerusalem) prophesied during the last decades of the kingdom of Judah until a few years after the Babylonian destruction of Jerusalem (approx. 627–583 BCE). His primary prophecy on the relationship between ethics and ritual is one of the most dramatic in the Jewish Bible, the renowned "Temple Sermon," at the beginning of the reign of King Jehoiakim (609 BCE), in chapter 7, verses 1–15.[58] For this prophecy, Jeremiah was put on trial for his life:[59]

(1) *The word which came to Jeremiah from the Lord, saying,* (2) *Stand at the gate of the House of the Lord, and there proclaim this word. . . .* (3) *Thus says the Lord of Hosts, the God of Israel: Mend your ways and your actions and I will cause you to dwell in this place* [or, I will dwell with you in this place]. (4) *Don't put your trust in lying words, saying,* "*The Temple of the Lord, the Temple of the Lord, the Temple of the Lord are these* [buildings]!" (5) *Instead, if you truly mend your ways and actions; if you truly execute justice between a man and his fellow;* (6) *if you do not oppress the stranger, orphan, and widow; if you do not shed innocent blood in this place; if you do not go after other gods to*

your own hurt, (7) then I will cause you to dwell in this place, in the land that I gave to your fathers from of old forever.

(8) See, you are relying on lying words that are of no avail. (9) Will you steal, murder, commit adultery, swear falsely, sacrifice to Baal, and follow other gods whom you have not known, (10) and then come and stand before Me in this House that bears My name and say, "We have been rescued!"—[rescued] in order to do all these abhorrent things!?! *(11) Is this House that bears My name a robbers' cave in your eyes!?!* I, too, have seen [what is going on]*—declares the Lord.*

(12) Just go to My place at Shiloh, where I had caused My name to dwell there formerly, and see what I did to it because of the wickedness of My people Israel. (13) And now, inasmuch as you have done all these deeds—declares the Lord—and though I have spoken to you early and persistently, you have not listened. Though I called to you, you did not respond. (14) Therefore, I will do to the House which bears My name, in which you trust—the place which I gave to you and to your fathers—as I did to Shiloh. (15) And I will cast you out of My presence as I cast out your brothers, all the offspring of Ephraim. (7:1–15)[60]

Different elements of this passage ensure that a wholesale denial of the cult is not Jeremiah's intent: if the people repent of their wicked ways, that is, stop doing evil and begin doing good, God will establish them in the Temple precincts (verse 3); improved ethical behavior and monotheism will result in permanent continuity of the people at both the Temple and the Promised Land (5–7); God's destruction of the ancient sanctuary at Shiloh due to wickedness[61] did not result in the end of the cult (12). Similarly, Jeremiah promises elsewhere that if the people sanctify the Sabbath, the full complement of sacrifices at the Temple shall continue.[62]

What then is the message of this passage? By the time of this prophecy, the Temple had stood for more than three hundred years, despite the invasion of the Pharaoh Sheshonq (tenth century BCE) and the Assyrian conquest (eighth century BCE). The people considered it inviolable. They believed that the Temple's continued existence was a divine guarantee that, no matter what happened, the Judahites were secure upon their land. Jeremiah radically challenged their belief system. He prophesied that the existence of Israel's most revered cultic institution was

NOT unconditional. Everything depended upon obedience to God, particularly with regard to the primary ethical commandments. To rely on the Temple's continuous presence was to "trust in lying words." It was justice and care for the underprivileged elements of society that were crucial—the poor widow, orphan, and resident alien—as well as the cessation of idolatry (5–6, 9). In ethical terms, Jeremiah principally resorts to the demands of the Ten Commandments—the prohibitions of theft, murder, adultery, and swearing falsely (9)—as the conditions necessary to avoid destruction of the Temple and exile (12–15).

Undoubtedly, the elimination of syncretism (the worship of other gods along with the God of Israel) is essential for the prophet, but so are the moral obligations. Either way, ritual in the face of immorality and idolatry is worthless. The Temple acquires its purity not intrinsically but on the basis of the ethical quality of those who worship there.[63] If the worshipers behave immorally, then the Temple is no more than "a robbers' cave" and thus of no value to God. Later, Jeremiah, like Isaiah and Micah before him, will promise an essential role for the Temple and its cult in the time of redemption that will succeed destruction and exile.[64]

Conclusions

The Torah, as mentioned above, does not palpably differentiate between ethical and ritual laws as to relative importance, even though indications exist that morality is of special significance. The prophets stand at a time when the Torah's laws were already known to the populace. What do they see? They look upon a society rife with moral corruption, where the people's behavior is influenced by the venality of the upper classes. At the same time, they see a cult meticulously observed but perverted from holiness to self-serving hypocrisy. The people treat God as a pagan deity, one who can be appeased with an overabundance of offerings. Within this pervasive environment of unethical behavior, the prophets repudiate the complex of rituals associated with holidays and holy places.

Those academics who claim that the prophets are pronouncing the illegitimacy of the cult per se are imposing modern notions of liberal religion or secular values upon the ancient world.[65] Just as atheism in the ancient world was inconceivable, so was a religious society without the rituals of worship.[66]

Even in modern secular democratic societies such as the United States, rituals are inherent. Ritual is, in fact, innate in all human societies. As a famous Jewish Bible professor once analogized,[67] it is a ritual in America that, on a wife's birthday, the husband will bring her a bouquet of flowers. Should the husband have been a good husband throughout the year, concerned with his wife's needs and personal growth, not taking her for granted, appreciative of her kindnesses and acting kindly to her, not going out with his buddies too often and not staying out too late, not coming home drunk and disorderly, careful and polite in his speech to her, faithful, etc., and then brings her roses on her birthday, she will gladly accept them as the symbol of a love that is manifested on a daily basis. However, should the husband not be particularly caring or attentive, taking her for granted, behaving in a churlish and unthinking fashion, going out too much for too long and with poor consequences, speaking harshly to her, being unfaithful, or any combination of the above (each person can make up his or her own list), and then bring her a bouquet on her birthday, she has the right to throw the roses in his face, saying, "The symbol of love is meaningless when it is not accompanied by loving behavior." So, too, is the message of the prophets. All the rituals of the cult, from prayer to sacrifice, are merely symbolic of the people's love of God. However, if the people do not demonstrate their love of God in their daily lives, then God rejects the cult, and punishment will ensue.

But how can the people behave lovingly to a God who needs nothing? The prophets respond, "Show love to the image of God, your fellow human who is also a member of your society." If the people obey the ethical laws of the covenant and treat each other with kindness, with predominant emphasis on the needs of the underprivileged elements of the community, then the rituals of prayers and sacrifices are accepted as symbolic of a love that is exhibited daily. On the other hand, if the people do not behave ethically toward each other, then cultic actions are of no significance. *The revolutionary message of the prophets is that ritual is both secondary to ethics and dependent upon moral behavior for its validity.*[68]

Again, it is important to remember that in Israel, ritual, rather than the people's gift to the Deity, is apprehended as God's present to the people, an act of munificence intended for their benefit. It enables the people to be drawn, as it were, into a more intimate relationship with God. The cult, though, is only a means to an end. To the prophets, the goal is the people's obedience to God's ethical commandments in order to create a just, righteous, and caring society. In such a society, ritual is not only accepted but redeemed.[69]

The prophets made one more pivotal advancement. Previously, the Torah's self-understanding of the Sinai treaty had resolved that the fate of the nation hinged upon whether or not the people obeyed all of covenantal law—civil, criminal, and cultic. In the books of the Former Prophets—Joshua, Judges, 1 and 2 Samuel, 1 and 2 Kings—the primary causes for national doom are the cardinal sins of worship of foreign gods and idolatry.[70] Now, however, the prophets articulate a radical criterion: in the eyes of God, the destiny of the people is determined first and foremost by their ethical behavior.[71]

These twin prophetic, ethical innovations—the primacy of morality over ritual and ethical behavior as the determining factor of national destiny—are unparalleled in the ancient Near East.

5

The Requirement of "Return"

The Development of Repentance from Torah to Prophecy (with a Note on Theodicy)

The previous chapters have emphasized the necessity of Israel's obedience to God's commandments as articulated in the Torah. Further, the prophets particularly accentuated the obligation to focus on ethical behavior. However, what happens when the people, as individuals or as a nation, disobey God? Is the prescribed punishment inevitable, or is it possible to mitigate the sentence or even eliminate it? The Jewish Bible, especially the Torah and the Prophets, affirms that through repentance, punishment may be moderated or even abolished.

But what is repentance? The modern definition of "to repent," according to the *Oxford English Dictionary*, is "To review one's actions and feel contrition or regret for something one has done or omitted to do; (esp. in religious contexts) to acknowledge the sinfulness of one's past action or conduct by showing sincere remorse and undertaking to reform in the future." Although this articulation will serve here as a starting point, the investigation herein will compel significant adjustment of the meaning of repentance in its application to ancient Near Eastern literature, as well as to that of the Jewish Bible.

It should be noted that what makes sincere repentance a highly virtuous activity is its response to immoral behavior. Repentance then becomes the signifier of a mature ethical outlook.

The Ancient Near East

The problem of repentance as an ethical category is compounded in ancient Near Eastern polytheism by two major factors—the capricious character of the gods (see chapter 1) and the lack of revelation of the gods' will. If the gods are not dedicated to ethical behavior, then the morality of repentance becomes a hit-and-miss proposition. And if one has no way of being certain what a god wants, then how is a person to know when a sin has been committed for which one must atone?

However, ancient Near Eastern literature is not of one cloth—not a surprising conclusion when one considers that the literature at our disposal was created over a period of two thousand years and is derived from numerous civilizations. The following pages will reveal some representative viewpoints.

Again, the morality of the gods is unpredictable. Nonetheless, a basic assumption of Old Babylonian texts (nineteenth–sixteenth century BCE) is that the gods ruled the universe in justice.[1] Thus all human suffering was viewed as punishment for some sin(s). Hence an individual was ultimately responsible for his or her own fate. If a person could keep on the correct side of the gods, no harm could befall him.

> Every day worship your god. Sacrifice and benediction are the proper accompaniment of incense. Present your free-will offering to your god, for this is proper toward the gods. Prayer, supplication and prostration offer him daily, and you will get your reward. Then you will have full communion with your god. . . . Reverence begets favor, sacrifice prolongs life, prayer atones for guilt.[2]

Nonetheless, that proposition was put to the test by the observation that personal piety could not guarantee a life of prosperity, because the travails of a devout individual were an undeniable occurrence.[3] This realization and its implications are illustrated in a famous Kassite period (sixteenth–twelfth century BCE) text, *Ludlul bel numiqi*, "I will praise the lord of wisdom" (also known as *The Poem of the Righteous Sufferer*).[4] In Tablet I, the sufferer recounts the many miseries and betrayals he has had to endure and the obvious conclusion that his gods have abandoned him. In Tablet II, as he reflects on his untenable position, he feels that he is unjustly treated.[5]

> Like one who has not made libations to his god, nor invoked his goddess when he ate, does not *make* prostrations nor recognize (the necessity of) bowing down, in whose mouth supplication and prayer are lacking, who has even *neglected* holy days, and ignored festivals, who was negligent and did not observe the gods' rites, did not teach his people reverence and worship, but has eaten his food without invoking his god, and abandoned his goddess by not bringing a flour offering, like one who has gone crazy and forgotten his lord, has frivolously sworn a solemn oath by his god, [like such a one] do I *appear.* (ll.12–22)

But that is not him! "For myself, I give attention to supplication and prayer: My prayer was discretion, sacrifice my rule. The day for worshipping the god was a joy to my heart . . . I had my land keep the god's rites, and brought my people to value the goddess's name" (ll.23–30).

He then confesses his lack of comprehension of the consequence of his pious behavior and of what the gods want from humanity. Indeed, the moral standards of humans and gods appear to have nothing in common with each other.[6]

> I wish I knew that these things would be pleasing to one's god! What is good for oneself may be offence to one's god, what in one's own heart seems despicable may be proper to one's god. Who can know the will of the gods in heaven? Who can understand the plans of the underworld gods? Where have humans learned the way of a god? (ll.33–38)

In Tablet III, in dreams, the sufferer is promised deliverance by the god Marduk, who finally receives his prayers and restores his health as well as apparently his former station. The sufferer in Tablet IV responds with prayers and sacrifices. However, the good and evil that come upon the human, whether due to the god's will or not, are inexplicable.

This lack of understanding of the relationship between one's behavior and the punishment of the gods, or what is acceptable human behavior to the gods, is mirrored in other texts.

> Mankind is deaf and knows nothing.
> What knowledge has anyone at all?
> He knows not whether he has done a good or bad deed.
> Where is the wise man who has not transgressed and [committed]
>   an abomination?[7]

A comparable perspective appears in *The Babylonian Theodicy* (originally written ca. 1000 BCE)—a dialogue between a sufferer and his friend.[8] The former does not understand why the gods do not protect those who are too weak to protect themselves, or why the strong so oppress others, nor why the firstborn is so favored over younger children. The friend counters by saying that prosperity is due to piety. "He who looks to his god has a protective spirit. The humble man who fears his goddess accumulates wealth." The sufferer contends that crimes among both animals and humans does pay and that these very criminals even neglect the gods, while he, who has been pious, suffers! "The prominent person who has multiplied his wealth, did he weigh out precious gold for the goddess Mami? [Have I] withheld offerings? I have prayed to my god." The friend counters that one cannot understand the minds of the gods. "You are as stable as the earth, but the plan of the gods is remote," although criminals do meet a bad end. The sufferer reiterates that his devotion to religion has gone unrewarded and has only led to his suffering. "In my youth I tried to find the will of my god; with prostration and prayer I sought my goddess. . . . The rogue has been promoted, but I have been brought low." The friend repeats that one cannot comprehend the gods' wisdom. "The mind of the god, like the center of the heavens, is remote; . . . people cannot know it." The sufferer claims that the rich and powerful are always favored in the false testimony they give against the impoverished, thereby grinding down the poor. Finally, the friend acknowledges that the injustice that men do is part of their nature due to the way they were created by the gods.

Narru, king of the gods, who created mankind, And majestic Zulum-
mar, who pinched off the clay for them, And goddess Mami, the queen
who fashioned them, Gave twisted speech to the human race. With
lies, and not truth, they endowed them forever. Solemnly they speak
favorably of a rich man. . . . But they treat a poor man like a thief,
They have only bad to say of him and plot his murder.

The sufferer, in response, can only plead that the gods reinstate their
protection over him.

For the author of this theodicy, the difficulty lies in the reality of the
oppression of the pious by the wicked. The sufferer thus refuses to accept
the idea that the gods protect the innocent. The acknowledgment by
the friend that the gods made humans liars and persecutors—thereby
ensuring their criminality and "vindicating" their punishment—
extinguishes the older belief that the divine creators rule the universe
in justice.[9]

The conviction that the gods were capricious or worse led Mesopotamians to take a jaundiced, even mocking view of the deities. Such a
perspective appears in *The Dialogue of Pessimism*, a conversation between
a slave and his master in which the master states that he wants the slave
to do something and the slave supports it. Then the master changes his
mind, and the slave supports that! In lines 53–61, the subject is sacrifice.
The master says,

"Fetch me water for my hands . . . so that I can sacrifice to my god."
Slave answers, "Sacrifice, sir, sacrifice. The man who sacrifices to his
god is satisfied with the bargain: he is making loan upon loan." Master:
"No, slave, I will by no means sacrifice to my god." Slave: "Do not
sacrifice, sir, do not sacrifice. You can teach your god to run after you
like a dog, whether he asks of your rites, or 'Do not consult your god,'
or anything else."[10]

It is true that not all the gods were perceived to be amoral. The *Nanshe
Hymn* (twenty-second century BCE) to the Sumerian god of social justice, Nanshe, affirms her (and her assistant, Hendursaga's) ethical judgment of human behavior,[11] as does the *Shamash Hymn* (from the library

of Ashurbanipal) concerning the Babylonian god of justice.[12] Further-more, the Hittite prayers constantly appeal to the gods' sense of justice.[13]

Nevertheless, the overriding inscrutability and unreliability of the gods leads man into despair. Ultimately, suffering means that the human must have sinned, and his only option is to admit his guilt and beg for mercy. At the same time, he realizes that he is not responsible for his sin, for it is human nature to offend the gods. As one scholar concludes, "The result is an anonymous guilt with no real sense of wrongdoing."[14]

The untenable nature of the human condition is compounded in the *Erra and Ishum* narrative (eighth century BCE; tablets found in Assyria and Babylonia).[15] Erra is a violent god who, in a threatening speech against Marduk, takes away human free will:

Tablet II

I.51 "The black-headed people will revile you . . ."
I.61–62 "a son will not ask after the health of his father, nor the father of his son. A mother will happily plot harm for her daughter."

Tablet III

I.7 "I shall sever the life of the just man who takes on parental responsibility.
I.8 I shall set up [at the head?] the wicked man who cuts off life.
I.9 I shall change the minds of people, so that the father will not listen to the son.
I.10 The daughter will speak words of rejection to the mother.
I.11 I shall make their words wicked, and they will forget their god."

In one of his responses to get Erra to forego his threat, Ishum, a god who tries to act as a peacemaker, says:

Tablet IV

II.104–7 "O warrior Erra, you have put the just to death.
You have put the unjust to death.
You have put to death the man who has sinned against you.

You have put to death the man who did not sin against you."

Erra responds by naming members of nations who will kill each other ruthlessly:

> I.131 "Sealanders shall not spare Sealanders . . . nor Assyrian Assyr-
> ian . . .
> I.134 . . . nor country country, nor city city,
> I.135 Nor shall tribe spare tribe, nor man man, nor brother brother,
> and they shall slay one another."

Erra destroys cities, mountains, and cattle. At last he rests and brazenly admits to the evil he has wrought.

> II.6–10 "What if I did intend the harm of the wrong I have just done?
> When I am enraged, I devastate people!
> Like a hired man among the flocks, I let the leading sheep out of
> the pen.
> Like one who does not plant an orchard, I am not slow to cut it down.
> Like one who plunders a country, I do not distinguish just from
> unjust, I fell [them both]."

Finally, Ishum flatters him.

> II.18–19 "What if you were to rest now, and we would serve you?
> We all know that nobody can stand up to you in your day of wrath!"

Erra is then appeased (II.20–22).

The utter capriciousness and unrestrained brutality of Erra (against which the other gods were powerless), coupled with the temporary elimination of human free will, illustrate how precarious and uncontrollable was the author's perception of man's existence.

Even though the Mesopotamian realized that he may not have been morally responsible for his sins against the gods, he still desperately tried—by sacrifice, prayer, magic, and confession—to persuade the gods to end his suffering. Nonetheless, since the penitent is not aware of the specific sins he has committed, his confession is imprecise—as in, for example, the *Prayer to Every God* (a Sumerian text from the library of Ashurbanipal; copied from an older original):[16]

> In ignorance I have eaten that forbidden of my god; In ignorance I have set foot on that prohibited by my goddess. O Lord, my transgressions are many; great are my sins. . . . The transgression which I have committed, indeed I do not know; The sin which I have done, indeed I do not know. . . . The lord in the anger of his heart looked at me. . . . When the goddess was angry with me, she made me become ill. The god whom I know or do not know has oppressed me.
>
> Man is dumb; he knows nothing; Mankind, everyone that exists, what does he know? Whether he is committing sin or doing good, he does not even know.

Exceptions in which crimes were specified, however, did exist. In many locales in the ancient Near East, adultery, as a social crime against the husband, was termed the "great sin" against the gods.[17] Further, among the Hittites, evidence exists of general categories of sins, such as breaking an oath to a god, or not fulfilling cultic obligations, or trespassing the sancta.[18] It makes sense that the suffering of a king and his people would be perceived as the consequence of the particular sin of disregarding an oath to a deity, for such negligence would be sure to bring along curses in its wake. In the *Plague Prayers of Mursilis* (a Hittite monarch in the fourteenth century BCE), the king confesses to oath-breaking:[19]

> the Hattians ignored their obligations; the Hattians promptly broke the oath of the gods. . . . The matter of the [broken] oath which was established [as a cause] in connection with the plague, offerings for those oaths I have made to the Hattian Storm-god, my lord. . . . Now, I have confessed before the Hattian Storm-god . . . [admitting]: "It is true, we have done it." . . . If a servant has incurred guilt, but confesses his guilt to his lord, his lord may do with him whatever he pleases. But because [the servant] has confessed his guilt to his lord, his lord's soul is pacified, and his lord will not punish that servant. I have now confessed . . . if ye demand from me additional restitution, tell me of

it in a dream and I will give it to you. . . . Let this plague abate again in the Hatti land![20]

Some Mesopotamian incantations did confess to specific acts.

I frivolously took a solemn oath in your name. . . . I promised and then reneged; I gave my word but then did not pay. . . . I spoke lies, I pardoned my own sins. . . . I coveted your abundant property, I desired your precious silver. I raised my hand and desecrated what should not be so treated. In a state of impurity I entered the temple.[21]

Another unusual Hittite exception comes from the *Instructions for Palace Personnel to Insure the King's Purity*:

You who are leatherworkers . . . take always oxhides and goatskins from the [royal] kitchen! Do not take any other! *If you take any other and tell the king about it, it is no crime for you.* I, the king, will send that abroad or give it to my servants. But if you conceal it and it becomes known afterwards, they will put you to death together with your wives [and] your children.[22]

In this one instance, confession of the actual crime (of taking not-permitted hides) before the king *and before the guilty confessor is apprehended* results in the abrogation of punishment.

Nonetheless, in ancient Near East literature, such confessions to explicit acts were extraordinary. It is also noteworthy that Mursilis's confession was designed to end the punishment that was ongoing, just as the general confessions were intended to end the supplicant's suffering. A few specific confessions also appear in the Egyptian New Kingdom, such as on the "Votive Stela of Neferabu with Hymn to Ptah," in which the author admits that he "swore falsely by Ptah, Lord of Maat . . . he does not overlook [i.e., forgive] anyone's deed! . . . he taught a lesson to me! . . . look on me in mercy!"[23]

A quite different circumstance occurred when the petitioner was faced with a scenario in which his goal was to avoid suffering. On such an occasion, some scholars have adopted a truly Orwellian term for the supplicant's words which deny any wrongdoing—"negative confession"! Thus in Egypt, in the *Book of the Dead* (ca. 1550 BCE), the deceased, in order to be judged meritoriously, denies having done some forty-two acts, such as sinning, lying, theft, and slander.[24] Similarly, on the fifth day of the Babylonian New Year's festival, the king enters the Temple of Bel (Marduk) and the high priest removes the king's scepter, loop, mace, and crown.[25] The high priest then

> goes out and strikes the cheek of the king. . . . He pulls . . . [him by] the ears; he makes him kneel down to the ground. . . . the king says the following once: "I did [not s]in, lord of the countries. I was not negligent toward you. [I did not des]troy Babylon, I did not command its overthrow. [I did not] . . . Esagil [the temple], I did not forget its rituals. [I did not s]trike the cheek of the privileged citizens . . . nor did I bring about their humiliation. . . . for Babylon; I did not destroy its walls."[26]

After the king has spoken, the high priest informs him that Bel will listen to his prayer, magnify his kingship, and destroy his enemy. The high priest restores the scepter, loop, mace, and crown to the king, and then he "strikes the cheek of the king. When [he strikes] his cheek, if his tears flow, Bel is favorable; if his tears do not flow, Bel is angry: the enemy will rise up and bring about his downfall."[27] The primary purpose of this ritual appears to emphasize the king's need to be faithful to his god, who provides the king with all his beneficence. Ergo the humiliation—the king is made to realize that he is nothing without his god's favor.

What does not happen at the Babylonian New Year's festival or in the *Book of the Dead* is any kind of repentance or remorse. To the contrary, the evidence shows that the supplicants are protesting their innocence and denying any misbehavior. Indeed, confession is the furthest thing from their minds, for it may well have resulted in punishment which would have been contrary to their goals.[28]

In sum, in Mesopotamia, unexplained suffering gave rise to the idea that the gods had an unfathomable will in terms of what they considered tolerable human behavior. More than that, humans were actually created with moral flaws so that their sinning was inevitable. The only thing that humans could do to relieve their suffering was to be pious in their rituals, confess their inescapable sins generally (specific sins rarely), and plead for mercy in their prayers, all the while knowing that they were not truly at fault. In Egypt, the deceased either confessed unspecified sins or denied any wrongdoing—all in an attempt to be awarded an acceptable afterlife. Confession for general sins combined with sacrifices, then, was the essence of repentance in the ancient Near East.[29]

The Torah Narrative

Admission of wrongdoing occurs two dozen times in the biblical narrative. Sometimes such confession is found in stories where admission of guilt is both divorced from a cultic context and not an attempt to fulfill God's command, but is self-motivated (usually in order to stop or avoid punishment).[30] Sometimes such confession implies that it is a Divine requirement attached to the cult.[31] That so many stories include elements of repentance is quite extraordinary in comparison with ancient Near East narratives—whether about gods or humans—in which remorse is rare.[32]

The longest and most remarkable story of repentance in the Jewish Bible is certainly that of Joseph and his brothers (Gen. 37–45, plus 50:15–21), which contains two exceptional episodes of repentance.

Genesis 38 relates the story of Judah and Tamar. The story assumes a custom in pre-Sinai revelation times of levirate marriage (which becomes Torah law in Deut. 25:5–10), whereby the widow of a man who died childless is given in marriage to his brother. Judah's eldest son dies childless, and Judah gives his wife, Tamar, to the next son. However, he, too, dies childless. Judah fears that Tamar is a jinx and so decides not to give her to his youngest son, under the pretext that he is too young (Gen. 38:11). When Tamar realizes that the youngest son has now become old enough for marriage, but that Judah is not fulfilling his duty by her (38:14), she takes matters into her own hands. She finds out where Judah is going, she dresses up as a prostitute (hiding her face underneath a veil), and sits down on the way Judah is traveling. Judah sees her and, not knowing her true identity, asks her for sexual intercourse.

"What," she asked, "will you pay for sleeping with me?" He replied, "I will send a kid from my flock." But she said, "You must leave a pledge until you have sent it." And he said, "What pledge shall I give you?" She replied, "Your seal and cord, and the staff which you carry." So he gave them to her and slept with her, and she conceived by him. (16–18).

Tamar returned then to her father's house where she had been staying. Judah, in the meantime, sends her a kid goat with a friend, who obviously cannot find her. Judah, unwilling to do harm to his reputation (verse 23), decides not to do a wide search for her in order to reclaim his paraphernalia.

About three months later, Judah finds out that Tamar is pregnant. Since she is technically betrothed to his youngest son, that means, in ancient terms, that she has committed adultery. He pronounces judgment—she is to be burned to death. As she is brought out, she has Judah's things delivered to him, saying,

"I am with child by the man to whom these belong. . . . Examine these: whose seal and cord and staff are these?" Judah recognized them and said, "She is more in the right than I, inasmuch as I did not give her to my son Shelah." And he was not intimate with her again. (25–26)

The story ends by Tamar giving birth to twins (27–30), one of whom will be the ancestor of King David (Ruth 4:18–22)!

Nonetheless, Judah's verbal admission that he was in the wrong and that Tamar was more righteous than he, plus his obvious cancellation of the death sentence, is a clear instance of sincere repentance.

The second and even more moving case of sincere repentance is the central motif of the story of Joseph and his brothers. Joseph's brothers, hating him for his tale-bearing, his egotistical dreams, and their father's favoritism (Gen. 37:2–4, 8), decide to kill him (18–19). But Judah, in order to save his life, persuades the brothers to sell Joseph as a slave to a caravan going to Egypt (28). The brothers then bring the coat their father gave Joseph, dipped in goat's blood, and Jacob makes the intended assumption that Joseph was eaten by a wild animal (31–33). Jacob is disconsolate, but the brothers show no remorse.

Many years pass, and Joseph, whose personality has matured by years in prison and the realization that his dream-interpreting "talent" is due to God, now has become the viceroy of Egypt owing to his interpretation of Pharaoh's dreams and his wise advice on how to save Egypt. When his older brothers suddenly appear before him, sent by Jacob to acquire food from Egypt due to the famine (predicted, unknown to them, by Joseph), Joseph recognizes them. They don't recognize him, for he is much older and dressed as a royal Egyptian. He realizes that he has an opportunity to see if they, too, have morally matured. He sets an elaborate scheme in action that will culminate with the brothers returning to Egypt with their youngest sibling, Benjamin, who is also Joseph's younger and only full brother. For Joseph knows that the reason that the brothers came down the first time without Benjamin is because he was kept at home by their father, for he now is his father's favorite—the only son left from Jacob's beloved dead wife Rachel. When Joseph forces the brothers to return with Benjamin, the question that will be resolved by Joseph's plot is: will the brothers abandon Benjamin in Egypt the way they abandoned Joseph, or will they do everything they can to save him?

As the brothers are unknowingly caught up in the progression of Joseph's scheme, they express guilt over their treatment of Joseph.

They said to one another, "Alas, we are guilty on account of our brother, because we looked on at his anguish, yet paid no heed as he pleaded with us. That is why this distress has come upon us." Then Reuben spoke up and said to them, "Did I not tell you, 'Do no sin against the boy'? But you paid no heed. Now comes the reckoning for his blood." (42:21–22)

Joseph then takes Simeon from them as surety that they will return with their brother, Benjamin. (Or will they abandon Simeon?)

Finally, after Judah convinces Jacob, they come back with Benjamin. Joseph still does not reveal himself to them, but arranges that his special goblet be packed secretly in Benjamin's bag and sends them on their way with all their victuals. Immediately, Joseph sends his house steward after them to lay the accusation that one of them has stolen Joseph's cup. They deny any such crime, but volunteer that anybody who has stolen the cup should die, and they will all become slaves to Joseph. The house steward, undoubtedly on Joseph's instructions, states that only the guilty person will become a slave and the rest will be free to go. When the goblet turns up in Benjamin's bag, they all rend their clothes (in mourning) and return with Benjamin to Joseph's house. The fact that they all return with Benjamin already shows that they do not intend to abandon him. How far will their resolve be carried?

When they arrive at his house, Joseph accuses all of them (44:15). Judah answers for the group, admits that God has uncovered their transgression, and offers them all as slaves to Joseph (16). Joseph, however, insists that only the guilty one shall be his slave, and the rest can go back in peace to their father (17). Judah then pleads on behalf of Benjamin and tells the viceroy that Benjamin is the only child left of his mother and that their aged father will die unless Benjamin is brought back to him (19–31). Therefore, Judah begs Joseph to let him stay to be his slave in place of Benjamin and let the other brothers bring Benjamin back (32–33). As the brothers are innocent of the theft of Joseph's cup, Judah's confession in verse 16 refers to the punishment the brothers are now receiving due to their past crime against Joseph.[33] Judah's plea and confession finally convince Joseph that his brothers have indeed changed, for they are unwilling to abandon Benjamin as they had abandoned him. Joseph then breaks down and reveals himself to his brothers (45:4–15).[34] The test is over.

Nowhere in the ancient Near East or the Bible is there another story such as this. The repentance of Joseph's brothers in their refusal to repeat their sin of abandoning Joseph by also abandoning Benjamin is a precursor to Maimonides' twelfth-century CE definition of complete repentance:

What constitutes complete repentance? He who is confronted by the identical situation wherein he previously sinned and it lies within his power to commit the sin again, but he nevertheless does not succumb because he wishes to repent, and not because he is too fearful or weak [to repeat the sin]. How so? If he had relations with a woman forbidden to him and he is subsequently alone with her, still in the throes of his passion for her, and his virility is unabated, and [they are] in the same place where they previously sinned; if he abstains and does not sin, this is a true penitent. (*Mishneh Torah*, "Laws of Repentance," 2:1)[35]

Joseph's brothers, under Judah's leadership, have fulfilled the *Oxford English Dictionary's* definition of "repent" found at the beginning of this chapter, the last criterion of which is "undertaking to reform in the future." For the first time in recorded history, a human has undertaken an inner transformation of his character that results in improved ethical behavior.[36]

Laws

An entirely new approach to human suffering is presented in the Torah.[37] In the ancient Near East, a person knew that the *cause* of suffering was divine, but one could never be sure *why* he was suffering—because the gods were capricious, or some trespass had occurred due to the gods' intentions being unfathomable, or human character resulted in sinning. That was not the case in the Torah. The Torah's assumptions were categorically opposed to those in the ancient Near East: God was an ethical judge. Due to revelation of the commandments, God's will was known; humans, by dint of their free will, could decide to be continually obedient to God. Thus if suffering was due to Divine punishment, then that punishment was justifiable.[38]

This new approach was the foundation of the Torah's laws on repentance, such as was expressed on the Day of Atonement (or Day of Purgation—Leviticus 16). Since God, within whom divinity was centralized, was known to be "good," then evil was perceived to be a product of human will and behavior only (and not of other deities). Ritual repentance for the combined sins of the nation, particularly the willful, purposeful sins, was carried out by cleansing the inner room of the sanctuary, the Holy of Holies (God's throne room; verses 16–17), of the contamination caused by the people's bad behavior. The cleansing process included the high priest's confession of the people's iniquities preceded by animal sacrifices and accompanied by a communal fast.[39] Thus the once-a-year rituals, confession, and public fast (a unique day of communal self-denial) was felt to represent sincere repentance resulting in Divine forgiveness (and averting severe Divine punishment on the entire nation). It should be noted that, unlike Babylonia, God is perceived as directly interested in the behavior of *all* the people as pertains to His judgment of the nation, and not just that of the king (see the Sinai treaty in chapter 2).

Forbidden acts that were *inadvertently* committed by the community (once they become aware of them) are expiated by purification offerings (animal sacrifices, Lev. 4:13–21), as are such acts done by the community's leaders (22–26) and commoners (27–35). The purpose of the sacrifices in these instances is not for the sake of forgiveness per se. These acts are forgiven because of their accidental nature and the offenders' remorse. Rather, the reason for the sacrifices is that the inadvertent sins of the community have the power to pollute as far as the incense altar (in the first room of the sanctuary), while accidental sins of individuals can only pollute the outer, sacrificial altar (and cannot enter the sanctuary), which is why expiation is made in those places (verse 18 as opposed to verses 30 and 34). Only on the Day of Atonement is expiation made in the Holy of Holies to purge it of the willful sins of individuals and the community, since only those rebellious acts had polluted that far. The principle is simply that God would not want to dwell in a dirty house, and the Israelites, as the only beings whose behavior could pollute the sanctuary, might, as it were, so disgrace "the House of God" that He would no longer choose to "live" there. Therefore, the purpose of the priests' rituals involving the sacrifices was to cleanse the sanctuary of human-produced evil in order to make it "inhabitable" for the Divine presence.[40]

Perhaps the greatest scholar of the rituals of the Torah, Jacob Milgrom, described the rite as "the priestly picture of Dorian Gray" and compared it to its ancient Near East context:

> A sin [by an Israelite] committed anywhere will generate impurity that, becoming airborne, penetrates the sanctuary in proportion to its magnitude. Israel's neighbors also believed that impurity polluted the sanctuary. For them, however, the source of impurity was demonic. Therefore, their priests devised rituals and incantations to immunize their temples against demonic penetration. Israel, however, in the wake of its monotheistic revolution, abolished the world of demonic divinities. Only a single being capable of demonic acts remained—the human being. The humans were even more powerful than their pagan counterparts: they could drive God out of God's sanctuary. . . .

God will not abide in a polluted sanctuary. . . . If the pollution levels
continue to rise, . . . God abandons the sanctuary and leaves the people
to their doom. . . .

Thus . . . the priestly doctrine of collective responsibility. Sinners may
go about apparently unmarred by their evil, but the sanctuary bears
the wounds, and with its destruction, all the sinners will meet their
doom.[41]

And what of the individual's role in repentance? According to the
Torah, no remorse or confession is acceptable *once a perpetrator has
already been apprehended,* for the Bible's innate and wise psychological
assumption is that such an expression of regret would be insincere and
simply a ruse in order to get a reduced punishment. (Why such expressions are not forbidden in modern criminal trials at the sentencing phase
is incomprehensible.) For example, the law is straightforward concerning property theft:

> *When a man steals an ox or a sheep, and slaughters it or sells it, he shall
> pay five oxen for the ox, and four sheep for the sheep.*[42] *. . . He must
> make restitution; if he lacks the means, he shall be sold for his theft.*[43]
> *But if what he stole—whether ox or ass or sheep—is found alive in his
> possession, he shall pay double. . . .*
>
> *When a man gives money or goods to another for safekeeping, and they
> are stolen from the man's house—if the thief is caught, he shall pay
> double. . . . In all charges of misappropriation—pertaining to an ox, an
> ass, a sheep, a garment, or any other loss . . .* he [who is convicted] *shall
> pay double to the other.* (Exod. 21:37–22:8)

In other words, with the exception of the theft and disposal of an ox or
sheep, a robber who is arrested must pay a double restitution to the
victim—the stolen object (or its value) plus a 100 percent fine.

But what happens if the perpetrator, *before he is caught,* feels guilty
over what he has done? In such cases, does the Torah make allowance
for individual remorse? The answer appears in Lev. 5:20–26:

The Lord spoke to Moses, saying: When a person sins by committing a sacrilege against the Lord in that he has dealt deceitfully with his fellow in the matter of a deposit or investment or robbery; or having withheld from his fellow or having found a lost object he has dealt deceitfully about it; and he swears falsely about any one of the things that a person may do and sin thereby—when one has thus sinned, and feeling guilt, he shall return that which he robbed or that which he withheld, or the deposit that was entrusted to him, or the lost object he found, or anything else about which he swore falsely; he shall restore it in its entirety and add one-fifth to it. He shall pay it to its owner as soon as he feels guilt. Then he shall bring to the priest, as his reparation to the Lord, an unblemished ram from the flock, or its assessment, as a reparation offering. The priest shall effect expiation on his behalf before the Lord so that he may be forgiven for whatever he has done to feel guilty thereby.[44]

This text in Leviticus is supplemented by Num. 5:5–8:

The Lord spoke to Moses, saying: Speak to the Israelites: When a man or a woman commits any wrong toward a fellow man [i.e., toward a person], *whereby he commits sacrilege against the Lord, when that person feels guilt, he shall confess the wrong that he has done. He shall make restitution in the principal amount and add one-fifth to it, giving it to him whom he has wronged . . .—in addition to the ram of expiation with which expiation is made on his behalf.*[45]

The above two passages show that a person who has stolen from or defrauded another, but who feels guilty *before he or she is caught,* must confess the crime and immediately make restitution to the victim of the object (or its value) plus a one-fifth fine. A one-fifth fine was imposed for inadvertent sins involving sacred objects (Lev. 5:15–16).[46] Then the culprit brings a reparation offering to the sanctuary. Extremely important ethical innovations are elucidated here concerning civil misdeeds:

- true repentance requires that the wrongdoer not only confess his or her crime but also make restitution to the victim;
- repentance mitigates the penalty payable to the victim. The unre-

pentant perpetrator is required to pay the value of the object plus a 100 percent fine to the victim. However, the repentant perpetrator only compensates the victim with the value of the object plus a 20 percent fine;

- thus the repentance of perpetrators reduces the effect of an intentional crime to that of an accidental one;
- a reparation offering is made by the perpetrator at the sanctuary, which results in (a) cleansing the part of the sanctuary polluted by the culprit's act, and (b) obtaining Divine forgiveness. The reparation offering was an *ethical* obligation, because in the Torah a crime against a human is a crime against God;
- the restitution to the victim *precedes* the reparation offering at the sanctuary. Therefore, compensation to the victim takes precedence over reparation to God![47]

This last innovation reverses the sacrificial norm in the ancient world that offerings to the deity take priority over the needs of humans. Only in the case of repentance in the Torah's laws do obligations to humans—in the form of restitution to victims—delay the duty to God. For the first time in the ancient world, repentance as an act of social justice is perceived as required by God and perhaps places sacrifice in a secondary position, even though that sacrifice is necessary to cleanse the contamination that one has caused in God's sanctuary.[48] To put it differently, in the case of restitution as part of repentance, one's ethical responsibility to one's fellow human takes priority over one's ethical responsibility to God.

The Prophets

The primary verb that dominates prophetic expression of repentance comes from the root *shuv*, "to return, to turn away from, to turn toward." In Milgrom's words,

This root combines in itself both requisites of repentance: to turn from evil and to turn to good. The motion of turning implies that sin is not an eradicable stain but a straying from the right path and that by the effort of turning, a power God has given all men, the sinner can redirect his destiny.[49]

Thus prophetic "repentance" really refers to a religious or covenantal "return."[50] As such, it appears some eighty-five times in prophetic books (twenty-seven times in Jeremiah alone), as opposed to thirty times in the rest of the Jewish Bible,[51] a margin of approximately three to one.[52] It is not simply a return to God in a spiritual sense but a turning away from evil deeds and a return to how God wants one to behave (Jer. 18:11, *"Turn back from your wicked ways, and mend your ways and your actions!"*), a return to the "way" of the Lord (Jer. 5:4, *"for they do not know the way of the Lord"*)—to His commandments, His instructions, and the stipulations of the Sinai treaty (Hosea 8:1, *"because they have transgressed My covenant and have rebelled against My torah"*).

What are the precise components of this "return"?[53] While the eighth-century BCE prophets Amos, Hosea, and Isaiah all use the term, perhaps the best response to this question may be found in Jer. 3:12–13 (a late seventh-century BCE text):

"Return, O backsliding Israel," speech of the Lord, "I will not be angry with you . . . for I am kind. . . . I shall not hold a grudge forever. Only recognize your transgression for you have rebelled against the Lord your God, and you have scattered your ways to strangers [that is, foreign gods] *under every leafy tree, and you have not obeyed my voice"— speech of the Lord.*

In analyzing this brief passage, one can detect four consecutive elements in the process of "return":

1. *"Return, O backsliding Israel"*: God opens the door to repentance by calling to His people to return to Him.[54] No comparable appeal by a god appears in ancient Near Eastern literature outside the Bible. As has been shown above, if the gods want to bring suffering upon a person, a city, or a kingdom, they issue no warning or indication that this misery is because of sin or just

the arbitrary wheel of destiny. In the prophets, in contradistinction, such appeals occur some thirty times![55]

Why does God call the people to repent? Because He is a being of kindness.[56] His anger at the people's wrongful behavior is only temporary.[57] God does not hold a grudge the way people do.[58] What God really wants is for the people to repent so that punishment will not be required. As Ezekiel says (18:21–23):

"If a wicked man repents of all the sins that he committed and keeps all My laws and does what is just and right, he shall surely live; he shall not die. . . . Is it My desire that a wicked man shall die?" says the Lord God. "It is rather that he shall turn back from his [evil] ways, and live."

It is on this ethical basis that the call to Israel to return to God is issued.

2. *"Recognize your transgression"*: Or "know" your sin.[59] Certainly, what is spoken of here is not some neutral understanding, but rather one born from the ethical emotion of regret for wrongdoing. The same verb is used by Jeremiah elsewhere in this sense (2:19, 23):[60]

Let your evil reprove you, let your backslidings rebuke you, and know and see how bitterly evil is your forsaking of the Lord your God. . . . How can you say, "I am not defiled, I have not gone after the Baalim"? Look at your deeds in the valley, know what you have done!

Here, the example of the sin that the people are to acknowledge and regret is the worship of foreign deities. This is characteristic of Jeremiah's early prophecies. However, Jeremiah 7 castigates the people also for their ethical crimes. Regret for sin is often accompanied by confession and expressions of remorse, such as in Jer. 31:18–19.[61]

I have surely heard Ephraim [North Israel] lamenting, "You have chastised me, and I am chastised, like a calf that has not been broken. Bring me back that I may return [to You] for You are the Lord, My God. For after I had turned [away from You], I became regretful, and after I became aware [from the verb "to know"] [of my sin], *I smote my thigh* (a sign of remorse). *I am ashamed and humiliated, for I bear the disgrace of my youth."*

3. *"For you have rebelled against the Lord your God"*: The implication of these words is that the people must stop their deliberate sinning. A "rebellious" sin is one that is done intentionally in wanton defiance against God.[62] Cessation of such sins is essential if one truly wishes to return to God, as in Jer. 26:2–3.

Thus said the Lord, "Stand in the court of the House of the Lord and speak to [the men of] all the towns of Judah, who are coming to worship in the House of the Lord. . . . Perhaps they will listen and turn back, each from his evil way, that I may renounce the punishment I am planning to bring upon them for their wicked acts."

4. *"and have not obeyed My voice"*: The inference here is that the return to God is not complete until the people fulfill His will by obeying His commandments and instructions.[63] In other words, after they cease to do evil, they must now do good, as in Amos 5:4–6, 14–15:

Thus said the Lord to the House of Israel: "Seek Me and you will live. . . ." Seek the Lord and you will live.

Seek good and not evil, that you may live, and that the Lord, the God of Hosts, may truly be with you. . . . Hate evil and love good, and establish justice in the gate;[64] perhaps the Lord, the God of Hosts, will be gracious to the remnant of Joseph (North Israel).

Similarly, Isa. 1:16–17:

Wash yourselves clean; put away your evil doings from My sight. Cease to do evil; learn to do good. Seek after justice; aid the wronged. Judge the rights of the orphan; argue on behalf of the widow.

Jeremiah 26:4–6, the continuation of the verses cited in point 3 above, focus on the necessity of following God's commands in the Torah.

Thus said the Lord: "If you do not obey Me, following My Torah that I have set before you, heeding the words of My servants the prophets [to repent] whom I have been sending to you per-

*sistently . . . then I will make this House like Shiloh, and I will
make this city a curse for all the nations of the earth.*"[65]

To summarize, the four elements of the process of repentance are (1)
an act of God's caring by giving people the option to repent in order to
avoid destruction and/or exile; (2) acknowledgment of sin accompanied
by remorse; (3) cessation of evil, of disobeying God; (4) return to God's
ways by obedience to His commandments.

The previous section showed that the Torah's laws concerning repentance deal both with the individual as part of the society as a whole
(Leviticus 16, Yom Kippur—the Day of Purgation) and the individual
within his or her own immediate context (Lev. 4, 5; Num. 5—inadvertent
sins or sins converted from intentional to accidental). The latter context requires the guilty party not only to repent to God but also to
repent to the victim through confession and compensation. That two-
pronged approach is characteristic of the Torah's legal traditions, which
view the individual's actions as affecting both one's own life and the
destiny of the community, for the laws are also the stipulations of the
Sinai covenant.

This two-sided approach does *not* appear in prophetic literature. The
prophets perceive each individual within the context of the covenant,
perhaps because they see destruction and possibly exile on the horizon
threatening the entire society. Therefore, the prophets concentrate on
repentance in terms of the impact that it can have to ward off Divine
punishment on the polity.[66] In other words, once Israel has sinned, and
while the people still dwell in a divinely ordained state in the land of
Israel, they must repent in order to avoid destruction and exile.[67] Unlike
the Torah's laws, the prophets do not mention the obligation of the guilty
party to confess to and compensate the human victim. This may simply
be due to their acceptance of Torah law, and their silence does not indicate any opposition to it. However, another factor is at play here. As
stated above, the overarching prophetic term for repentance is *shuv*,
"return." To whom or to what can one return? Only to God and to His
commandments/paths (that is, the way of life in accord with His revealed
will), for the prophets claimed that both were abandoned by the Israelites. Because of the prophetic focus on using the term *shuv* in reference

to a spiritual return to God, one couldn't very well talk about a similar kind of spiritual "return" to a human.

Of course, by fulfilling the third and fourth elements of the prophetic process of repentance to God—ceasing to do evil and obeying God's instructions—gain will accrue to former victims, a kind of "collateral benefit," although certainly these are key objectives in the Divine goal of creating a just and righteous society.[68]

As mentioned above, in prophetic thought, if the people truly repent, God promises to respond by accepting the people back without any punishment whatsoever for their past sins, as in Jer. 18:6–8:[69]

> *"Behold like the clay in the hands of the potter, so are you in My hands, O House of Israel! At one moment I may decree that a nation or a king-dom shall be uprooted and pulled down and destroyed; but if that nation against which I have made the decree turns back from its wickedness, I will relent concerning the punishment I planned to bring on it."*

This prophetic innovation goes beyond the Torah's laws, for in those laws, repentance mitigates the punishment but does not eliminate it altogether.[70] The prophets, however, expanded the power of repentance and, therefore, of God's forgiveness by decreeing that true "return" abol-ishes the possibility of punishment. Such ethical graciousness could not have been imagined by the other peoples of the ancient Near East.

A Note on Theodicy

It must be noted that the dominant approach in the Jewish Bible to com-prehending God's stated expectations of Israel's relationship to Him, and His reaction to the Israelites' behavior, is reward and punishment. If the people are obedient to God, they will be rewarded; if disobedient, punishment will ensue. This system not only prevails in the Torah and the Prophets but also in the historiographic books: Joshua, Judges, Samuel, Kings, Ezra, Nehemiah, and Chronicles.[71] Repentance adjusts this system in favor of the Israelites. It gives the people another oppor-tunity to comply with God's instructions and thus to receive His bounty rather than to be sentenced to disaster. The images that lie behind this structure are that of the God-Israel relationship perceived as Judge-judged, Parent-child, and King-subject. In reality, this system of equitable Divine retribution is one of theodicy, the justification of the good God in the face of the existence of evil.[72]

The above arrangement, in turn, is based upon the ubiquitous scriptural reiteration of God's goodness.[73] Thus God is good, His creation is good, His will as crystallized in His commandments is good, human obedience to that will is good, the reward for that obedience is good, and repentance is good.

Unfortunately, the one variable in this equation is human obedience to God. Disobedience is, by definition, evil, and the recompense for that disobedience, that is, Divine punishment that results in human suffering, is also termed "evil," as in Jer. 18:8, 11:

> *if that nation turns back from its evil* [behavior] [Hebrew, ra'ah], *I will relent concerning the punishment* [ra'ah] *I planned to bring on it. . . . Thus said the Lord: 'Behold, I am forming disaster* [ra'ah] *against you and laying plans against you. Turn back each of you from your evil* [ra'ah] *ways.*

That people have free will to choose good or evil is a biblical assumption and the source of tension between the Divine command and its human fulfillment. In the Noah story, humanity is seen as basically selfish, and it is a biblical axiom that *"there is no man who does not sin"* (1 Kings 8:46).[74] So human inclination toward evil results in evil actions, that is, disobedience to God's will. The direct result of the people's evil is their suffering (God's just punishment), which, too, is termed "evil," as in Jeremiah 18 above. Of course, God has warned the people of this suffering in the "curses" of the Sinai treaty in Lev. 26:14–39 and their rewording in Deut. 28:15–68.

However, these two fundamental concepts—that of God's goodness and of human inclination to evil, with their respective implications—are not always accepted in the Jewish Bible itself. It is an irony of biblical thought that just as the acknowledgment of human evil arises out of human experience, so it is human experience of a different kind that raises the greatest challenge to that concept. For if human suffering results from God's just response to human evil, then how can it be that the wicked prosper and the righteous suffer? Indeed, the challenge to the system of Divine reward and punishment primarily takes the form of bewildered questioning, often bitter, often painful. In Jer. 12:1, the prophet says, *"You are righteous, O Lord, though I contend with You. Yet I would bring charges against You:—Why does the way of the wicked prosper? Why are the workers of treachery at ease?"* (Also Ps. 10:1–2, 13), *"Why, O Lord, do You stand aloof, heedless in times of trouble? The wicked in his arrogance hounds the needy. . . . Why should the wicked man scorn God, thinking that You will not call* [him] *to account?"* (Similarly Job 10:1–3), *"I am disgusted with life. . . . I will speak to the bitterness of my soul. I say to God, 'Do not condemn me; let me know what You charge me with. Does it benefit You to oppress, to despise the toil of Your hands, while smiling on the counsel of the wicked?'"*

It is instructive that only rarely do these expressions of unjust human suffering take an accusatory, rather than a pleading, tone toward God, such as Jer. 15:18, *"Why must my pain be perpetual, my wound incurable, resistant to healing? You have been to me like a spring that fails, like waters that cannot be relied upon."* A most poignant enunciation of complaint against God for the unjust sufferings of the people appears in Ps. 44:18–25.

> *All this has come upon us, yet we have not forgotten You, or been false to Your covenant. Our hearts have not gone astray, nor have our feet swerved from Your path, though You have crushed us. . . . If we forgot the name of our God and spread forth our hands to a foreign god, God would surely search it out, for He knows the secrets of the heart. It is for Your sake that we are slain all day long, that we are regarded as sheep to be slaughtered. Rouse Yourself; why do You sleep, O Lord? . . . Why do You hide Your face, ignoring our affliction and distress?*[75]

The Psalmist's accusation of God here is based upon the people's innocence. Particularly meaningful is the question *"Why do You sleep, O Lord?"* because the Psalmist well knows that God is beyond nature and has no need of sleep. However, his question is purposely insulting. He is speaking to God as if the Lord were a pagan deity who is a natural being and therefore needs to sleep (and eat, drink, etc.)! The Psalmist is so desperate that he is willing to risk God's wrath in order to arouse His justice.

The above questioning of God's justice is peculiar to those who believe in ethical monotheism and the first to be asked by such believers. We have already seen, via the ancient Near East texts brought at the beginning of this chapter, that the ancient Near Eastern deities were perceived to be capricious. Thus they could not be expected to consistently behave in any kind of just manner; it was rare that a human understood why a god was causing suffering. Evil was a common reality in the ancient Near East world because different deities had different roles (some are demonic, others are more caring), humans erred unknowingly, humans were ignorant about the mystery of the gods' will, and the gods created humans with moral flaws.[76] Ethical monotheists, though, require an acceptable response to unjustified evil in order to maintain their belief in the goodness of God, and therefore in God, period. Thus the above questions led to a new construction of theodicy: the vindication of God's goodness despite the apparent existence of *unjustifiable* evil. The Jewish Bible provides numerous responses, each dependent upon the individual author:

- Evil is a result of the actions of wicked people against the righteous or innocent—a theme in Psalms, such as 11:2, *"For behold, the wicked bend the bow, they set their arrow on the string to shoot from the shadows at the upright."*[77] In other words, God has given all humans freedom of choice, which means that some people will choose to do evil to others. The Psalmists, however, never abandon the hope that the success of the wicked and the pain of the righteous is only a temporary condition that God will eventually correct: *"Away from me, all you evildoers, for the Lord heeds the sound of my weeping. . . . All my enemies will become despondent and stricken with terror"* (Ps. 6:9–11).[78]
- The temporary nature of the suffering of the righteous (perhaps in pain in their organs) is seen also in their being "tested" by God: *"You have visited me at night, tested my heart, refined me, and found nothing amiss"* (Ps. 17:3).[79]

   The idea of the suffering of the righteous due to a Divine test leads into the narrative introduction to the book of Job (an entire book devoted to the problem of theodicy), chapters 1 and 2. Job is *"blameless and upright."* He would even sacrifice sin-offerings to God on the off-chance that his children had sinned (Job 1:1–5).[80] On a *"day that the divine beings presented themselves to God"* (verse 6), the Lord points out Job's greatness, his reverence of God, and his shunning of evil to the *satan*—Hebrew for "adversary" (verse 8; the *satan* is not God's adversary but that of humans). The "adversary" is here presented as a kind of cynical, hardboiled police detective who disbelieves the pure righteousness of any person. Hence he challenges God that Job is only upright because he has been rewarded with wealth, children, and good health (verses 9–11; 2:4–5). God, out to prove Job's righteousness to the *satan*, permits the latter to destroy (at least some of) Job's property, kill Job's ten children, and inflict Job with a severe case of boils (1:12–19; 2:6–7). Yet Job responds with two famous verses. The first is 1:21 (after his children have died): *"Naked came I out of my mother's womb, and naked shall I return there; the Lord has given, and the Lord has taken away; blessed be the name of the Lord."* The second verse, in reaction to his wife's urging that he should end his misery by blaspheming God and dying (2:9), is Job's rebuke followed by his rhetorical question in 2:10, *"Should we accept only good from God and not accept evil?"*

The notion that God uses Job as a pawn, causing him heinous suffering, in order to prove a point on a dare is surely odious to modern sensibilities. However, the scenario above conceals a deeper issue: does human loyalty to God result only from reward—expected or received—or is such loyalty due to a reverence for God that supersedes any material consideration—either positive or negative? That issue is also at stake in the rest of the poetic book of Job (3:2–42:6). Is God only justified, or deserving of human worship, due to equitable reward and punishment? If the righteous suffer for no just reason, is God still worthy of devotion? Perhaps the key vehicle for answering this question is the theophany out of the whirlwind (and Job's reaction) in chapters 38–42, yet scholarly interpretation of these chapters has been highly conflicting.[81] Without engaging the scholarly debate in depth, it seems that a reasonable conclusion from these chapters is that Job (and his friends)

speak from a very limited perspective, that of the human condition. Humanity is a mere speck on the cosmic windshield, that is,
people are ignorant or do not take into consideration the immea-
surable work of the Creator who is responsible for the entire universe and all life within it. First God expounds on His creation and
organization of nature. *"Where were you when I laid the earth's
foundations? . . . On to what were its bases sunk?"* (38:4, 6). This
Divine peroration continues with descriptions of God's control of
the sea (8–11), His command of the light of day (which entraps the
wicked, 12–15), the gates of death and darkness (16–18), precipita-
tion (snow, hail, rain, 22–30, 34–38), and the constellations (31–33).
God then turns to His provisions for the animal kingdom: the lion,
raven, mountain goat, wild ass, wild ox, ostrich, the horse, hawk,
and eagle (38:39–39:30). To all this, Job admits his own lack of
worth and renders himself speechless (40:3–5).

God then resumes His thunderous oration. *"Would you impugn
My justice? Would you condemn Me that you may be right?"* (40:8),
reminding Job that he has constantly stated that he is undeserving
of his suffering, for he did no wrong. God continues by rhetorically
asking Job to condemn and deal with all arrogant people, as God
does, thereby implying that Job himself is arrogant. For what
human can challenge the justness of God without that challenge
being an act of hubris (11–14)? On the same theme, God illustrates
His incomparable power by describing the gigantic and terrifying
aspects of the two monsters, Behemoth and Leviathan, which only
He tames (40:15–41:26). After hearing all this, Job finally responds
(42:1–6), *"Indeed, I spoke without understanding of things too won-
drous for me which I did not know. . . . By the ear I have heard you,
and now my eye has seen you. Therefore, I am disgusted* [with myself
or my own words] *and repent* [for what I said], [sitting] *on dust
and ashes."*[82] The purpose of God's speech over chapters 38–41
appears to be to induce humility in Job by pointing out His might
in creating and ordering the cosmos and His care for all living
things. In the face of such awesomeness, just retribution for human
behavior must sometimes take a backseat.

The ending narrative of the book, in which God restores Job's fortunes and gives him twice what he had before (42:10,12), plus another seven sons and three daughters (42:13), and more, seems contrived, as if his first children (1:2) could so easily be replaced. The message of this section seems to be that eventually the righteous will be rewarded. However, that hardly agrees with the preceding Divine theophany.

- Rarely is human suffering through illnesses explicated by natural causes. Such an exception appears concerning the good king Asa in 1 Kings 15:23: *"Only, in his old age, he became ill in his legs."* The Chronicler, though, as is his wont to explain all suffering as the result of sin, finds fault with Asa: *"In the thirty-ninth year of his reign, Asa became ill in his legs, yet ill as he was, he did not seek the Lord, but physicians"* (2 Chron. 16:12). This verse clearly indicates that Asa, by only consulting physicians without praying to God, perceived his illness as due solely to natural causes.

  Additionally, Ecclesiastes 3 views the ups and downs of life as being part of the Divine order of the universe, but not as God's response to human behavior.[83]

- The biblical concepts of corporate personality and collective responsibility gave rise to other reasons for the suffering of the innocent. Jeremiah, Ezekiel, and Lamentations all express the popular view that the people have suffered for the sins of their ancestors: Jer. 31:29 (with the difference of one letter, identical to Ezek. 18:2), *"Parents have eaten sour grapes and the children's teeth are set on edge"*; Lam. 5:7, *"Our fathers have sinned and are no more, and we have suffered [for] their iniquities."* The famous passage of Isaiah 53 is unique in its description of the righteous servant of God, whether an individual or a group, undergoing misery for the sins of the people.

  It is noteworthy that in the late biblical period, the temptation to evil is personified in the figure of the "adversary," *satan.* Aside from Job 1–2, an instructive comparison can be seen between 2 Samuel and the appearance of the *satan* in 1 Chronicles in clarifying how David came to the sinful decision to order a census of the people—sinful because a census would contradict God's promise to the patriarchs to make their descendants so numerous as to be uncountable (for example, Gen. 13:16). Here are the key opening verses from each text:

> 2 Samuel 24:1. *"The anger of the Lord again flared up against Israel; and He incited David against them saying, 'Go and number Israel and Judah.'"*
>
> 1 Chronicles 21:1. *"Satan arose against Israel and incited David to number Israel."*

Note that the Chronicler apparently cannot impute any evil to God, and thus replaces "the Lord" in 2 Samuel with *"Satan,"* that is, the adversary against humans. It is fascinating that the book of Samuel here has no such compunctions.

- The Scroll of Esther, a very late biblical book, does not even mention God! Nonetheless, the story's plot has too many "coincidences" to not assume that someone is pulling the strings behind the scenes: During Esther's youth, Queen Vashti is deposed, setting the scene for Esther's entrance (1:19). A "beauty contest" is held (to be judged by the king in his chambers) to determine the next queen, and Esther is taken as a "contestant" (2:8). None of the virgins who precede her win the king's heart before she is brought to his palace (2:16–17). Mordecai just happens to learn of a plot to kill the king (2:22; he reveals it to Esther, the two conspirators are killed, and Mordecai's deed is recorded in the king's records, vs. 23). Haman, enraged at Mordecai for not bowing to him, decides to kill both Mordecai and all the Jews. So he casts a "lot" and the date of genocide falls almost a full year away, time enough to undue his nefarious plans (3:5–7). When Mordecai beseeches Esther to go to the king to save the people, he raises the possibility that Esther's appointment as queen was no accident—*"and who knows if it was for a time such as this that you attained royalty?"* (4:14). When the king is unable to sleep, he orders his records to be read to him, and it just happens that what is related is Mordecai's informing on those who wished to assassinate the king (6:1–2). The message of the story then is that even when things look darkest, and God seemingly is nowhere to be found, He is working behind the scenes to save the innocent.
- Finally, in the apocalyptic section at the end of the book of Daniel

(perhaps the last words written into the Jewish Bible), the righteous will be resurrected to eternal life and the wicked to eternal revulsion (12:1–2): *"At that time, your people will be rescued—all who are found inscribed in the book. And many of those that sleep in the dust of the earth will awake, some to eternal life, and some to reproaches and eternal abhorrence."* This is the only text in the Hebrew Bible that may prefigure the concepts of the world to come and hell. "The world to come" is a common rabbinic vision of life after death that has the advantage of settling all accounts justly. For example, the Babylonian Talmud, Tractate Kiddushin 40b, records, "Rabbi Elazar the son of Rabbi Zadok said, 'The Holy One Blessed be He brings suffering on the righteous in this world so that they will inherit the world to come.'" In other words, the righteous are requited for their few bad deeds in this world so that they will be rewarded for their many good deeds in the world to come.[84]

The above survey is far from comprehensive, and it only presents in broad strokes some of the representative statements in the Jewish Bible on the problem of theodicy. It is noteworthy that no attempt is made to come up with one, single overarching perspective. Indeed, classical Jewish writing after the Bible—the Talmud, midrashic works, Jewish philosophic writings—will enunciate numerous explanations for the suffering of the righteous and the prosperity of the wicked. Perhaps the reason for so many viewpoints is the consciousness of the authors of the Tradition that theodicy is such a thorny problem that no one position will suffice for everybody. Rather, each person must find his or her own path to the acceptance of Divine sovereignty even when just retribution is absent.

The Jewish Bible still believes in a God of just reward and punishment, even if present reality does not always support that faith. Eventually Judaism will evolve to the more mature perspective that one obeys the commandments not because one expects or seeks reward but because it is what one should do. Thus in the first chapter of the Mishnah of *Pirkei Avot* (literally, "Chapters of the Fathers"), 1:3, Antigonus of Socho (third century BCE?) is cited as stating, "Be not like servants who serve the master in order to receive a reward; instead, be like the servants who serve the master not in order to receive a reward. And let the awe of Heaven be upon you."[85]

6

The Establishment of Hope

The Prophetic Promise of Redemption

The previous chapter on repentance emphasized that the prophets required the Israelites to return to God and His ways in order to avoid destruction and exile. Nevertheless, according to the Jewish Bible, what if the people do not repent, and destruction and exile become unavoidable and eventually overpower the people? Does this tragedy spell the end to the God-Israel relationship? Must the people wander in exile forever—without God, without land, without hope—and finally lose their identity through assimilation? Are the people of Israel to become just one more small nation—like Moab, Edom, Ammon, Aram, Philistia—who flourished for a time and then disappeared into the mists of the past? [1]

Or, despite destruction and exile, does the Bible posit a positive eschatology, an optimism about the people's future destiny in which God redeems Israel from exile?[2] Will the relationship of the people worshiping God in its land be reestablished? Will the grand experiment to create a just Israelite society continue? If so, how will the people maintain their national religious identity in exile? As will be seen, it was the prophetic vision of redemption and restoration that instilled the people with their belief and hope that God had not abandoned them, but would ultimately save them and return them to their land and to their relationship with Him.

However, before we can claim an Israelite prophetic innovation, we must examine ancient Near East literature for evidence of a faith in an ultimate positive destiny.

The Ancient Near Eastern Background

The oldest ancient Near East texts available that relate to restoration are Sumerian laments on the destruction of the Third Dynasty of Ur, which ruled over southern Mesopotamia, a victim of invaders at the end of the third millennium BCE. The *Lament for Ur* states that the chief gods were responsible for the destruction, but it does not provide a reason.[3] The chief goddess of Ur, Ningal, pleads with them to no avail:

> After they had pronounced the utter destruction of Ur . . .
> On that day verily I abandoned not my city;
> My land verily I forsake not.
> To Anu the water of my eye verily I poured;
> To Enlil I in person verily made supplication.
> "Let not my city be destroyed," verily I said unto them; . . .
> "Let not its people perish" . . .
> Verily Anu changed not this word;
> Verily Enlil with its "It is good; so be it" soothed not my heart . . .
> The utter destruction of Ur verily they directed;
> That its people be killed, as its fate verily they decreed.

Ningal's plea above illustrates the complete lack of mercy with which the chief gods decide upon Ur's destruction, neither for her tears nor for the death of the people.

The lament closes with Ningal's prayer for the restoration of Ur, directed to the chief god of Ur, the moon god Nanna:

> From days of old when (first) the land was founded.
> O Nanna, have worshipful men, laying hold of your feet,
> Brought to you their tears over the silent Temple, their chanting
>   (allowed) before you;

So with the dark-headed people cast away from you, let them (yet)
    make obeisance to you,
With the city laid in ruins, let it yet tearfully implore you,
(and) O Nanna!—With your restoring the city, let it rise into view
    again before you,
And not set as set the bright stars. . . .
The personal god of a human has brought a greeting gift,
a (human) supplicant is beseeching you.
O Nanna, you having mercy on the country,
. . . you having, according to what your heart prompts,
Absolved, O Nanna, the sins of that man,
The man who beseeches you, an anointed one, may you bring your
    heart to relent toward him,
And having looked truly upon the supplicant who stands here for them,
O Nanna, whose penetrating gaze searches to bowels,
May their hearts, that have suffered (so much) evil appear pure to you.
May the hearts of your ones who are in the land appear good to you,
And, O Nanna!—in your city again restored they will offer up
    praise for you!

Ningal's prayer for restoration here is not to the great gods but to the chief god of Ur, Nanna. (Prayers for redemption are also included in laments in the Jewish Bible.)[4] Perhaps he will have mercy on the remnant. The few humans who have survived have given up neither their piety nor their hope. The goddess's prayer, as it were, is said on their behalf.[5]

The *Lamentation over the Destruction of Sumer and Ur* contains a similar description of why Ur met its end:

The gods An, Enlil, Enki, and Ninmah decided its fate.
Its fate, which cannot be changed, who can overturn it—
Who can oppose the commands of An and Enlil?[6]

In other words, no reason is given for the destruction of Ur other than the decision of the gods. This decision is then challenged by Sin (another name for Nanna), who confronts his father, the great god Enlil, concerning the illogic of his decree:

> O father who begot me, why have you turned away from Ur, the
>   city that was built for you? . . .
> The boat with first-fruit offerings no longer brings the first-fruit
>   offerings to the father who begot me. . . .
> Enlil, my city of Ur, which is all alone, return to your embrace. . . .
> Oh, the righteous temple! . . . Oh, its people, its people!

Enlil answers:

> My son, . . . why do you concern yourself with crying? . . .
> The judgment of the assembly cannot be turned back. . . .
> Ur was indeed given kingship (but) it was not given an eternal reign.
> From time immemorial, since the land was founded, until the pop-
>   ulation multiplied,
> Who has ever seen a reign of kingship that would take precedence
>   (forever)?
> The reign of its kingship had been long indeed but had to exhaust itself,
> O my Nanna, do not exert yourself (in vain), leave your city!

Enlil gives two responses to Nanna—first, that what the gods' assembly
has decreed cannot be turned back and, second, that nothing lasts forever. No human reign is permanent! Nanna's tears are in vain. He must
accept the situation as is. Nonetheless, after one last plea from Nanna,
the lamentation nears its end with Enlil's assurance that Ur will be reestablished:

> Enlil then provides a favorable response to his son:
> Ur shall be rebuilt in splendor, may the people bow down (to you),
> There is to be bounty at its base, there is to be grain. . . .
> May Ur . . . be restored for you!
> Having pronounced his blessing, Enlil raised his head toward the
>   heavens, saying:
> May the land . . . be organized for Nanna,
> May the road(s) of the land be set in order for Sin! . . .
> By order of An and Enlil (abundance) shall be bestowed!

The lament then concludes with a prayer to the great gods for numerous favorable blessings, each one followed by the words "may An not change it." Among others, these blessings include the total retreat of the enemy (characterized as "the storm"), the gods treating the people with justice, travel on the roads, water in the Tigris and Euphrates, rain and good crops, fish and fowl in the marshes, agricultural produce, a fully populated land, rebuilt cities, and that everybody be cared for. The last words are addressed to Nanna.

O Nanna, your kingship is sweet, return to your place!
Let its people lie down in safe pastures, let them copulate!
. . . O Nanna—oh, your city! Oh, your temple! Oh, your people!

The description of restoration in this lament embodies within it elements that will reappear in biblical prophecies of redemption over a thousand years later—agricultural abundance, repopulation, rebuilt cities, restitution of kingship (here, to the chief god of Ur), justice, peace and prosperity. However, due to the huge disparity in time and geography, it is difficult to conceive of a way in which this Sumerian text could possibly have been known to biblical writers. On the other hand, that these themes appear in both places is unsurprising, since it is a common phenomenon to construct a future on the recollection, or image, of an idealized past—and the notions of agricultural plenty, populated land, teeming cities, justice, peace and prosperity would be common ideals throughout the ancient Near East.

Two major differences should be noted between these Sumerian texts and their later biblical counterparts. In Sumer, the ones identified as pleading with the great gods for restoration, and to whom the great gods respond, are always lesser deities. The human voice, as it were, is not heard, for such voices would have been below the purview of the gods. Not so in the Bible. Second, no exile is mentioned and, therefore, no return from exile—the dominant theme of restoration prophecies in the Jewish Bible.

One last Sumerian text is the *Lament for Isin* in which its chief goddess, Nininsina, laments the destruction of her temple and pleads with Enlil that it be restored:

> My father, may it be restored! When? May it be restored! You
>   decreed it!
> My father Enlil, may it be restored! . . .
> I—let me go into my house, let me go in, let me lie down. . . .
> I—let me go into my storehouse, let me go in, let me lie down. . . .
> I—let me lie down to sleep in my house, its sleep was sweet . . . its
>   bed was good.[7]

Here, the goddess begs for the restoration of her temple, which presumably would not occur without the restoration of the city, for who would rebuild the temple and provide her comforts if not the people of the city? Nonetheless, she appears to be concerned only with her own desires and not at all with the needs of the people.[8]

Egypt also provides some "prophetic" texts on restoration. However, these, like the other texts below, are apparently fake prophecies, that is, they present themselves as prophecies of the future, but in reality praise the reign of a current monarch.[9] One such text is *The Prophecies of Neferti*, a political statement composed apparently at the court of Amenemhet I (1990–1960 BCE), but purporting to originate in the court of Snefru (Fourth Dynasty, ca. 2613–2589 BCE).[10] After listing a variety of calamities (due to enemies, nature, social upheaval) that have beset the land, Neferti, a wise scribe, "predicts" the arrival of a redeemer king, Ameny. This is a purposely poorly concealed reference to the king to whom Neferti speaks, Amenemhet I, whose short name is, indeed, Ameny:[11]

> Then a king will come from the south,
> Ameny, the justified, is his name. . . .
> He will unite the Two Mighty Ones,[12] . . .
> Rejoice, O people of his time,
> The son of man will make his name forever and ever.
> They who incline toward evil,
> Who plot rebellion. . . .
> The Asiatics will fall to his slaughter,
> The Libyans will fall to his flame,
> The rebels to his wrath, the traitors to his might. . . .
> Then order will come into its place

While wrongdoing is driven out.[13]
Joyful will be he who will observe and he who will serve the king.

This ideal king (Amenemhet I) did unite Upper and Lower Egypt, drive away the enemies, and restore order.[14] The notion of a future king who will punish the wrongdoers of the nations and provide order and protection also appears in some biblical prophecies of redemption.[15]

Five later Akkadian texts, too, have been identified by scholarship as speaking of some level of restoration. However, these five texts are also written "after the fact," that is, they are not prophecies of the future but "predictions" of the past, and they were written either in support of a current monarch or to describe the deeds of a past one.[16] The two oldest among these are the Shulgi and Marduk prophecies (perhaps both late second millennium BCE). In the former, Shulgi, a king and a god who founded Nippur, discusses the kings who will succeed him. After Nippur is destroyed, he states,

By the order of E[nlil], the [r]eign of the king of Babyl[on] will
    come to an end. . . .
A certain one . . . will a[rise] . . . he will restore Girsu and Lagash.
    He will renew. The [san]ctuary of the gods will be (re)built. . . .
[. . . the sanctu]ary of Nippur . . . Isin . . . will be (re)built.[17]

Since the text comes some thousand years after the reign of Shulgi, its purpose apparently is to validate a reigning king.[18] However, the text indicates a reasonable desire that demolished temples will be rebuilt—in similarity to certain later biblical prophecies.

In the *Marduk Prophecy*, the god Marduk is depicted as describing his travels until he returns to Babylon.[19] At that point,

A king of Babylon will arise, and he will renew the temple. . . . He
    will lead me and bring me into my city Babylon . . . forever.
. . . he will see the goodness of the god. . . . his [rei]gn will be long.
That prince will be strong. . . .
That prince will make the land feed on the splendor of his
    grass(lands). His days will be long. . . .

He will cause the temples to shine like gems. All the gods he will
bring bac[k]. He will gather in the scattered land an[d] make
firm its foundations. . . .

The rivers will bring [fi]sh; field (and) mead[ow] will be full of
yield; the grass of [wi]nter (will last) to summer; the grass of
summer will last to winter. The harvest of the land will prosper;
the market will be favorable. Evil will be set right; disturbances
will be cleared up, evil will be brought to light. . . . Brother will
love brother; a son will rever[e] his father like a god. . . . Compassion will be established among the people. . . . That prince
[will ru]le [all the lands.] I an[d] all the gods, having befriended
him, will destroy Elam.[20]

Rather than predicting a future ideal king, the text was apparently written toward the end of the reign of Nebuchadnezzar I (1126–1103 BCE) in
order to serve as "a propaganda piece" to support his campaigns and to
glorify his reign.[21] As such, it is not comparable to the biblical prophecies of redemption which originate prior to the return to the land under
Persian rule, even though those prophecies will look forward to agricultural increase and a just society.

Three "after the fact" texts come from the seventh century BCE and
later: *Text A (Prophecies)*; the *Uruk Prophecy*; the *Dynastic Prophecy*.
Text A is the most obscure, but apparently originates in seventh century
BCE Assyria and tells of events that took place five centuries earlier. It
contains themes of agricultural increase, good kingship, and a more
ethical society, similar to the *Marduk Prophecy* above.[22] The late fourth
century BCE *Dynastic Prophecy* resembles the apocalyptic passages of
Daniel.[23] In the *Uruk Prophecy*, after the reign of several bad kings, one
finds the following (lines 11–18),

After him a king will arise in the midst of Uruk who will render
judgments for the land and will establish decisions for the land. He
will establish the rites of Anu in Uruk. . . . He will rebuild the temples of Uruk and restore the houses of the gods. He will renew Uruk . . .
and will refill the rivers and irrigated fields with abundance and pro-
ductivity. After him, his son will arise as king in Uruk and rule the

entire world. He will exercise authority and kingship in Uruk, his dynasty will stand forever. The kings of Uruk will exercise authority like the gods.[24]

This text was most probably written at the end of the reign of Nebuchadnezzar ("a king will arise") or at the beginning of the brief reign of his son, Awel-Marduk (562–560 BCE), in order to support him ("his son will arise as king"). However, the latter was assassinated by his successor, Neriglissar.[25] Once again, one sees the themes of a king establishing order, the restoration of the cult, agricultural abundance, and a permanent dynasty (symbolizing social order and peace)—all typical ideals of common ancient Near East society.

It appears that in the extant material, the only genuine texts portraying restoration are the Sumerian laments, while the others represent fictionalized depictions. What then do all these texts have to say about an eschatology (a vision of a divinely molded future that is radically different than normal human life)? As Paul Hanson states, in the Mesopotamian's perception,

> The rise and fall of empires reflected decisions in a divine assembly which was not bound by any historical sequence. One decision leads to the rise of Akkad to hegemony over the city states, another to its fall. The same pattern leads to the rise of Ur, and then to its fall; again to the rise of Babylon, and its fall. No common line connects these separate threads in an unbroken development. They are but separate episodes reflecting isolated decisions in the divine assembly.[26]

Hartmut Gese concluded concerning the Mesopotamian conception of history that there was "no thought of the development of one condition out of another in the course of time, let alone the idea that history has a goal and a purpose."[27] In short, even though people in the ancient Near East certainly had an understanding of what an ideal world and kingship might look like, no evidence exists that they knew of, or looked forward to, such a divinely ordained future—with the possible exception of the ancient Sumerian *Lament over the Destruction of Sumer and Ur.*[28]

Redemption in the Jewish Bible

Unlike the relative paucity of materials in the ancient Near East, future redemption is a ubiquitous theme in the Jewish Bible, emphasized primarily in the Latter Prophets but appearing also in the Torah, Psalms, Lamentations, Daniel, Ezra-Nehemiah, and Chronicles.[29] The material is wide and varied and too much to deal with here in an exhaustive analysis. This section, therefore, will seek to focus on only certain aspects: the literal socio-legal understanding of the Hebrew terms for "redemption" and their transference into a metaphor of the God-Israel relationship; the conceptual meaning of future redemption—the characteristics of that eschatological age; the circumstances (that is, the conditional elements) necessary for redemption to occur; and the significance of the prophetic legacy on redemption for future generations.

The Socio-Legal Terminology of Redemption and Its Transference to Metaphor

"Redemption" in the Jewish Bible is both a technical term and an eschatological concept. As a technical term, the Hebrew verbs *ga'al* and *padah* are used in socio-legal contexts generally referring to the rescue of an individual or his property from a difficult circumstance by means of a monetary payment, such as property sold for debt or debt-servitude.[30] The redeemer (*go'el*) was always the nearest adult male relative who was responsible for the economic well-being of his kin, inasmuch as the latter lacked sufficient means to redeem himself or his property. A special case was the "blood-redeemer" who avenged murder and, by extension, all severe harm inflicted on a relative.[31]

From the literal socio-legal understanding of the "blood-redeemer," a transference to a theological metaphor refers to God as redeemer of the people of Israel. Such an idea lies at the basis of Jacob's blessing of his grandchildren Ephraim and Manasseh (Gen. 48:16) in its reference to *"the angel who redeemed me from all evil."* However, the archetypical act of Divine redemption was God's saving of Israel from Egyptian bondage. In Exodus 6:6, God redeems the Israelites from their suffering in Egypt and delivers them from slavery, in order to make them His people (6:7) and to bring them to the Promised Land (6:8). In the Song of the

Sea, the redeemed people are brought to God's pasture and ultimately to His sanctuary in Canaan (Exod. 15:13–17). Similar redemptive language appears in Deuteronomy, Samuel, Micah, Psalms, and Nehemiah.[32] (A great many other passages refer to the Exodus from Egypt, but use other language besides that of the Hebrew words for redemption.)

Given the awesome significance in the biblical consciousness of God's saving of Israel from Egypt, that event becomes the model for future redemption, as in Jer. 16:14–15 (repeated in 23:7–8):

> *Assuredly, the days are coming—declares the Lord—when it shall no more be said, "As the Lord lives who brought the Israelites out of the land of Egypt," but rather, "As the Lord lives who brought the Israelites out of the northland, and out of all the lands to which He banished them." For I will bring them back to their land, which I gave to their fathers.*

It is not surprising then that since the Hebrew words for redemption were used to describe the rescue from Egypt, they would also be used for the concept of restoration from destruction and exile. Indeed, thirty-five of the thirty-six mentions of future restoration using the Hebrew words for redemption appear in prophetic texts (twenty-four of these in Second Isaiah, Isa. 34–35, 40–66, written during the Babylonian exile and its immediate aftermath).[33]

One of the conclusions that can be drawn concerning the connection between the socio-legal context of the redeemer (*goʾel*) and the use of that root in reference to both the exodus from Egypt and God's future restoration of Israel from exile is that the operative image is actually that of the "blood-redeemer." After all, God's redemption of His people involves no monetary payment for debt, as in most of the social-legal contexts of redemption. Further, in the Torah's law, *"the blood-redeemer himself shall put the murderer to death"* (Num. 35:19, 21), and he comes *"in hot anger"* (Deut. 19:6) to avenge his beloved relative's death. That portrait is similar to the depiction of God as the redeeming, vengeful warrior in Second Isaiah, for example, Isa. 63:2–4, 6–7, 9, 11–13, 16:[34]

> Why is your clothing so red,
> Your garments like his who treads grapes?

"I trod out a vintage alone; . . .

I trod them down in My anger, trampled them in My rage;

Their life-blood bespattered My garments, and all My clothing was
stained.

For I had planned a day of vengeance, and My year of redemption
arrived. . . .

I trampled peoples in My anger. . . ."

I will recount the kind acts of the Lord. . . . For all that the Lord has
wrought for us,

The vast bounty to the House of Israel that He bestowed upon them

According to His mercy and His great kindness. . . .

In His love and pity He Himself redeemed them. . . .

Where is He who put in their midst His holy spirit?

Who made His glorious arm march at the right hand of Moses?

Who divided the waters before them . . . Who led them through
the deeps

So that they did not stumble . . . ?

Surely You are our Father:

Though Abraham regard us not, and Israel recognize us not,

You, O Lord, are our Father;

From of old, Your name is "Our Redeemer."

The graphic depiction here of God's warrior image on behalf of Israel
may not accord well with modern sensibilities. Nonetheless, for the
remnant of a people whose loved ones had been killed, whose land and
kingdom had been destroyed, and who lived at the sufferance of their
captors in exile, this portrayal of God as their beloved father-redeemer
could not fail to provide comfort. A more powerful image of God's
caring and saving love for His people would be hard to find.[35]

The Conceptual Meaning: The Eschatological Age of Redemption

What will be the components that will comprise the eschatological age?

A. God is the one who will initiate both the process of redemption
   of His people and will enact it: Amos 9:14, "*I will restore My
   people Israel*"; Zeph. 3:20, "*At that time I will bring you and at*

[that] *time I will gather you . . . when I restore your fortunes before your eyes—said the Lord"*; Jer. 31:7, *"For thus said the Lord: Cry out in joy to Jacob. . . . Sing aloud in praise, and say: The Lord has saved your people, the remnant of Israel."*[36]

B. The most common denominator that is presented as an essential element in the age of redemption is the return of the exiles to their land—without which, of course, no restoration could occur: Amos 9:15, *"I will plant them upon their soil"*; Isa. 11:12, *"He will hold up a signal to the nations and assemble the banished of Israel, and gather the dispersed of Judah from the four corners of the earth"*; Ezek. 36:24, *"I will take you from among the nations and gather you from all the countries, and I will bring you back to your land."*[37]

C. Once back in their land, the people would enjoy miraculous agricultural harvests, increased flocks and cattle, and amplified population: Amos 9:13, *"A time is coming—declares the Lord— when the plowman shall meet the reaper, and the treader of grapes him who sows the seed; when the mountains shall drip wine and all the hills shall wave [with grain]"*; Hosea 2:24, *"And the earth shall respond with new grain and wine and oil"*; Joel 4:18, *"And in that day, the mountains shall drip wine, and the hills shall flow with milk"*; Jer. 31:27, *"A time is coming—declares the Lord—when I will sow the House of Israel and the House of Judah with the seed of men and the seed of cattle."*[38] The verse from Amos echoes the reward for obedience to the commandments foretold particularly in Lev. 26:5,[39] *"Your threshing shall overtake the vintage, and the vintage shall overtake the sowing."* Leviticus 26:9 also mentions increased human population, and Deut. 28:4,11 refers to that as well as increased cattle.

D. The people will dwell securely in the land, with none to make them afraid that the experience of destruction and exile will be repeated: Amos 9:15, *"I will plant them upon their soil, nevermore to be uprooted from the soil I have given them—said the Lord your God"*; Hosea 2:20, *"In that day . . . I will banish bow, sword, and war from the land. Thus I will let them lie down in safety"*; Zech. 14:11, *"Never again shall destruction be decreed, and Jerusalem *shall dwell secure.*"[40] Here, too, security resembles the reward mentioned in Lev. 26:5, *"You shall dwell securely in your land."*[41]

E. The Davidic monarchy would be restored and under just rulers: Amos 9:11, *"In that day, I will raise up the fallen booth of David; I will mend its breaches, raise up its ruins, and will build it as in the days of old"*;[42] Isa. 11:1–5, *"But a shoot shall grow out of the stump of Jesse.*[43] *. . . The spirit of the Lord shall alight upon him: a spirit of wisdom and insight, a spirit of counsel and valor, a spirit of knowledge and reverence for the Lord . . . but he shall judge the poor with righteousness . . . and slay the wicked with the breath of his lips. Justice shall be the girdle of his loins"*; Jer. 23:5, *"See, the days are coming—declares the Lord—when I will raise up a righteous branch of David. He shall reign as king and prosper and he shall do what is just and right in the land"*;[44] Ezek. 34:23, *"Then I will raise up upon them a single shepherd to tend them—My servant David. He shall tend them, he shall be a shepherd to them."*[45]

The fact that most of the above prophecies focus on the king's justice and righteousness is an important component in facilitating the future just society.[46] However, not all prophets look to the future renewal of the Davidic dynasty. Obadiah (ca. 585–550 BCE), verse 21, depicts the reinstitution of the judges as future human rulers, while kingship is only God's: *"Deliverers will ascend Mount Zion to judge Mount Esau, but kingship will belong to the Lord."*[47] Second Isaiah has a different vision.[48] In 55:3–5, he prophesies, *"And I will make with you an everlasting covenant, the enduring loving-loyalty [hesed] promised to David. As I appointed him a leader of the peoples, a prince and commander of the peoples, so you shall summon nations you did not know, and nations that did not know you shall come running to you. For the sake of the Lord your God, the Holy One of Israel has glorified you."*

In the above passage, the assurance of God's lasting loyalty to David, promised in the books of 2 Samuel and Psalms,[49] has now been transferred to the people! This prophecy accords well with Second Isaiah's other statements that kingship resides only in the Lord.

F. The cult and priesthood would be reconstituted in Jerusalem:

Jer. 33:18, *"Nor shall there ever be an end to the line of the levitical priests before Me, of those who present burnt offerings and turn the meal offering to smoke and perform sacrifices"*; Ezek. 37:26,28, *"and I will place My Sanctuary among them forever. . . . And when My Sanctuary abides among them forever, the nations shall know that I the Lord do sanctify Israel."*[50]

As prophesied in Isaiah and Micah, the nations will come to worship the Lord in Jerusalem.[51] This theme reappears in Second Isaiah (the anonymous prophet of the latter half of the sixth century BCE)—Isa. 56:7, *"For My House shall be called a house of prayer for all peoples."*[52] It is also found in Zechariah in both chapter 8 and chapter 14 (chapters 9–14 are apparently a late fifth century BCE addition to the book of Zechariah.)

Urged on by the late sixth-century BCE prophecies of Haggai and Zechariah and witnessed by historiographic texts, the promise of the reestablishment of the cult was fulfilled with the completion of the building of the Second Temple in 515 BCE.[53]

G. The covenant between God and Israel would be renewed and all Israel would obey God's Torah: Covenant and Torah appear together in Jer. 31:31–34:

See, a time is coming—declares the Lord—when I will make a new covenant with the House of Israel and the House of Judah. It will not be like the covenant I made with their fathers, when I took them by the hand to lead them out of the land of Egypt, a covenant which they broke. . . . For this is the covenant that I will make with the House of Israel after those days—declares the Lord: I will put My torah into their innermost being and inscribe it upon their hearts, and I shall be their God and they shall be My people. No longer will they teach each other saying to one another, "Know the Lord," for all of them from the least of them to the greatest shall know Me—declares the Lord, for I will forgive their iniquities and remember their sins no more.[54]

Note that the content of the new covenant is the same as the Sinai one— the Torah. The only thing that has changed is the method of transmission. Rather than being given externally, it will be given internally, thereby ensuring that the people will never again sin against God. Thus they will never again have to endure destruction and exile.[55]

The idea that the covenant at the time of redemption will guarantee peace and security also appears in Hosea, Ezekiel, and Second Isaiah.[56] This idea, too, may be derived from the guarantee of God's continued covenantal relationship with Israel based upon the blessings of reward for keeping the commandments in Lev. 26:9, *"and I will maintain My covenant with you."*[57]

- That God's Torah will be obeyed in the future is a theme in other prophecies besides the Jeremiah one mentioned above: Isa. 2:3-4 // Mic. 4:2-3, *"And many peoples shall go and say: 'Come, let us go up to the Mount of the Lord, to the House of the God of Jacob; that He many instruct us in His ways and that we may walk in His paths.' For torah shall come forth from Zion, and the word of the Lord from Jerusalem. Thus He will judge among the nations."*

Even though this text speaks of "many nations," it is inconceivable that Israel would not be included. Rather, they are already there, and therefore do not have to make a special journey up to Jerusalem. A later commentary on this passage is found in Second Isaiah—Isa. 51:4,7, *"for torah shall go forth from Me, and My justice for the light of peoples. . . . Listen to Me, you who know righteousness, O people within whose heart is My torah,"* that is, the reference to the Torah going forth from God and justice among the nations. On the other hand, the reference to the Torah within the people's heart most probably is derived from Jeremiah 31.[58]

- Ezek. 44:24 states that the priests in the eschatological age shall keep God's Torah. The well-known role of the priests to teach God's Torah to Israel is fulfilled by the returnees to Zion after the exile, as witnessed by Haggai.[59]
- In the conclusion of a prophecy on the coming, even apocalyptic, cataclysm in which the wicked will be destroyed and the righteous saved, Mal. 3:22 emphasizes the necessity of the Torah: *"Be mindful*

of the torah of Moses My servant, whom I commanded at Horeb laws and statutes for all Israel."

It is hardly a coincidence that when Ezra and Nehemiah sought to rejuvenate the people's commitment to their religion, they held massive public readings of the Torah (Nehemiah 8). In a public penitential prayer following the readings, God's eternal loyalty to the covenant is affirmed: *"our God, the great, mighty, and awesome God, who stays faithful to His covenant"* (Neh. 9:32). The people then make a formal pledge to God to obligate themselves to follow the entire Torah, *"And the rest of the people . . . join with their noble brothers, and take an oath with sanctions to follow the Torah of God, given to the hand of Moses the servant of God, and to observe fully all the commandments of the Lord our Master, His statutes and laws"* (10:29–30).[60]

The Conditions Required for Redemption to Occur

Is the eschatological age conditional on certain required elements? The previous chapter illustrated the necessity of repentance to avoid destruction and exile. However, after destruction has occurred and in the middle of exile, must the people repent of their past sins in order to effect Divine redemption? Or does the punishment wipe out the crime? What role do God's mercies play? Or do other motivational factors exist? This section will seek to provide answers.

Future Redemption in the Torah

It is axiomatic in academic scholarship that future redemption is referred to three times in the Torah: Lev. 26:40–45; Deut. 4:29–31; 30:1–10. In each passage, the people, overwhelmed by the destruction and exile that has overcome them due to their disobedience to God's laws/treaty stipulations, are depicted as penitent. Yet upon closer examination it turns out that while redemption is explicitly predicted in Deuteronomy 30, it is at best only hinted at in Leviticus 26 and Deuteronomy 4.

Leviticus 26:3–39 is an extensive list of blessings and curses that will come upon the people depending upon their obedience to God's commandments/laws/stipulations of the Sinai covenant. Several verses then address the aftermath of the realization of the curses:

> (40) *And* [the survivors] *shall confess their iniquity and the iniquity of their fathers, in that they committed sacrilege against Me and, more-over, that they continued in opposition to Me—*(41) *so that I, in turn, had to continue in opposition to them and disperse them in the land of their enemies—then their uncircumcised heart shall be humble and then they shall accept their punishment in full,* (42) [then] *I will remember My covenant with Jacob; also My covenant with Isaac and also My covenant with Abraham I will remember, namely, I will remember the land* (43) . . . *as they accept their punishment in full* . . . (44) . . . *while they are in the land of their enemies I will not spurn them or loathe them so as to destroy them, annulling My covenant with them: for I the Lord am their God.* (45) *But I will remember in their favor the covenant with the first* [or former] *ones whom I freed from the land of Egypt in the sight of the nations to be their God: I am the Lord.* (Lev. 26:40–45)[61]

Note that confession and contrition precede God's remembering the covenant with the ancestors and the later Sinai covenant. At the same time, it seems the intention of vs. 44 to say that God does not intend to annul His covenant with them (even though their disobedience means that the people annulled God's covenant; see vs. 15), so God's mercy may be here intimated. Again, no restoration is mentioned, although God's remembering the covenant *"in their favor"* is certainly a good sign.

As part of Moses' speech to the Israelites on the plains of Moab, Deu-teronomy 4 reiterates the obligation of the people to obey God's laws. Verses 25–28 particularly emphasize that idolatry will result in destruc-tion and exile. Verses 29–31 then depict what will happen next:

> *And you shall search there for the Lord your God and you will find* [Him], *for you will seek Him with all your heart and soul. When you are in distress and all these things shall befall you, in the days to come you will return to the Lord your God and obey Him. For the Lord your God is a compassionate God: He will not fail you nor will He destroy you; He will not forget the covenant that He made by oath with your fathers.*[62]

In similarity to the previous passage from Leviticus 26, these Deuteronomy verses depict the people's repentance to God in exile. However, the Hebrew term used here for repentance is from the root *shuv*, that is, the spiritual "return" characteristic of prophetic language. Again, like Leviticus 26, Deuteronomy 4 references God's remembering the covenant He made with the ancestors.[63] And again no mention of restoration appears. Restoration may be a logical intimation, but its absence is noteworthy.

The only other occurrence of the usage of the root *shuv* as spiritual "return" to God takes place in Deut. 30:1–10, again as the people's repentance in exile, but this time as a clear condition for restoration:

> *When all these things befall you—the blessing and the curse that I have set before you—and you take them to heart amidst all the nations to which the Lord your God has banished you, and you return to the Lord your God, and you obey His voice with all your heart and all your soul according to all that I command you this day—you and your children, then the Lord your God will restore your fortunes and will have mercy upon you. He will bring you together again from all the peoples where the Lord your God has scattered you . . . and the Lord your God will bring you to the land that your fathers possessed, and you shall possess it . . . Then the Lord your God will circumcise your heart and the heart of your offspring to love the Lord your God with all your heart and all your soul in order that you may live . . . You will return and obey the voice of the Lord, and you shall do all His commandments that I command you this day. And the Lord your God will grant you abounding prosperity in all your undertakings, in the issue of your womb, the offspring of your cattle, and the produce of your soil . . . since you will obey the voice of the Lord your God to keep His commandments and His laws that are recorded in this book of the Torah—for you shall return to the Lord your God with all your heart and soul.[64]*

It should be noted that the above passage contains many of the elements that appear in prophetic descriptions of the eschatological age—God will initiate and enact redemption; the exiles' return to the land (a reversal of the curse of exile in 28:64); enjoyment of agricultural harvests, increased flocks, cattle, and population (a restatement of the blessings in 28:4a); the people would obey the commandments of the Torah (the reason for the blessings in 28:1–2). The only elements that do not appear are the promise of permanent safety; the restoration of kingship, priesthood and worship; and the renewal of the covenant. Even though the promise of permanent safety and the renewal of the covenant are not specifically mentioned, they are intimated. Certainly, the restoration of the positive relationship between God and Israel is plainly stated. Further, God's circumcision of the heart of the people implies that obedience to His commandments will become part of the people's nature. If so, then they will not sin any more and thus will no longer live in fear of the punishment of destruction and exile. Many academic scholars have noted the similarity between this passage and late passages in Jeremiah and, therefore deem this passage exilic or even post-exilic (in similarity to the ancient Near Eastern "after the fact" texts mentioned above). However, the fact that this passage does not mention the restoration of the priesthood and sanctuary (which does occur after the return to the land) and, on the other hand, that God's circumcision of the heart is mentioned (which does *not* occur) argues against a post-exilic date.

It is also clear that "return" to God—mentioned four times—is a condition for redemption. To summarize these three Torah passages:

- All three passages speak with assurance of the exiled people's repentance (Deuteronomy 4 and 30) or regret and confession (Leviticus 26);
- The possibility of redemption is, at best, only intimated in two of the passages (Lev. 26; Deut. 4);[65]
- Only Deuteronomy 30 actually predicts redemption and posits repentance as a condition, even though it is assured;
- Deuteronomy 30 contains most of the elements that appear in prophetic descriptions of the eschatological age, but these elements actually reflect the blessings in Deut. 28. These eschatological elements do not include either the restoration of the cult or monarchy.

One other significant observation: the fact that the only times in the Torah that the root *shuv* is used in reference to repentance occurs *after* the full punishment of destruction and exile has taken place is in stark contrast to those prophetic texts in which it is primarily used to *avoid* such punishment. Therefore, it may be correct to say that the depiction of repentance in the two Deuteronomy passages is incomplete, as is the portrayal of the age of redemption.[66]

Future Redemption in the Eighth-Century BCE Prophets

Amos (ca. 775–750 BCE) was the first prophet to predict national destruction and exile.[67] Even though he refers to the people's failure to repent while still in the land (4:6–11), he does not mention repentance as a condition in the future age. In his understanding, only the wicked Israelites will die during the time of destruction and exile (9:9–10): *"For I will give the order and shake the House of Israel through all the nations, as one shakes* [grain and stones] *in a sieve, and not a pebble falls to the ground.*[68] *All the sinners of My people shall perish by the sword."* Since the following verses portray restoration, the implication is that the righteous will survive. Thus repentance is superfluous.

Hosea (ca. 750–725 BCE), however, vacillated. Sometimes he prophesied a redemption dependent upon repentance—3:5, *"Afterward, the Israelites will repent* ["return"] *and seek the Lord their God and David their king—and they will come trembling*[69] *to the Lord and His goodness in the days to come";* 14:2–3 (after destruction—verse 1), *"Return, O Israel, to the Lord your God, for you have fallen because of your sin. Take words with you and return to the Lord"* (and God responds, verse 5, *"Generously I will take them back in love, for My anger has turned away from them"*). Other times, he predicted a redemption in which repentance was absent, but God's love for His people comes to the fore—2:16–17, 21, *"I will speak coaxingly to her and lead her through the wilderness and speak to her tenderly . . . she shall respond as in the days of her youth, when she came up from the land of Egypt. . . . And I will espouse you to Me forever";* (after calling Israel, *"My son,"* 11:1, and the prediction of destruction in verse 6, God says) 11:8–9, *"How can I give you up, O Ephraim? . . . How can I make you like Admah, render you like Zeboiim?*[70] *. . . all My tenderness is stirred. . . . I will not turn to destroy Ephraim. "* Note that these prophecies in Hosea 2 and 11 portray the people as either God's beloved wife or son.

In other words, sometimes Hosea seems to have felt that Israel did not deserve the benefits of God's love unless it repented, and sometimes it seems that God's love simply overwhelmed His senses. It is not accidental that when repentance is not a condition for redemption, the text reveals God's love for Israel, for it is that intimate emotion that provides the condition for redemption.

Hosea, more so than Amos, was the first of the literary prophets to live on the edge of national disaster: Assyria's destruction of North Israel and the ensuing exile (Assyria began taking captives from North Israel in 732 BCE). Thus the need to delineate the motivation for redemption was more critical for him than Amos. Unlike Amos, Hosea conceived of no innocent remnant. With no prophetic models to follow, and given the tempestuous times in which he lived and how they must have played upon his psyche, it is not surprising that Hosea's views of the redemptive process fluctuated.

Isaiah ben Amoz (ca. 740–700 BCE) conceived of a surviving remnant who, nevertheless, would repent, Isa. 6:13: *"But while a tenth part yet remains in it* (that is, in the land), *it* (the remnant) *shall repent"*; 10:21, *"Only a remnant shall return, only a remnant of Jacob, to Mighty God."* This is even true of Egyptians after destruction, 19:22, *"The Lord will first afflict and then heal the Egyptians; when they turn to the Lord, He will respond to their entreaties and heal them."*[71]

Although Micah (circa 725–700 BCE) has a few isolated prophecies of redemption, the only hint of a reason for restoration is God's own commitment and emotional attachment to His people.[72] After a description of the destruction of the land by invaders from Assyria and Egypt as punishment for the people's sins (7:12–13), 7:18–20 states:

Who is a God like You, forgiving iniquity, and passing by treachery for the remnant of His heritage? [The One Who] did not sustain His anger forever, because He delights in lovingkindness. He will once more have compassion on us; He will trample on our iniquities. And You shall hurl into the depths of the sea all their sins. You shall give truth to Jacob, kind loyalty to Abraham, which You swore to our fathers from the days of old.[73]

The rhetorical question concerning God's incomparability (obviously, no one is like God) is only one of many in the Hebrew Bible.[74] Here,

God's exceptionality is illustrated by His forgiveness even of willful sin, the temporary nature of His anger, and his loyalty and compassion—all in relationship to His people.[75]

Future Redemption in Jeremiah

Jeremiah's (ca. 640–583 BCE) thoughts on the relationship of repentance to redemption progress through three stages. First, during the reign of Josiah (641–609 BCE),[76] the young prophet believed that Israel's repentance and God's mercy were the determining conditions for redemption—3:12–13, 22; 4:1:[77]

> Go, make this proclamation toward the north,[78] and say: "Return, O backsliding Israel," speech of the Lord, "I will not be angry with you . . . for I am kind. . . . I shall not hold a grudge forever."

> "Return, O backsliding children, I will heal your backslidings."

> "If you return, O Israel," speech of the Lord, "then you shall return to Me. If you remove your abominations from My presence, you will no longer wander [off your land]."

The second stage occurred between 597 and 587 BCE in prophecies of redemption to the Judean exiles who were taken with King Jehoiachin to Babylon,[79] and it comprised a subtle shift as the element of Divine mercy outweighed that of the people's repentance. Note how in the following passage the emphasis is on God's redemption, and the people's repentance appears at the very end, almost as an afterthought (24:5–7).[80]

> Thus says the Lord, the God of Israel: ". . . so will I single out for good the Judean exiles whom I have driven out from this place to the land of the Chaldeans. I will look upon them favorably, and I will bring them back to the land; I will build them and not overthrow them; I will plant them and not uproot them. And I will give them a heart to know Me,[81] for I am the Lord. And they shall be My people and I will be their God, for they will return to Me with all their heart."

If the people will return to God with all their heart, why is it necessary for God to give them a heart to ensure their obedience? The incongruity of the text may illustrate the prophet's own ambivalence. It appears that Jeremiah had begun to despair of the people's ability to return to God of their own accord. Yet even though God's promise of redemption takes center stage, the prophet is still unable to give up all hope for repentance.

About that same time, Jeremiah sent a letter to the Jehoiachin exiles (29:1–7), the importance of which should not be underestimated. Not only does he urge them to lead a normal life, *"Build houses and live in them, plant gardens and eat their fruit, take wives and beget sons and daughters . . . and let them bear sons and daughters. Multiply there, do not decrease"* (vv. 5–6), but he actually devises an ethical constitution for living in exile, *"And seek the welfare of the city to which I have exiled you and pray to the Lord in its behalf; for in its well-being you shall have well-being"* (vs. 7). The letter continues with a prophecy of redemption, verses 10–14:

> *For thus said the Lord: "When Babylon's seventy years are completed, . . . I will fulfill to you My promise of favor to bring you back to this place. For I am mindful of the plans I have made for you . . . plans for your welfare . . . to give you a hopeful future. When you call Me, and come and pray to Me, I will give heed to you. You will search for Me and find Me, for you will seek Me wholeheartedly. I will be found by you . . . and I will restore your fortunes. And I will gather you from all the nations . . . to which I banished you . . . and I will bring you back to the place from which I exiled you.*

Although this passage speaks of the exiles calling to God, praying to Him, and seeking Him, these intimations of repentance are both assured and secondary to the main factor. That dominating factor, as in Jeremiah 24, is God's caring promise of restoration. Highly significant, here, is the seventy years' interval before redemption—three generations. The people are required to accept delayed gratification. Hope for their own redemption is all but taken away, but is guaranteed for their grandchildren. That more mature hope, once inculcated by the deportees, will enable the community to maintain their identity and belief in God despite the rigors of the exile—until the hour of restoration.

Jeremiah's third and final stage takes place either on the eve of the destruction of Jerusalem in 587 BCE or shortly thereafter.[82] In one of the most famous of prophetic passages, Jeremiah envisions a new covenant between God and Israel, 31:31–36:

> *"Behold, the days are coming," speech of the Lord, "when I will make a new covenant with the House of Israel and the House of Judah. It will not be like the covenant I made with their fathers, when I took them by the hand to lead them out of the land of Egypt, a covenant which they broke, even though I had been their husband . . . but this is the covenant I will make with the House of Israel after those days.*[83] *. . . I will put My Torah within them and will write it on their heart. I will be their God and they shall be My people. No longer will they teach one another and say to one another, 'Know the Lord,' for they shall all know Me, from the least of them to the greatest," speech of the Lord, "for I will forgive their iniquities and no more remember their sins." Thus says the Lord, Who established the sun for light by day, the laws of moon and stars for light by night . . . whose name is Lord of Hosts: "If these laws (of nature) should ever be annulled by Me . . . only then would the offspring of Israel cease to be a nation before Me for all time."*[84]

As mentioned above (in the discussion on the characteristics of the age of redemption), the only difference between the new covenant and the one given at Sinai is the method of transmission. The Torah, that is, the covenant stipulations/laws, is to be Divinely injected into the people's hearts. Following the will of God will now become part of the people's nature. Therefore, there will be no need for anybody to teach anybody else how to obey God. All this will come about after their sins are wiped out, *"for* (that is, because) *I will forgive their iniquities."* That this forgiveness is a purification is evidenced from a parallel Jeremiah redemption passage, 33:6–8, *"I will heal them. . . . I will restore the fortunes of Judah and Israel. . . . And I will purify them from all the iniquities that they sinned against me, and I will pardon all their iniquities that they sinned against me, and which they rebelled against me."*

Thus the people have now been purified, just as they were purified (by their own actions) before the Sinai covenant (Exod. 19:10–15). Note that the new covenant passage contains no hint of repentance.

Why does the now-aged prophet drop any semblance of repentance from his final prophecies of redemption? For some forty years, Jeremiah fought losing battles to convince his people to turn from their obdurate ways. He learned that *"the heart is deceitful above all things and incurable"* (17:9). The prophet was well aware that, left to their own devices, there was no surety that those who would experience redemption would not eventually repeat the crimes of their ancestors. And what of their children? Jeremiah was fearful that the restored people, like their forefathers, would begin to disobey God and be incapable of repentance: *"Can the Cushite change his skin or the leopard its spots? Just as much as you, who are trained to do evil, could do good"* (13:23); *"the sin of Judah is inscribed with an iron stylus, engraved with a point of adamant on the table of their heart"* (17:1).

And then what? After experiencing the tragedy of the destruction of Jerusalem (and exile) on his own flesh, as it were, Jeremiah could not conceive of the whole catastrophic cycle of redemption to disobedience to destruction and exile repeating itself.[85] Thus he prophesied a new reality. By God's gracious act of inserting the Torah into their nature, the people will be compelled to obedience to the Divine commandments and never again suffer the disaster of God's punishment. This point is brought home in the new covenant passage by the juxtaposition of the verses that speak of the permanence of the obedience to the (laws of the) Torah within the people and the permanence of the existence of the people as identical with the laws of nature.[86]

If repentance is no longer Jeremiah's requirement for redemption, what is? Perhaps other prophecies of the prophet can suggest an answer: Jer. 30:10–11, 15–18,

> *"Have no fear, My servant Jacob . . . I will deliver you from far away, your offspring from the land of their captivity. . . . I will make an end of all the nations among which I have dispersed you. But I will not make an end of you, I will not leave you unpunished, but will chastise you as justified. . . .*

I did these things to you because your iniquity was so great and your sins so many. . . . Those who despoiled you shall be despoiled . . . but I will bring healing to you and cure you of your wounds," speech of the Lord. . . . Thus says the Lord: "I will restore the fortune of Jacob's tents and have compassion on his dwellings."[87]

Also, 50:19–20, *"I will lead Israel back to his pasture . . . In those days and at that time," speech of the Lord, "the iniquity of Israel shall be sought, and there shall be none; the sins of Judah, and none shall be found; for I will forgive those who I allow to survive."*

In the above passages from Jeremiah, chapters 30 and 50, two motivations for redemption assert themselves:

a. Punishment for sin obviates the necessity for repentance as a precondition for redemption. In other words, the enactment of the sentence wipes out the crime.
b. The punishment resulted in Israel's great suffering which, in turn, arouses God's merciful response to end His people's misery and restore them to their land.

Future Redemption in Ezekiel

Ezekiel prophesied during the first part of the Babylonian exile (593–571 BCE).[88] He never indicated that repentance was the determinant of national redemption.[89] Only in one prophecy does a possibility of repentance appear to have any role at all during the time of redemption—11:17–20:

Thus said the Lord God: "I will gather you from the nations . . . where you have been scattered, and I will give you the soil of Israel. When they arrive there, they will remove all its loathsome and abominable things (idols) from it. I will give them a single heart and a new spirit into you; I will remove the heart of stone from their flesh and give them a heart of flesh, so that they follow My laws and keep My statutes. They shall be My people and I will be their God.[90]

The above passage envisions God's deliverance without any preconditions. Only *after* the people return to the land do they abolish idolatry from it—a kind of repentance, perhaps, that in any case succeeds restoration (and does not precede it). This behavior is similar to other passages in Ezekiel that emphasize how redemption will elicit remorse and shame, such as 20:42–43: *"when I bring you to the soil of Israel . . . there you will recall your ways and all the acts by which you defiled yourselves; and you will loathe yourselves for all the evils you committed."*[91]

Note, however, that the placement of a new heart and spirit into the people that will impose obedience to God's laws is reminiscent of Jeremiah's new covenant passage, as well as Jer. 32:37–40:

> *I am gathering them from all the lands to which I have banished them in My anger . . . and I will bring them back to this place and let them dwell in security. They shall be My people and I will be their God. I will give them a single heart and a single path to revere Me for all time to benefit them and their children after them. I will make them an eternal covenant that I will not turn away from them, to treat them well; and I will put into their heart reverence for Me, so that they do not turn away from Me.*

The "single heart" of Ezekiel 11 was apparently influenced by Jeremiah 32,[92] and the "new spirit" was most probably Ezekiel's interpretation of Jeremiah's "new covenant," as illustrated by Ezek. 36:22–32, 37–38, which also provides a new motivation for redemption:

> *Thus said the Lord God: "Not for your sake will I act, O House of Israel, but for My holy name, which you have caused to be profaned among the nations to which you have come. I will sanctify My great name which has been profaned among the nations. . . . And the nations shall know that I am the Lord . . . when I manifest My holiness before their eyes through you. . . . I will gather you from all the countries and I will bring you back to your soil . . . you shall be purified from all your impurities. . . . And I will give you a new heart and put a new spirit into you; I will remove the heart of stone from your flesh and will give you a heart of flesh. . . . Thus I will cause you to follow My laws and faithfully keep My statutes. Then you shall dwell in the land which I gave to your*

*fathers, and you shall be My people and I will be your God. And when
I have saved you from all your impurities, I will summon the grain and
make it abundant. . . . I will make the fruit of your trees and the crops
of your fields abundant, so that you shall never again be humiliated
before the nations because of famine. Then you shall recall your evil
ways . . . and you shall loathe yourselves for your iniquities and your
abominations. Not for your sake will I act . . . let it be known to you!
Be ashamed and humiliated because of your ways, O House of Israel!" . . .
Thus said the Lord God: "Moreover, in this I will respond to the House
of Israel and act for their sake: I will multiply them like flocks of humans,
like flocks of sheep for sacred offerings, like the flocks of Jerusalem during
her festivals, so shall the ruined cities be filled with flocks of people. And
they shall know that I am the Lord."*

This eschatological passage, with its emphasis on the shame of the people
and their profanation of the name of God among the nations, is a new
concept in biblical prophecy, as is the reason for redemption: just as
exiled Israel is the cause of the profaning of God's name, the redemption of the people in their land will result in the sanctification of God's
name.[93] God's redemptive acts will result in the nations' acknowledgment of His greatness, vs. 36: *"And the nations that are left around you
shall know that I the Lord have rebuilt the ravaged places and replanted
the desolate land."* So, even though Ezekiel shows the influence of Jeremiah, his motivation for redemption is exceptional.

Nonetheless, verses 37–38 indicate that God also acts on behalf of the
people, *"I will respond to the House of Israel and act for their sake."* Indeed,
elsewhere Ezekiel indicates that God will rescue the people out of His
mercy for them, 34:12, 16, 28, 29:

*"As a shepherd seeks out his flock when some [of the animals] have
gotten separated, so I will seek out My flock, I will rescue them from all
the places to which they were scattered. . . . I will look for the lost, and
I will bring back the strayed; I will bandage the injured and I will
strengthen the sick. . . . They shall no longer be a spoil for the nations . . .
they shall dwell secure and untroubled . . . they shall not have to bear
again the taunts of the nations."*[94]

Ezekiel, then, draws on two motivations for redemption:

a. God's concern for the sanctification of His name that has been profaned by Israel's exile among the nations;

b. God's caring for His abused people.

Future Redemption in Second Isaiah (Isaiah 34-35, 40-66)

The anonymous prophet, known as Second Isaiah, whose words are found in the latter half of the book, delivered numerous prophecies of redemption in chapters 35 and 40–66, some in exile and some after he had accompanied his people back to their homeland.[95] (King Cyrus of Persia conquered Babylon in 539 BCE and encouraged the Judahites to return to their land.)[96] Second Isaiah's prophecies contain many motives for redemption.[97]

A. Divine mercy: As stated earlier in this chapter on the "blood-redeemer," God is the redeemer of Israel, who redeems His children (43:6, *"Bring My sons from afar, and My daughters from the end of the earth"*), for He is their father (63:16 and 64:7, *"You are our Father"*) and their mother (66:13, *"As a mother comforts her son, so I will comfort you"*).[98] God also redeems Israel for He is "her" husband, 54:6–8: *"For the Lord has called you back, as a wife once deserted and despondent. 'Can one reject the wife of one's youth?'—said your God. 'In a fit of rage I deserted you, but with vast mercies I will gather you back . . . '* said the Lord your Redeemer."[99]

Other texts also speak to God's protective attachment to Israel. He is *"the Mighty One of Jacob,"*[100] *"the Holy One of Israel,"*[101] and their *"savior"*[102] who *"helps"* Israel.[103] Additionally, Israel is the *"chosen"* of God,[104] whom God *"created."*[105] Further, God is their caring shepherd—40:11, *"Like a shepherd He pastures His flock: He gathers the lambs in His arms, and carries them in His bosom"*—and their Redeemer-King—44:6, *"Thus said the Lord, the King of Israel, and their Redeemer, the Lord of Hosts."*

Unquestionably, these various ways and images in which the

intimate relationship between God and Israel are presented
speak to the Deity's mercies upon His people, which are aroused
due to the harshness of exile. So a prophecy against Babylon,
47:5–6, states, *"O Fair Chaldea, nevermore shall they call you
Mistress of Kingdoms. I was angry at My people. . . . I put them
into your hands, but you showed them no mercy; upon the aged
you made your yoke extremely heavy."*[106]

B. God's Concern for His Name: At the same time, reminiscent of
Ezekiel, God also acts for His own sake—43:25, *"It is I, I who—
for My own sake—wipe your rebellious acts away, and will
remember your sins no more"*—and for the sake of His name—
48:9,11, *"For the sake of My name, I control My wrath, and* [for
that of] *My glory, I hold Myself in check, not to destroy you . . . For
My sake, My sake, do I act, lest* [My name] *be dishonored!"*

C. Repentance: The only possible mention of repentance in chapters 40–48 (which the vast majority of scholars agree were said
in exile) may occur in 44:22: *"I have wiped away your rebellious
acts like a cloud and your sins like a mist. Return to Me, for I have
redeemed you!"* The obvious question is if God has wiped out
their sins and is redeeming the people, then why do they have to
repent? It may well be that normal prophetic repentance is not
meant here, but perhaps a simple turning toward God of the
exiled, downtrodden people. The next verse may emphasize that
what is being spoken about is a turning to God that is an uplift-
ing of the people's spirits, verse 23, *"Exult, O heavens, for the
Lord has acted! Shout aloud, O lowest depths of the earth! Break
into songs of joy, O mountains . . . for the Lord has redeemed
Jacob and has glorified Himself through Israel."* On the other
hand, it is possible that the call to return to God is meant for the
people to show thanks for His coming redemption or contrition
for past sins.[107]

Isaiah 55:5–7 is a call for repentance that appears within a prophecy of redemption (apparently delivered in exile): *"Seek the Lord while
He can be found! Call to Him while He is near! Let the wicked give up his
way, the sinful man his plans. Let him return to the Lord, and He will have*

compassion on him, to our God for He freely forgives." As verse 12 speaks about the return of people to the land, verses 5–7 are apparently a call to repentance similar to Jeremiah's (in Jer. 29:10–14, above), in which repentance seems to be secondary to God's promise of redemption.

Isaiah 58:1–14 is a call to repentance, to moral behavior, and to Sabbath observance and is one of the most moving ethical passages in the Jewish Bible.[108] If the people obey God's will, then He will respond to their prayers, cause them to flourish, and rebuild their ruined cities.

> *Raise your voice like a ram's horn! Declare to My people their rebellious transgression and to the House of Jacob their sins! (The people say:) "Why, when we fasted, did You not see? When we mortified ourselves, do You pay no heed?" (God responds:) Because on your fast day you attend to your business and oppress all your laborers. . . . Is such as this the fast I desire? A day for humans to mortify themselves? Is it . . . lying in sackcloth and ashes? Is not this the fast I desire: to unlock fetters of wickedness . . . to let the oppressed go free and snap every yoke? It is to share your bread with the hungry and to take the homeless poor into your home. When you see the naked, clothe him, and do not ignore your own kin. Then shall your light burst through like the dawn and your healing spring up quickly. . . . Then, when you call, the Lord will answer; when you cry out, He will say: "Here I am." If you banish perversion from your midst, the pointing finger and evil speech . . . then . . . you shall be like a well-watered garden. . . .*
>
> *Men from your midst shall rebuild the ancient ruins. . . .*
>
> *If you refrain from trampling the Sabbath underfoot, from pursuing your affairs on My holy day; if you call the Sabbath "Delight," . . . then you shall find your delight in the Lord. . . . I will let you enjoy the heritage of your father Jacob. The mouth of the Lord has truly spoken.*

Now that the people have returned to their land, the prophet reinstitutes the older system: to receive God's benefits, the people must repent of their evil deeds and heed the prophetic message of the primacy of morality over ritual.[109]

Post-Exilic Prophets

Nothing in the later prophecies of redemption of Haggai and Zechariah added new themes to those that had already appeared in the earlier prophets. Haggai and Zechariah (chapters 1–8) focused primarily on the foundation of the redeemed community in their own days—the building of the Second Temple as well as the leadership of the high priest Joshua and the hoped-for Davidic heir Zerubbabel.

Although a major concern for Malachi (ca. fifth century BCE) is the poor cultic offerings, he (like Second Isaiah's prophecies from the time after the return to the land) requires repentance and obedience to all the commandments. In 3:5, his overriding concern is ethical:

"I will close upon you in judgment, and I will be a relentless witness against the sorcerers, adulterers, those who swear falsely, those who cheat laborers of their wages, and those who subvert [the cause of] *the widow, the orphan, and the resident alien—those who do not revere me," said the Lord of Hosts.*

Like Amos, Malachi's prophecy of the future depicts a time when the righteous will be saved and the wicked destroyed, 3:18–20:

And you shall come to see the difference between the righteous and the wicked, between him who serves God and him who does not serve Him. For lo, that day is coming, burning like an oven. All the arrogant and all the doers of evil shall be straw, and the day that is coming . . . shall burn them to ashes. But for those who revere My name, a sun of righteousness with healing shall shine upon you.

The final words of the book (and the Jewish Bible's prophetic collection) present a unique condition for that future time.[110] After a command in verse 22, *"Remember the Torah of Moses My servant, which I commanded him at Horeb with laws and statutes for all Israel,"* verses 23–24 state, *"Behold, I am sending you Elijah the prophet before the coming of that great and terrible day of the Lord. He shall turn the heart of the parents to the children and the heart of the children to their parents, lest I come and strike the earth with utter destruction."*[111] Here, reconciliation between parents and children (a theme in Malachi 1:6; 2:10; 3:17) is required or else nobody will survive "the day of the Lord."[112] Perhaps these last verses are saying that for people to be considered righteous—and therefore worthy to be saved—they must not just be good to others but must also be in good relationship with their parents and children.

Summary of the Conditions for Redemption

The conditions for the people's future redemption vary with each prophet. All the prophets, of course, understand that redemption is a Divine act.

- Amos and Malachi envision a redemption for the innocent or righteous, as the wicked will have been destroyed.
- Micah views redemption dependent upon God's mercies for His people.
- Hosea, Jeremiah, Ezekiel, and Second Isaiah all see God's mercy for His people, to whom He is emotionally attached, as a dominant factor aroused, at least in part, by the harsh treatment undergone by the nation. However, for Hosea, Jeremiah, and Second Isaiah, sometimes the people's repentance plays a major role, and in Jeremiah and Second Isaiah, sometimes a secondary role. (Jeremiah 24 is particularly similar to Deuteronomy 30.)
- Isaiah ben Amoz apparently prophesies that redemption is dependent upon repentance.
- Ezekiel and Second Isaiah also contain a different motivation for redemption—God's unhappiness with the defamation of His name.

If Jeremiah, Ezekiel, and Second Isaiah are taken as forming a continuous line from the latter part of the seventh century BCE to the latter part of the sixth, a pattern emerges. As long as destruction had not overtaken Judah, prophecies of redemption still contained the precondition of repentance, dovetailing with the standard prophetic calls for repentance to avoid Divine punishment. However, once Jerusalem had been destroyed and the full exile was under way, redemption was seen as totally dependent upon God's beneficence. It appears that the effect of the cruelty of destruction and the severity of exile served in large measure to wipe out the need for repentance and arouse God's mercies. The manifestation of the punishment is a motivation for divine forgiveness and purification of the people. In the throes of the exile, the very demand to repent in order to effect national redemption might have been more than the people could have borne. Instead, God extends to His people His love and mercy, for He is emotionally attached to them. Together they are, depending on the metaphor, Parent and children, Husband and wife, caring Shepherd and sheep, or King and loyal servants. The covenant is everlasting, as is the Torah.

With the Persian defeat of Babylon in 539 BCE and the advent of the actual restoration to the land, once God is perceived to have begun the process of redemption, the requirement of repentance begins to reappear. Finally, with the people again settled in their homeland, the demand to return to God regains its pre-exilic prominence. Now the gift of a new covenant and a new heart, which would have obviated the need for repentance, since it would have eliminated the possibility of sin, would recede into the consciousness of the people to await future needs.[113]

Conclusions

The surfeit of details in this chapter concerning redemption was presented to make a statement: in contrast to the ancient Near East, the Jewish Bible has highly advanced concepts of redemption, but those concepts developed over centuries and under a variety of experiences. Only in one ancient Sumerian lament—more than a millennium before biblical prophecies—is there any sense of a divine promise for the positive future of a city and its people. As one well-known scholar, John Bright, put it:

> Israel's eschatological hope cannot itself be explained in terms of borrowing, if only because not one of the ancient paganisms . . . ever developed anything that can properly be spoken of as an eschatology. Being polytheisms . . . dedicated to serve the well-being of the existing order, without sense of a divine guidance of history toward a goal in accordance with a long-range purpose announced in advance, they could hardly have done so. . . . However much Israel may have bor-

rowed from the world of her environment, it is impossible that her eschatological hope, or her peculiar orientation toward the future, could have had its origin there.[114]

At the beginning of this chapter, the question was begged: why is it that of all ancient Near Eastern peoples, only the Israelites (to be sure, in their Judahite form) survived, not just as a nation but also as a religious people? The answer is to be found in Israel's prophecies of redemption. These prophecies, building upon past sacred traditions—the Divine promise to the patriarchs, the Exodus, the Sinai covenant with its Divine law and Torah—guaranteed to the people that no matter what happened, no matter how severe the punishment of destruction and exile, God would redeem His people.

It is even possible to pinpoint the precise prophecy, the exact historical circumstance, and the very prophet who transmitted the necessary seed of hope that would blossom inside the people's hearts and enable them to survive the tribulations of exile. Ironically, that prophet would be Jeremiah. This is ironic because Jeremiah is primarily known as a prophet of doom, the prophet who foretold the destruction of Jerusalem and the Babylonian exile. How do we know that he was the key prophet of redemption? The Jewish Bible tells us so at the beginning of Ezra and at the end of 2 Chronicles (36:22–23).[115] Ezra 1:1–3 reads,

> *In the first year of King Cyrus of Persia,* [in order] *to fulfill the word of the Lord spoken by Jeremiah, the Lord roused the spirit of King Cyrus of Persia to issue a proclamation throughout his realm by word of mouth and in writing as follows: "Thus said King Cyrus of Persia: The Lord God of Heaven has given me all the kingdoms of the earth and has charged me with building Him a house in Jerusalem, which is in Judah. Anyone of you of all His people—may his God be with him, and let him go up to Jerusalem that is in Judah and build the House of the Lord God of Israel."*

In other words, both Ezra and Chronicles state that it was Jeremiah's prophecy of redemption that is fulfilled with the restoration of the people to the land. Which prophecy? Probably the reference is to the letter that

Jeremiah wrote to the Jehoiachin exiles in 29:10–14. Further, we have seen that Jeremiah's prophecies of redemption influenced the two great prophets of the exile, Ezekiel and Second Isaiah. Thus it may be determined that it was particularly Jeremiah's prophecies of redemption, supplemented by Ezekiel and Second Isaiah, which implanted the hope that gave the people enough strength to maintain their religious and national identity throughout the exile and into their return to the land. It is possible that the northern Israelite tribes assimilated in the Assyrian exile precisely because they had neither prophets nor prophecies of redemption to accompany them.

As the books of Haggai, Zechariah, and Malachi make clear, the Judahite community redeemed from exile were not the beneficiaries of *all* the promises of redemption. The people were reconstituted in their land, the Temple was built, and the ritual reinstituted. But the Davidic kingship was never reestablished, and peace and prosperity proved elusive. Nonetheless, the Covenant was renewed and the obligation to fulfill the commandments of God's Torah remained an eternal part of the people's existence.

Over time, the unfulfilled aspects of redemption were remembered and became an indelible aspect of the people's perception of the future. Therefore, no matter what calamities were visited on the descendants of those Judahites and those who joined them—who would now be known as Jews—the hope for a better future in their own land endured. That hope and those ancient prophecies of redemption would be adopted and reinterpreted to become the basis of a new religion, Christianity. For the Jews, even throughout a much longer exile, that hope would be constantly there and alive. As in Jeremiah's ethical message to the Jehoiachin exiles, it urged the people to work for the benefit of the communities in which they found themselves and to make the world a better place for all humanity.

Thus the prophetic hope for redemption would become one of the most important influences of the Jewish Bible on the history of western civilization.

Conclusion

The previous chapters have demonstrated a multitude of meaningful ethical ideas and pragmatic innovations that represent a rebellion against ancient Near Eastern thought. To mention only some of them:

A comparison of Mesopotamian and biblical creation stories concluded that humans were conceived to emulate God as good rulers of the earth, not slaves to the gods' physical needs and self-centered desires. Further, men and women were created equally in the "image of God" which in turn meant that human life was sacred. God's rest on the Sabbath was transformed into the first universal labor law. Indeed, that all members of society, even slaves, ceased work one day a week was a unique democratizing enactment. An assessment of the biblical flood story in contrast with Mesopotamian ones established that God rules the world with justice, and that evil is not demonic but the result of unrestrained human selfishness. Nonetheless, humans are capable of exercising their free will to behave ethically.

An analysis of the biblical understanding of the Sinai revelation to the people determined that, as a people in a treaty with God, each individual is equal in responsibility—the future of the society is even dependent upon the behavior of the individual. Additionally, as a people subject to a God-given law, the community becomes responsible for the fate of the individual, giving rise to the concept of mutual individual and communal responsibility. Moreover, since human life is sacred, human life and property are not commensurable. Furthermore, as God is the source of goodness, ethical values are holy and become law; one is required to help others and even act lovingly toward them. Such love is implicit in the understanding that God's instruction (*torah*) to Israel signifies a parent-child relationship, which implies that Divine punishment for misbehavior is only corrective, but the relationship is permanent. Thus hope for the future becomes a fixture of the relationship.

An examination of the treatment of the resident alien and the poor—the two most underprivileged members of society—reveals that the Torah, unlike all other ancient Near East legal collections, creates a host of laws on their behalf. The resident alien was transformed into a divinely, legally protected member of society with wide-ranging benefits and significant parity with the average citizen. The result is the elimination of xenophobia. Similarly, each member of society is obligated to care for and sustain the poor, which includes the widow and orphan. New laws are established for their benefit, which are unattested even by the most ethical considerations of ancient Near East wisdom literature.

A survey of prophetic texts uncovered a revolutionary message: religious ritual is both secondary to ethics and dependent upon moral behavior for its validity. The superior importance of obedience to God's ethical commandments is for the purpose of creating a just, righteous, and caring society. Therefore, ethical behavior becomes the determining factor in national destiny.

However, what if someone did not behave ethically but committed a crime? The Jewish Bible responds with two primary processes of repentance. First, the Torah legislates numerous ethical innovations concerning repentance for civil misdeeds, including that the wrongdoer—*before* he or she is apprehended—must not only confess his or her crime but must make restitution and pay a penalty to the victim. Further, since every crime against a human is a crime against God, a reparation offering is made by the perpetrator at the sanctuary. However, the restitution to the victim *precedes* the reparation offering—therefore, compensation to the victim takes priority over reparation to God! The prophets, on the other hand, focus on repentance as "return" to God and His commandments in order for the society to avoid destruction and exile. As in the Torah, even the possibility of repentance is viewed as an act of Divine mercy. The prophets, though, go beyond the Torah by expanding the power of repentance and, therefore, of God's forgiveness by decreeing that true "return" eliminates punishment altogether.

Finally, when destruction and exile are realized, in contrast to the paucity of material in the ancient Near East, the Jewish Bible's prophetic literature provides numerous texts that portray highly advanced concepts of redemption. These texts all promised that God would return the exiles to their homeland. Various texts prophesied that the people would then dwell there securely forever, enjoying abundant agricultural harvests, increased flocks and cattle, and amplified population; the Davidic monarchy would be restored under just rulers and the cult would be reinstituted in the Temple in Jerusalem; the covenant would be renewed and the people would obey the Torah. All the prophets understood that redemption was a merciful Divine act, although some prophecies saw God as motivated by the people's repentance and some by the people's suffering in exile. What is certain is that prophecies of redemption provided the hope necessary for the Jewish people to endure not only the Babylonian exile but also future exiles and historical tragedies (those same prophecies would be reinterpreted and serve as the basis for Christianity). Particularly, one of Jeremiah's prophecies urged the people to work for the benefit of the communities in which they found themselves—a message that would be converted into a directive to make the world a better place for all humanity.

What is there about the Jewish Bible that presents so many ethical innovations in such a variety of areas—from concepts of creation of the cosmos and humanity to national identity and social justice to an individual's sacrifice and repentance to a people's hope for the future? All is explained through one fact and one fact alone, the Jewish Bible's understanding of the one God. As a great scholar stated, the Jewish Bible is "the manifesto of the monotheistic revolution."[1] In contrast to all the rest of the literature of the ancient Near East, the biblical texts in which these ethical advances are found all posit a good, just, caring God who created the world and humankind and chose to reveal His will to the people of Israel and their prophets. Truly, the Torah itself displays awareness of its ethical uniqueness in the ancient world, as Moses is quoted in Deuteronomy 4:7–8, "For . . . what great nation has laws and statutes as righteous as all this teaching that I set before you this day?"[2]

And if you ask, "Who was the source of all these unique ethical ideas and concepts of moral behavior?" those same biblical texts provide only one answer—"God."

Notes

Abbreviations

ANET   *Ancient Near Eastern Texts Relating to the Old Testament.* 3rd ed. with supplement. Edited by James Pritchard (Princeton: Princeton University Press, 1969).

BWL   W. G. Lambert, *Babylonian Wisdom Literature* (Oxford: Oxford University Press, 1960).

COS   *The Context of Scripture: Canonical Compositions, Monumental Inscriptions, and Archival Documents from the Biblical World.* 3 vols. Edited by William W. Hallo (Leiden: Brill, 1997–2002).

Introduction

1. More than thirty years later, Milgrom would publish an accessible summary for the interested layperson of his magisterial scholarly commentary on Leviticus in the Anchor Bible series. That summary is *Leviticus: A Book of Ritual and Ethics.*

2. Because it was the original language of the Old Testament, Hebrew was often a required classical language in colleges in the eighteenth and nineteenth centuries.

3. The description here is taken from Larsen, "The 'Babel/Bible' Controversy and Its Aftermath," 95–100. Assyriology is the study of the archaeology, history, literatures, and languages of ancient Mesopotamia.

4. See Arnold and Weisberg, "A Centennial Review of Friedrich Delitzsch's 'Babel und Bibel' Lectures."

5. Finkelstein, "Bible and Babel," 368–370.

6. Finkelstein, "Bible and Babel," 372.

7. Baines, "Society, Morality, and Religious Practice," 190.

8. *Tanakh* is a Hebrew acronym: T = *Torah* (also known as the Pentateuch or the Five Books of Moses: Genesis, Exodus, Leviticus, Numbers, and Deuteronomy); N = *Neviim* (Prophets: Former Prophets—Joshua, Judges, 1 and 2 Samuel, 1 and 2 Kings, and Latter Prophets—Isaiah, Jeremiah, Ezekiel, Hosea, Joel, Amos, Obadiah, Jonah, Micah, Nahum, Habakkuk, Zephaniah, Haggai, Zechariah, Malachi); Kh = *Ketuvim* (Writings: Psalms, Proverbs, Job, The Song of Songs, Ruth, Lamentations, Ecclesiastes, Esther, Daniel, Ezra, Nehemiah, 1 and 2 Chronicles).

9. It is important to realize that what are being compared here are *literatures* and not *histories*. Questions of historical truth—whether of creation, the flood, the Sinai revelation, etc.—are not the subject of this book. The issue that is being addressed here is how important biblical texts understand reality and the ethics of monotheism.

10. One can ask, of course, the same question about the physical finds of archaeology (tombs, pottery, palaces, temples, etc.). However, for the purposes of ideology and ethics, the knowledge that can be garnered from writings is far greater and more detailed.

11. The following analysis has made considerable use of Shemaryahu Talmon's excellent article, "The 'Comparative Method' in Biblical Interpretation—Principles and Problems," esp. 414–16. See also Hallo, "Ancient Near Eastern Texts and Their Relevance for Biblical Exegesis": "Given the frequency of different settings of ancient Near Eastern texts . . . it is useful to recognize such contrasts as well as comparisons or, if one prefers, to operate with negative as well as positive comparison."

12. See Tigay, "On Evaluating Claims of Literary Borrowing," 253–55.

1. The Jewish Bible's Unique Understanding of God

1. See, most recently, the wide variety of relevant material published in the three-volume compilation edited by William W. Hallo, *The Context of Scripture: Canonical Compositions, Monumental Inscriptions, and Archival Documents from the Biblical World.*

2. See *The Religion of Israel*, Moshe Greenberg's translated and abridged edition of Yehezkel Kaufmann's trailblazing eight-volume Hebrew opus.

Much of the formulation expressed herein I learned as a teaching assistant in Shalom Paul's class in biblical religion in the early 1970s.

3. This is true whether one believes (as do Orthodox Jews) that most of the Torah has one author or (in accord with the documentary hypothesis) that the creation story in Gen. 1:1–2:3 is the product of P (the Priestly source or school). Most academics who hold with the documentary hypothesis view P as both a source and an editor (responsible for editing Genesis–Numbers). In this scheme, both the Genesis creation story and the Ten Commandments come from P.

4. All references here to the Babylonian creation epic are based upon the classic translation and study by Alexander Heidel, *The Babylonian Genesis*. It should be noted that many creation traditions exist in the ancient Near East. *Enuma Elish* (and Utnapishtim afterwards) is used here for demonstrative purposes, and due to its popularity, in the many comparisons and contrasts to the creation story of Gen. 1:1–2:3. The result, as will be noted in the text, is that the biblical stories were written with the Babylonian ones in mind. Scholarly attempts have also been made to show connections between Egyptian creation stories and Gen. 1:1–2:3, although these connections appear to be less than the Babylonian ones. Two obvious similarities to Egyptian stories are the existence of primordial waters and creation by divine speech. See the graduate paper by Tony L. Shetter, "Genesis 1–2 in Light of Ancient Egyptian Creation Myths." I thank Dru Johnson for this reference. One interesting Egyptian parallel to the Genesis 1 creation story appears in "The Instruction to [King] Merikare" (based on copies from as late as the fourteenth century BCE, but may have originated as early as the last part of the third millenium BCE. *COS*, 1: 65–66), although it is doubtful that this story influenced the Genesis 1 creation story:

> Well tended is mankind—god's cattle.
> He [the god] made sky and earth [Gen. 1:1] for their sake,
> He subdued the water monster [a similar motif to Tiamat in *Enuma Elish*],
> He made breath for their noses to live [Gen. 2:7].
> They are his images [Gen. 1:26–27], who came from his body.
> He shines in the sky for their sake;
> He made for them plants and cattle,
> Fowl and fish to feed them [Gen. 1:26, 28–29, 9:2–3].
> He slew his foes, reduced his children,
> When they thought of making rebellion.

He makes daylight for their sake [Gen. 1:14],
He sails by to see them.
He has built his shrine around them,
When they weep he hears.
He made for them rulers in the egg,
Leaders to raise the back of the weak.
He made for them magic as weapons
To ward off the blow of events,
Guarding them by day and by night.
He has slain the traitors among them,
As a man beats his own son for his brother's sake,
For god knows every name.

The selection above has intriguing similarities to Genesis creation stories (see the brackets), even while placing the god squarely within the norms of ancient Near Eastern paganism—note the references to the god as the sun and magic. Further, ambiguity abounds, so humans are called both the "god's cattle" and "his images, who came from his body." Nonetheless, the god here is clearly the benefactor of humanity. Compare Tigay, "On Evaluating Claims of Literary Borrowing," 252. It is worthwhile here to quote at length Jon Assman's commentary on the above passage ("Monotheism and Polytheism," 23):

This is not only an extremely anthropocentric view of creation, it is also a monotheistic view of the divine. The text speaks of God; other gods are not mentioned. This kind of monotheism, however, is not a matter of religion, but of genre and perspective. If one looks at the world in the way that this text does, the principles of plurality and differentiation disappear, and the ultimate unity of the divine appears. This perspective is characteristic of the genre of wisdom literature, a forerunner of moral philosophy that reflects in a very general way on the fundamentals of human existence. Egyptian wisdom literature generally speaks of god instead of specific gods. This is not only a generic term, to be filled in by a specific god as the case may be (a god instead of the god), but a specific term referring to the sun-god and creator, as in the Instruction of Merikare. In the perspective of moral philosophy, this is the only god that really counts, the one god on which everything else (including the other gods) depends. Such a "monotheism of perspective" is conventionally termed henotheism to distinguish it from monolatry as a monotheism of cult, worship, and commitment, whereas the term *monotheism* is reserved for a combination of both: the transformation of a henotheistic perspective into a full-fledged religion or vice versa, the transformation of a monolatrous cult (which recognizes the existence of other gods but worships only one) into a religion adopting the henotheistic perspective in which the other gods do not exist at all.

In Egypt, the henotheistic perspective of wisdom literature and the polytheism of cult coexist without any apparent conflict.

5. No written versions of *Enuma Elish* precede the first millennium BCE. Most academic scholars date any narratives about Sinai to the tenth century BCE or later. Genesis 1 is dated by most academics to anywhere from the late pre-Exilic period to the early post-Exilic period. However, the fact that Genesis 1 reflects old, detailed Israelite traditions is obvious from such texts as Exod. 2:1–3 (which relies on both Genesis 1 and the Noah story) and Isa. 11:6–9 (eighth century BCE), which depicts a future universal vegetarianism and harmony between humans and animals. Ideal futures are often reminiscent of ideal pasts. Note that the antiquity of Genesis 1 may also be supported by a ninth-century BCE Aramaic text from northeastern Syria (today) about the dedication of a statue of a Syrian god which contains cognates for both Hebrew terms used in Gen. 1:26–27: "image" and "likeness" (COS, 2:153–54n10).

6. *Enuma Elish*, Tablet IV, line 14. This quote and those in the next paragraph are all from Lambert, "Mesopotamian Creation Stories."

7. *Enuma Elish*, Tablet IV, lines 96–102.

8. *Enuma Elish*, Tablet IV, lines 137–40.

9. Rare texts such as Ps. 74:12–17 (compare 89:7–12) represent mythological borrowings from other cultures that depict God as warring against the sea and sea monsters at the time of creation. However, even here these elements do not signify any real challenges to God's omnipotence. These unusual texts are "merely episodes, evidences of divine power that were suitable embellishments for hymns" (Kaufmann, *The Religion of Israel*, 292n2).

10. This majestic view of man is pointed out by Rabbi Joseph B. Soloveitchik in his brilliant article, "The Lonely Man of Faith."

11. *Ruach* can mean either "wind" or "spirit." The Latin *spiritus* originally meant wind. The invisibility of wind probably gave rise to its spiritual meaning.

12. See Unterman, *From Repentance*, 49, 187. Other "mother" images of God appear in Jer. 31:20 and Isa. 66:13.

13. Similarly, see Sarna, *JPS Torah Commentary: Genesis*, 12–13, regarding the verse's meaning as it relates rulership to 'image' of God.

14. See in chapter 2 for the discussion on the Sinaitic treaty.

15. Gen. 16:2–6; 21:10–12; 27:46–28:2; 30:1–3, 16; 31:4–16. Note also the equality of the lovers in the Song of Songs where, if anything, the woman's voice predominates.

16. The *"wayward and rebellious son who does not heed the voice of his father and the voice of his mother"* can be brought by both parents to the court and is subject to the death penalty (Deut. 21:18–21; compare Prov. 19:26).

17. See chapter 2 on the significance of the metaphor of *torah* in depicting the parent-child relationship.

18. Frymer-Kensky, *Studies in Bible and Feminist Criticism*, 166–67.

19. See Hasel, "Sabbath."

20. The earliest such statement I found is in Heidel, *Babylonian Genesis*, 125.

21. Similarly, see the depiction of creation in Ps. 8:4–9. This point is made also in the context of covenant in an excellent work by Joshua Berman, *Created Equal: How the Bible Broke with Ancient Political Thought*. Loewenstamm, "Beloved Is Man in That He Was Created in the Image" showed, on the basis of two Assyrian texts (eighth–seventh century BCE), that the biblical conception of the human as royalty in the creation story was practically identical to the Assyrian understanding of the king as the statue (the cognate for the Hebrew *tzelem*, "image") of the god. Note how the Jewish Bible democratizes the idea. I thank Shalom Paul for this reference. Comparably, see Curtis, "Man as the Image of God in Genesis in the Light of Ancient Near Eastern Parallels." Theoretically, one may think that the majestic view of humans in Genesis 1 could be challenged by the statements in Lev. 25:42 and 55 that the Israelites are God's servants or slaves (the Hebrew word *eved* can mean either). However, the context is how the Israelites are to treat those of their fellows who are temporarily slaves/servants, and these statements serve as motivating reminders that God is the ultimate master who redeemed them from Egypt. Thus one is not permitted to treat another Israelite harshly (verses 43 and 54), as did the Egyptians (Exod. 1:13, 14). In like manner, Lev. 25:23 refers to the Israelites as resident aliens in God's eyes, meaning that they are not permitted to sell off any piece of the Land permanently, since God is the Land's ultimate owner.

22. All references to this Babylonian flood story are based on another classic work by Alexander Heidel, *The Gilgamesh Epic and Old Testament Parallels*.

23. Finkelstein, "Bible and Babel," 365–66, claims that there is nothing sub-

stantially different between the "noise" heard by Enlil and that heard by God emanating from Sodom and Gomorrah (Gen. 18:20–21; 19:13), that is, both are due to the wickedness of mankind. However, the Babylonian text clearly indicates that the noise is due to human overpopulation! Finkelstein does make a good point, though, that in the late Assyrian version of the Atrahasis epic (seventh century BCE), Atrahasis pleads with the gods on behalf of his fellow men concerning a plague that is sent upon them before the flood. Again, the purpose of the analysis here is not to reject the idea that moral views existed in the ancient Near East.

24. For other connections between the biblical creation and flood stories, see Sarna, *JPS Torah Commentary: Genesis,* 49–50.

25. See Frymer-Kensky's excellent comparison of the Babylonian flood stories with that of Noah in "The Atrahasis Epic and Its Significance for Our Understanding of Genesis 1–9." The fickleness of the Babylonian gods here has recently been analyzed in a detailed article by Jacob Klein, "A New Look at the Theological Background of the Mesopotamian and Biblical Flood Stories."

26. What God does "regret" is the making of humans who end up behaving so violently (Gen. 6:6–7). Rather than hinting that God is not omniscient in terms of the future, in keeping with the pedagogical character of the Bible this description of God's interior thinking/emotions is probably designed simply to teach us a lesson about humanity's proclivities.

27. Frymer-Kensky, "The Atrahasis Epic," 152–54.

28. No demons exist in the Hebrew Bible. The figure of Satan (Hebrew for "adversary") is not that of a divine power of evil. Rather, he is an angel who only appears (and rarely) in the last writings of the Bible and acts to incite humans to behave contrary to God's desires (Job 1–2; 1 Chron. 21:1), similar to the serpent in Gen. 3:1–5. Job 1–2 is exceptional in terms of permitting unjustified suffering, if only temporarily. See the excursus on theodicy at the end of chapter 5 below.

29. See, for instance, Jer. 18:11–12, 18 where "thinking thoughts" means "devising plans."

30. See also Josh. 24:15, 22; 1 Kings 18:21; Isa. 66:3–4; Prov. 1:29. The brief discussion here in no way attempts to identify any philosophic perspective on free will. Rather, it is merely pointing out a basic assumption of the text.

31. This is in accordance with the ancient Rabbinic statement that God gave humans the evil inclination and the Torah as the antidote. See Babylonian Talmud, *Kiddushin* 30b.

32. Some might wish to claim that the only assurance here is that God will not

destroy the world again by flood but that other worldwide catastrophes are possible. Such a claim takes the Bible out of its context. In biblical times, only a flood could cause such a catastrophe, and it could not occur without Divine sanction. Volcanoes, earthquakes, droughts, locusts, and other plagues were always known to be geographically limited and temporary. No one in those days knew of the possibility and consequences of a massive meteor strike or fantasized about an alien invasion.

33. Goetze and Levy, "Fragment of the Gilgamesh Epic from Megiddo."
34. I thank Professor Yair Zakovitch for this formulation.
35. I thank Marvin Sweeney for this example.
36. Walton, *Ancient Israelite Literature in Its Cultural Context*, 19–42, casts doubts on the possibility that the Bible's creation and flood stories were written in cognizance of the ancient Near East ones. However, he doesn't consider that the biblical stories may have been written to counteract those of the ancient Near East.

2. The Revelation at Sinai

1. Irving Greenberg, in *The Jewish Way*, 24–25, 64, claims that the Exodus from Egypt was the most important event in the Bible. However, according to the Jewish Bible, the Sinai revelation was unquestionably that event which best defined the God-Israel relationship–and therefore Israel's self-identity and history—according to most of the Torah, the historical writings, prophecy, and Psalms.
2. This aspect may be already recognized in the Bible itself. See Deut. 4:32–33: *"You have but to inquire about bygone ages that came before you, ever since God created man on earth, and from one end of the heaven to the other, has anything as great as this ever happened or has its like ever been heard of? Has any people ever heard the voice of a god speaking from the midst of fire, as you have heard, and survived?"* Also see Deut. 4:34–36). This idea enters innocently into the Rabbinic midrash that universalizes it: the story that God first offered the Ten Commandments to (and was rejected by) each of the nations before approaching Israel.
3. I thank Marvin Sweeney for this characterization.
4. Unterman, "The Social-Legal Origin for the Image of God as Redeemer *go'el* of Israel," 399. I thank Ed Greenstein for pointing out to me that the covenant and law metaphors reflect the text's true understanding of the God-Israel relationship. That is probably also true for the idea of the "kingdom of priests and a holy nation" and the parent-child relationship implicit in the idea of *torah*. Of course, the text considers Israel to be not

God's biological child but rather God's adopted firstborn. Adoption formulas are well known in both the ancient Near East and the Jewish Bible.

5. The seminal study on these similarities was written by George E. Mendenhall, "Covenant Forms in Israelite Tradition." For a more recent overview, see "Covenant" by Mendenhall and Gary A. Herion in the *Anchor Bible Dictionary*. See also Unterman, "Covenant." Some scholars have tried to relate the biblical Sinai covenant, especially as found in Deuteronomy, to later (seventh century BCE) Assyrian treaties. However, Assyrian treaties lack certain elements found in both Hittite and the Sinai treaties, which attests to the antiquity of the idea in Israel. See the meticulous analysis by K. A. Kitchen, *On the Reliability of the Old Testament*, 283–94. The Hittites are thought to be a people of Indo-European origin who settled in what is today Turkey. They established one of the great ancient Near East empires of the second millennium BCE.

6. Exod. 20:8–23:33; Deut. 5:12–18; and see 5:28 on.

7. Note that in the treaty that Joshua makes with the people to obey God (Josh. 24, and see 25 there), the people declare themselves to be witnesses (22). Joshua also designates a particular stone as a witness (27).

8. Pss. 99:5; 132:7–8; 1 Chron. 28:2.

9. Compare Josh. 8:30–35.

10. See Nehemiah 8. It should be noted that Moses, Joshua, and Ezra (in Nehemiah 8) are not kings. The emphasis here is on the examples of public readings. It should further be noted that Joshua's treaty with the people (Joshua 24) is one that he, not God, is making with them, although this event may be perceived to be a renewal of the Sinaitic treaty.

11. Note that in Exod. 24:10–11, the elders of the people see God! How can this be, when to see God is death? *"Yet He did not raise His hand against the nobles of the Children of Israel"* (see also Exod. 33:20; Judg. 13:22; Isa. 6:5). This one exception to that rule in the Bible must be due to the necessity of a ceremonial meal which ratifies the treaty before the Treaty-maker. It may also be that the nobles did not see the "face" of God, as in Exod. 33:20: *"But,"* He said, *"you cannot see My face, for man may not see Me and live."*

12. This fact also holds for other biblical treaties that God makes with people, such as the unconditional treaty that God makes with Abraham (Gen. 15:18) and Phineas (Num. 25:12–13) as well as the treaty with David (Ps. 89:4–5, 29, 35–36, on the basis of 2 Samuel 7). One Phoenician inscription exists that may be evidence that another ancient culture had the concept of a treaty with its gods, but even if true, the content of any such treaty has

not been found. Further, the seventh century BCE origin of this inscription is no proof that it preceded the Israelite concept of a divine treaty. See Zevit, "A Phoenician Inscription and Biblical Covenant Theology."

13. I thank Shalom Paul for pointing out to me that the Sinai treaty structure is the first allusion to God's kingship in the Torah's narrative. Further, God's kingship is implied by Exodus 19:6 (where the treaty is mentioned in verse 5), "and you shall be to me a kingdom of priests." If the people are the subjects in the kingdom, then who else can be the king other than God? It should be noted that God's kingship is already mentioned in poetry at the end of the Song of the Sea (Exod. 15:18) and in Num. 23:21 and Deut. 33:5, all ancient texts. In Ps. 44:5, 18; 74:12, 20, God's kingship is cited along with the (Sinai) treaty (and perhaps also Ps. 95:3, 7, where "if you would obey His voice today" echoes Exod. 19:5).

14. I thank Marvin Sweeney for this observation.

15. The one exception is the treaty made by Arnuwanda I of Hatti with the Men of Ismerika. See Beckman, *Hittite Diplomatic Texts*, 13–17. However, these men were apparently not a people but rather soldiers sworn to protect and defend the king's interests.

16. "You" in the plural form (referring to each member of the people) appears in Exod. 19:4–6 and is responded by the "we" form in verse 8. In the Ten Commandments, "you" in the singular is used supposedly in reference to the entire people. However, each action described is that done by an individual (Exod. 20:7, 10, 12–14). This point is made brilliantly by Berman, *Created Equal*, 40–44. Berman's book is the best analysis to date on the egalitarian aspects of biblical covenant and law (particularly that found in Deuteronomy), and this egalitarianism was a forerunner of the Enlightenment's democratic ideals. At the same time, it is necessary to recognize the patriarchal elements of biblical society. Women are totally excluded from participation in the priesthood and the military and generally ruled out of landownership, the judiciary, and the kingship (Berman, *Created Equal*, 13–14). Women also seem to be excluded from the holiday pilgrimages to the sanctuary: "*Three times a year all your males shall appear before the Master, the Lord God of Israel*" (Exod. 34:23; Deut. 16:16), although they are included in the public reading of the Torah every seventh year on Sukkot (the Feast of Tabernacles), according to Deut. 31:12. It is questionable how many laws are directed only for men to carry out, even if they are also of benefit to the women. So in the Ten Commandments, in an uncommon example, one is enjoined not to covet his neighbor's wife—hardly an injunction directed to a woman. At the same time,

women, unstated, are presumed to be included in the requirement not to
work on the Sabbath.

17. In reference to Deuteronomy, compare Berman, *Created Equal*, 196n94.

18. Most of the conclusions in this section in relationship to ancient Near
East and biblical law are based upon Shalom Paul's lectures and his seminal work, *Studies in the Book of the Covenant in the Light of Cuneiform
and Biblical Law.*

19. These collections derive from four different empires: Sumerian (Ur-
Nammu and Lipit-Ishtar), Babylonian (Eshnunna and Hammurabi),
Hittite (the Hittite Laws), Assyrian (Middle-Assyrian Laws). Transla-
tions for these and more minor collections may be found in Roth, *Law
Collections from Mesopotamia and Asia Minor.* Roth's dating is used
here. All references to specific laws are taken from Roth.

20. See Wilson, "Authority and Law in Ancient Egypt," 5–7.

21. Paul, *Studies*, 8–9. Indeed, some of ritual laws were to be known secretly
only to the priests (9n1).

22. Roth, *Law Collections*, 76, 80–81, 133–35.

23. Most scholars are of the opinion that the laws in these collections were
already societal legal norms which are simply adopted by the king. In
any case, the king claims authorship of the laws.

24. After all, the stela was placed in the temple. It may be assumed that only
priests had access to it. See Paul, *Studies*, 38.

25. However, the law collections were apparently based on earlier ones,
indicating a scholastic tradition, not a public one. See Eichler, "Examples of Restatement in the Laws of Hammurabi," esp. 365n2.

26. Indeed, no Israelite king is ever said to author a law code. See Moshe
Greenberg, "Some Postulates of Biblical Criminal Law," 11. However,
kings might issue decrees that go against Torah norms (1 Sam. 8:14–18;
compare 1 Kings 4:7; 5:27–30).

27. Exod. 20:1, 19; 30:11; 31:1; 34:10; Lev. 1:1; 4:1, 14; 6:1; Num. 5:5, 11; 6:1, 22;
8:1. Since all of Deuteronomy is Moses' speech summarizing the past
forty years and preparing the people for their entry into the Promised
Land, Moses' recapitulation of the laws simply mentions their Divine
origins. For example, "to keep the commandments of the Lord your
God that I am commanding you" (Deut. 4:2), "I taught you the rules
and laws which the Lord commanded me to do so" (verse 5), "and keep
His rules and His commandments which I command you this day"
(verse 40), "this day the Lord your God commands you to do these rules
and laws" (26:16), and so forth. Divine authorship is also emphasized by

the use of the first person singular within the laws (the Ten Commandments; Exod. 21:13; 22:22–23, 26, 28–30; 23:7, 13–15; Lev. 6:10; 11:44–45;
17:10–12, 14; 18:2–5, 26, 30; 19:2–4, 30–32, 34, 36–37; Num. 6:26–27; 10:10;
15:2, 18, etc.). It should be noted that the idea that law originated with
God influenced Christianity in terms of the Ten Commandments and
the Golden Rule. However, papal law was not perceived as divine. Islam
was also influenced, but it saw law as coming from both God and
Mohammed.

28. Paul, *Studies,* 31.
29. Known in the field of biblical law as apodictic style, direct address was
    used sometimes in nonlegal texts, such as Hittite treaties, moral direc-
    tives, and wisdom literature (see Paul, *Studies,* 112–24).
30. Paul, "Biblical Law," 72–73. Greenstein, "Biblical Law," 100, also empha-
    sizes the caring nature of biblical law: "Typically, biblical law cares about
    people, whereas Mesopotamian law worries about money." There, on
    Exod. 22:25–26, he states that the text refers "to God's personal concern
    for the indigent borrower."
31. Paul, *Studies,* 38.
32. See also Neh. 8 and compare 2 Kings 23:1–3. The contrast between Exod.
    21:1 and Hammurabi's epilogue may settle a difference of opinion
    between two famous medieval Jewish commentators in favor of Rashi
    (Rabbi Solomon ben Isaac, eleventh century), who states that *"before
    them"* refers to the people, as opposed to Nachmanides (Rabbi Moses
    ben Nachman, thirteenth century), who opines that it refers to the
    judges. In later Jewish practice, the seventh year public reading eventu-
    ally became a reading of the entire Torah that took place in the syna-
    gogue on a weekly basis and was completed once every three years.
    Within the past two thousand years, a larger portion is read in the syna-
    gogue every week so that the reading of the entire Torah takes place
    annually (which culminates in the "Rejoicing of the Torah" celebration
    at the end of Sukkot).
33. For example, Lev. 1:1; 4:1; 12:1; Num. 6:1; 15:37–38; 35:9–10. Compare
    Exod. 24:3. See Moshe Greenberg, "Three Conceptions of the Torah in
    Hebrew Scriptures," 14–15, and his emphasis that publication of the law
    was done orally.
34. Repeated, in nearly identical words, in Deut. 11:19.
35. Paul, *Studies,* 31. The metaphors are so interwoven that sometimes
    scholars characterize the Torah's law as "covenantal law."
36. For the significant exception of vicarious punishment, see below. Fur-

thermore, the civil and criminal laws, for example, in Hammurabi's collection, apply differently to people of various classes. Biblical law has no such class structure. I thank Marvin Sweeney for this formulation.

37. Certain laws indicate reward to the individual for obedience, such as honoring parents (Exod. 20:12), giving to the needy (Deut. 15:10, compare Deut. 24:12, 19), and sending away the mother bird before taking the nestlings (Deut. 22:6–7).

38. Greenberg, "Some Postulates of Biblical Criminal Law," 11–12.

39. For example, Jer. 33:11; Pss. 25:7–8; 34:9; 73:1; 100:5; 135:3; 136:1; 145:7–9; Ezra 3:11; 1 Chron. 16:34. The morality of God is a ubiquitous theme in the Jewish Bible. So when Moses asks to be shown God's glory, He replies, *"I will cause all my goodness to pass before you"* (Exod. 33:19). See also the parallel of Amos 5:4, 6 with 14, *"Seek Me that you shall live," "Seek the Lord that you shall live,"* and *"Seek good and not evil in order that you will live."*

40. See also Neh. 9:13: *"You gave them right laws and true instructions, good statutes and commandments."*

41. Compare Deut. 5:28–30; 6:24; 10:12–13; 12:28; 30:15–20; 1 Sam. 15:22; 1 Kings 8:36; Mic. 6:8. The idea that God's "way" requires ethical behavior in order to receive benefits is already stated at the beginning of the Sodom and Gomorrah episode. God reveals to Abraham His intentions: *"for I have singled him out, that he may command his children and his posterity to keep the way of the Lord by doing righteousness and justice, in order that the Lord will bring upon Abraham what He has promised him"* (Gen. 18:19).

42. This section relies on Moshe Greenberg's, "Some Postulates of Biblical Criminal Law" and "The Biblical Grounding of Human Value."

43. This is also the law in Lipit-Ishtar 9, which does not, however, delineate between day and night.

44. This is also the case in the Hittite laws 57–70, 101–3, 119–43 (and see Lipit-Ishtar 9 and Eshnunna 6).

45. In Nathan's famous parable to David (which David thinks is a real case) on his taking of Bathsheba, David's desire is to kill the thief, but he decides in accordance with this law (2 Sam. 12:1–6).

46. For example, Exod. 21:33–36; 22:4–5.

47. See Westbrook, "Punishments and Crimes," 550.

48. See Greenberg, "Some Postulates of Biblical Criminal Law," 20–21.

49. This is also true of sexual crimes, as opposed to the ancient Near East. See Greenberg, "Some Postulates," 21–23.

50. See also Lev. 24:19, *"so it will be done to him."* Exod. 21:29–32 is the case of the known goring ox—a case of negligent but unintentional, homicide, in which the defendant is not directly involved. As such, it is a special case, the only case in which ransom is permitted (30). However, verse 31 states unequivocally that vicarious punishment is not permitted: *"So, too, if it gores a son or a daughter,* [the owner] *shall be dealt with according to the same statute."* See Moshe Greenberg, "More Reflections on Biblical Criminal Law," esp. 9–15.

51. See Greenberg, "Biblical Grounding of Human Value," 42–48.

52. Far from being hidden, it is known that this epic was recited to the statue of the god Marduk in Babylon during the New Year's festival in the Neo-Babylonian empire. It was also adopted by the Assyrians. See Greenberg, "Biblical Grounding of Human Value," 42.

53. In this section, most of the understanding of the biblical concept of the people's holiness is taken from the teachings of Jacob Milgrom, the preeminent scholar on the ideology behind biblical ritual. His magisterial three-volume Anchor Bible commentary on Leviticus is unrivaled (*Leviticus 1–16, 17–22, 23–27*), to say nothing of his other books and more than two hundred articles.

54. Some source theorists ascribe this text to JE. For example, see Propp, *Exodus 19–40*, 142. However, other theorists see it as J, or E (Schwartz, "Israel's Holiness: The Torah Traditions," 50), or a redactor. In general, it seems that greater uncertainty exists among the source theorists concerning older narratives than later ones.

55. See Walton, *Ancient Israelite Literature in Its Cultural Context*, 127.

56. Schwartz, "Israel's Holiness: The Torah Traditions," 47–48. The Hebrew root for "holiness," *qdsh,* appears as a verb, noun, and adjective more than 850 times in the Tanakh. Wright, "Holiness (OT)," 237.

57. Temples, depending upon the particular locale, also had economic and political functions and could contain libraries. See Ward, "Temples and Sanctuaries—Egypt," and Robertson, "Temples and Sanctuaries—Mesopotamia." Additionally, Ancient Near East priests had functions as diviners, mourners, musicians, and exorcists (Milgrom, *Leviticus 1–16*, 52). None of these were functions of the Israelite priest, although the high priest—by use of the Urim and Thummim—could apparently petition God for a yes or no response to an important question. For a general overview of the functions of the Israelite priesthood, see Milgrom, *Leviticus 1–16*, 52–57, and Schiffman, "Priests."

58. Lev. 10:11; Deut. 17:8–11; 24:8; 33:8–10; 2 Kings 12:3; 17:27–28; Mic. 3:11 (a

rebuke); Jer. 18:18 (rebuke); Ezek. 7:6; 44:23; Hag. 2:11; Mal. 2:7; 2 Chron. 15:3; 17:9.

59. Similarly, in Exod. 4:22, Israel is termed the "firstborn" of God. In the ancient Near East, it was not uncommon for the firstborn to inherit two portions to every other son's single portion (Middle Assyrian Laws B1; Deut. 21:17) and also to take responsibility for the family. If Israel is God's firstborn, then the implication is that every other nation is a lesser son. So for Egypt to attempt to destroy Israel is a rebellion against God's designation and a usurpation of Divine authority. Thus Egypt's brutal enslavement of Israel becomes justification for the tenth plague, the death of the firstborn (see Exod. 4:23).

60. Stated explicitly in Lev. 25:42, 55.

61. Exodus 31:13–17 makes the Sabbath the sign of both God's sanctification of Israel (13) as well as a sign of His treaty with the people (16–17), just as circumcision was the sign of the patriarchal treaty that God made with Abraham (Genesis 17).

62. The people's holiness is also reiterated and expanded upon in Deuteronomy (7:6; 14:2, 21; 26:18–19). There (unlike Leviticus), Israel's holiness is a result of God's election and decision to make the people His treasured possession (again reiterating Exod. 19:6). However, this holy status is dependent upon the people's obedience to the treaty/laws. See Weinfeld, *Deuteronomy and the Deuteronomic School*, 226–28. Inasmuch as the treaty/laws contain both ethical and ritual elements, and Deuteronomy has a distinct humanistic disposition (Weinfeld, 282–97), Israel's holiness here, too, is ethically informed. Milgrom, *Leviticus 17–22*, 1384 (and see 1349–64), attributes Lev. 17–27 (H, the Holiness code that presumes P) to the eighth century BCE. Milgrom's commentary on Leviticus 19 alone runs to 130 pages!

63. Lev. 19:3, 9–18, 20–22, 29, 32–36.

64. Indeed, Lev. 19 deliberately alludes to the Ten Commandments, while reversing their order in verses 3–4: *"You shall each revere his mother and his father, and keep My Sabbaths; I am the Lord your God. Do not turn to idols or make molten gods for yourselves; I am the Lord your God"* (see also 11–12, theft and swearing falsely, and the second half of 36, which appears at the beginning of the Ten Commandments).

65. Milgrom, *Leviticus 17–22*, 1403. As is well known, Lev. 19:18 had great influence in early Rabbinic material. See Rabbi Akiba's statement (Sifra Kedoshim 4:12) and Hillel's (BT Shabbat 31a; JT Nedah 9), and the New Testament (Matt. 7:2; Luke 6:13; Rom. 13:8–10). It is interesting that Hillel's version is already found in Tobit 4:15, and the same idea appears in

Confucius's teachings (fifth century BCE). See Chan, "Confucian Thought: Foundations of the Tradition," esp. 17. Biblical law concerning the resident alien is ethically unique in the ancient Near East and will be dealt with in chapter 3.

66. Both here and its only other occurrences in the Bible, 1 Kings 5:15 and 2 Chron. 19:2. See Milgrom, *Leviticus 17–22*, 1403, 1653–56.

67. Joseph Telushkin makes a similar point about American law in *Biblical Literacy*, 461.

68. Milgrom, *Leviticus 23–27*, 2442–43.

69. Milgrom, *Leviticus 23–27*, 1400.

70. Lev. 20:26; Milgrom, *Leviticus 23–27*, 1604–6. Milgrom also points out that God's holiness is differentiated from the holiness of the people (or any other holy thing) in Leviticus (and all P and H texts, according to him) by the very spelling of the different usages of the word *qadosh*. Every time *qadosh* refers to God, it is written with full spelling. Otherwise, it is "defective."

71. Lopez and Fabry, "*tora* instruction, teaching," 15:612.

72. "*This Torah*," Deut. 1:5; 4:44; 27:3, 26; 28:58; "*This book of the Torah*," 28:61; 29:20; 30:10; 31:26. See Unterman, "Torah," 1083.

73. In later Judaism, the term came to mean not only the Pentateuch ("the written Torah") but also the Talmud ("the oral Torah"). Indeed, all of Jewish tradition is referred to as Torah. Unterman, "Torah," 1084; Lopez and Fabry, "*tora* instruction, teaching." 639.

74. Propp, *Exodus 19–40*, 148, assigns Exod. 24:12 to E, that is, eighth century BCE or earlier (p. 730).

75 All the laws from Lev. 1:1 through Num. 9:14 are stated as given at Sinai. See Milgrom, *Leviticus 1–16*, 139. It is probable that the reference to the plural *torot* in the story of Jethro in Exod. 18:16, 20 is also a reflection of Sinai, as Moses informing the people of God's laws and teachings presupposes the Sinai revelation. This view was first espoused by Rabbi Eleazar of Modiim (Mechilta Amalek 3; B.T. Zevahim 116a), and was followed by Rashi, Ibn Ezra, and Rashbam.

76. Unterman, "Torah."

77. The only possible biblical texts outside of Proverbs in which *torah* appears not in reference to God are the difficult "*This is the torah of man, Lord God*" of 2 Sam. 7:19, and Ps. 78:1 in which the Psalmist uses wisdom language (2), thereby representing himself as a sage teaching. See on Prov. 13:14 in the text.

78. Prov. 28:4–5, 9.

79. Other references to parents as teachers are Prov. 6:23; 7:1–2; 28:7; 31:26, 28.

80. Compare Prov. 29:18, which is admittedly ambiguous. It may either refer to the wisdom of a sage or that of a father (17), or even to God's instruction.

81. See Unterman, "Torah," 1084, Lopez and Fabry, "*tora* instruction, teaching," 633–34, and Liedke and Peterson, "*tora* Instruction." They opine that the *torah* of the parents, especially the mother, "was the ultimate origin" of the concept of Divine *torah* (1416). Indeed, in Proverbs, the child must obey the teachings of the mother, not just the father, 1:8; 6:20, and the mother is also regarded as contributing to the child's education (6:20; 10:1; 15:20; 19:26; 23:22–25; 30:17).

82. See Crenshaw, *Education in Ancient Israel*, and his earlier "Education in Ancient Israel." Crenshaw's position disagrees with that of Andre Lemaire, "Education," 2:308. However, as Crenshaw concludes (at the end of his chapter on "Schools in Ancient Israel," 112), "inscriptions leave little doubt that schools existed in Israel from about the eighth century, if not earlier, but they do not clarify the nature of these places of learning." He opines that, at the most, these schools belonged to "a few scribal guilds." Public schools only developed in the late Second Temple period, in accord with Rabbinic tradition (113). On the other hand, in the book's conclusion, he states "the primary teachers . . . were parents, and the home provided a natural setting for their instruction" (279, see also "Education in Ancient Israel," 614). Indeed, everywhere in the Bible in which children are depicted as being educated, it is the responsibility of the parents (for example, Exod. 10:2; 12:26–27; 13:8, 14–15; Deut. 4:9; 6:7, 20–25; 11:19; 32:7, 46, etc.). It is also conceivable that some kind of formal learning was required for priests' sons.

83. See Fox, *Proverbs 1–9*, 80. See also Nel, "The Concept of 'Father' in the Wisdom Literature of the Ancient Near East," and Weinfeld, *Deuteronomy*, 305.

84. Jacobsen, *Treasures of Darkness*, esp. 145–64.

85. Jacobsen, *Treasures of Darkness*, 158–59.

86. Jacobsen, *Treasures of Darkness*, 164. Numbers 21:29 (part of the "Heshbon Ballad," verses 27–30) seems to present the only exception, "*You are vanished, people of Chemosh. He has made his sons refugees and his daughters captive.*" In this verse, the people of Chemosh, the national god of Moab, are termed "his sons . . . and his daughters." It should be noted, however, that this is a Hebrew ballad, i.e., it presents the viewpoint of the Israelites, and therefore might not have been Moabite theology, but rather a transposition from Israelite theology. Note, too, that

the indeterminate, assumed "He" might refer to God (compare Amos 2:1–3). However, as Shalom Paul suggests to me, (a) the reference to sons and daughters is simply a Biblical way of referring to the male and female population (in this case) of Moab, and (b) this may be a circumstantial clause which should then be translated as "his sons are rendered . . . " (as per NJPS in accord with the interpretation of Rashi–the famous eleventh-century French Rabbinic exegete). Num. 21:29 is paraphrased in Jer. 48:46, *"Woe to you, O Moab! The people of Chemosh are devastated, for your sons are taken captive, and your daughters into captivity."* The fact that this verse in Jeremiah is unquestionably addressed to Moab may be indicative of the prophet's conviction that Chemosh is no more than an idol (as in Jer. 48:7).

87. 2 Sam. 7:14; Ps. 2:7; 89:27–28.

88. Propp, *Exodus 1–18,* 191, 195, assigns this statement and the following verse to documentary source E. Shalom Paul, "Adoption Formulae: A Study of Cuneiform and Biblical Legal Clauses," has shown that all the references to the Davidic king as the son of God, as well as Exod. 4:22, Jer. 3:19 and 31:8, are based on adoption formulae in ancient Near East family law. I find his evidence more convincing than that of Fensham, "Father and Son as Terminology for Treaty and Covenant," who tries to make the case that the father-son metaphor comes from ancient Near Eastern treaty terminology. The Jeremiah passages will be dealt with below in the text.

89. Noted by Yosef Bechor Shor (twelfth century, France). For God's care for other nations as similar to His care for Israel, see Amos 9:7.

90. The firstborn in Israel (Deut. 21:17) and in much of the ancient Near East legally inherited two portions of the father's estate to every other son's single portion. See Tigay, *The JPS Commentary: Deuteronomy,* 195–96 (and the footnotes cited there). This situation also apparently applies to Jacob's gift to Joseph in Gen. 48:22. The firstborn son also received the father's blessing and inherited succession to authority (Gen. 27:29, 37; 37:21–22; Elisha's metaphoric inheritance from Elijah–2 Kings 2:9). See Unterman, "Firstborn, first fruits, firstling."

91. Similarly, Reuven loses his firstborn status to Joseph, due to his sleeping with his father's secondary wife, Bilhah. See Gen. 35:22; 49:3–4; I Chron. 5:1. Absalom's intercourse with David's, his father, concubines was a blatant act of revolt (2 Sam. 16:21–22). For a similar idea of God punishing those who wish to destroy His first fruits (as opposed to firstborn), see Jer. 2:3.

92. See also Deut. 32:5, 19 ("sons and daughters") and 20 which contain apparent references to Israel as God's children.

93. Similarly, the usage of the Hebrew verb *qnh* in Exod. 15:16 prompts Propp, *Exodus 1–18*, 540, to suggest the translation there of *"the people which you begot."* Deut. 32:18, despite the use of the masculine singular in reference to God, actually uses language which most often refers to the *mother* having labor pains and giving birth. Tigay, *Deuteronomy*, 307. See below in the text for references to God as mother.

94. For this sense of the compassion of a father upon his children, see Ps. 103:13.

95. See also Deut. 32:5, 19.

96. This phrase is similar to Joseph expressing compassion for his full brother, Benjamin (Gen. 43:30), and the mercy of the true mother for her son at the judgment of Solomon (1 Kings 3:26).

97. See also Hosea 2:1.

98. Also, Isa. 1:2, 4.

99. Unterman, *From Repentance*, 183n16.

100. See also verse 4, another statement of God wishing the people to call Him "my Father," and yet they are disloyal. Additionally, see Jer. 3:22, *"Return, O backsliding children, I will heal your afflictions"* in which Jeremiah may be following Hosea in depicting God's healing of His offspring. The exact same words begin verse 14, in a later prophecy of redemption (Unterman, *From Repentance*, 125–26). In 4:22, when the people are called, *"foolish children, and not intelligent. They are wise to do evil but do not know how to do good,"* Jeremiah may be showing familiarity with Hosea 13:13, cited above in the text.

101. The analysis here of Jeremiah 31 is taken from Unterman, *From Repentance*, 47–49.

102. Jer. 31:20 is often mistranslated. The Hebrew word for "womb" is *may-a-yim*, which often means "innards." However, in context, it can only mean "womb," as it does in Gen. 25:23; Isa. 49:1; Ps. 71:6; Ruth 1:11, and the nearly identical phrase in Songs 5:4. Further, the word for "mercy" is understood biblically to be derived from the most common word for "womb"—the Hebrew roots of both words are identical. The idea of God as mother also appears in Gen. 1:2 and Isa. 49:14–15; 63:16 (see below in the text). See Unterman, *From Repentance*, 187n59.

103. Similarly, Ps. 103:13, *"As a father has mercy upon his children, so the Lord has mercy upon those who revere Him."*

3. Providing for the Disadvantaged

1. Westbrook, "Social Justice in the Ancient Near East," 149.
2. Olyan, *Rites and Rank*, 63.
3. It seems that antisemitism may be the one undying hatred, for even after the Holocaust, the hatred of the Jews has been transported into Muslim lands and has morphed there (and among other antisemites) into hatred of both the Jews and the State of Israel.
4. Hallo, cos, 2:334. No scholarly consensus exists on the exact translation of this law. For example, Vargyas, "Immigration into Ugarit," 399–400, translates "woman innkeeper" instead of "tapster."
5. cos, 1:224. A question exists whether the key noun is to be translated "deportee" or "foreigner." We will follow Moshe Weinfeld's translation of the latter on page 77 of "Judge and Officer in Ancient Israel and the Ancient Near East." Weinfeld compares the Hittite text to Deut. 10:18 in his commentary *Deuteronomy 1–11*, 439. Both #44 and #45 following emphasize the need for the border commander to keep an eye on the fields allotted to these foreigners and the harvest.
6. cos, 1:121. It is accepted in academic scholarship that this Egyptian text influenced Proverbs 22:17–24:22.
7. Today the term "wisdom" as applied to a type of Mesopotamian and Egyptian literature is considered imprecise by many scholars in the field, if not a misnomer. This literature is concerned more with "skills," "competence," and "knowing things." "Wisdom literature" probably derives from biblical studies in reference to Proverbs, Job, and Ecclesiastes and assumes a religious ethical piety. Herein, it reflects more common usage. Thus the "sage" in Egypt is more properly the "knower of things." See Lichtheim, *Moral Values in Ancient Egypt*, 1–8.
8. The discussion here on the metics is taken from Christiana van Houten, *The Alien in Israelite Law*, 39, but it is easily replicable.
9. Normally, one would not make conclusions on the basis of the lack of evidence, since such absence may simply be due to the fact that we do not have complete law libraries from the ancient world. However, given the sole reference from Eshnunna in the huge amount of material that we do have, it would be very surprising if the kingdoms and empires that produced the extant law collections and other legal materials (mentioned in chapter 2) had made laws for the protection of foreigners housed within their societies. This understanding is supported by a citation in Milgrom, *Leviticus 17–22*, 1705, of a paper given by the ancient

Near Eastern specialist M. A. Dandamayev (I have not succeeded in locating the original paper or any other references to it). Milgrom states that "Dandamayev (1990) described the legal status of aliens in sixth-century Mesopotamia. They were deprived of civil rights, they could not be members of the . . . city assembly . . . , own property, or have access to the Babylonian temples. . . . Instead, the aliens made up their own assemblies." Further, Susanne Paulus, "Foreigners under Foreign Rulers: The Case of Kassite Babylonia," concludes (9–10):

> The regulations found in the treaties and the examples discussed here make evident that there was no legal status of "foreigner" in the treaties, but that the treatment of this group depended on whether they were still subjects of a foreign king (merchants, messengers) or whether they tried to become the subjects of another king (fugitives).
>
> The same evidence comes from laws and legal texts, where a special status of "foreigner" also does not exist. An interesting exception can be found in the Middle Babylonian curse formulas . . . where the possibility is listed that malefactors . . . instigate others to act against the law instead of them. For example, "(if someone), because he fears these curses written of the stele, instigates a stranger . . . , a foreigner . . . , a son of nobody, a deaf one, a simpleton, an awkward one, or an ignoramus . . ." Here foreigners are treated together with mentally disabled people and those who did not know the rules of society, thus proving once more that being "foreign" was a social rather than legal status.

Finally, Jose E. Ramirez Kidd, *Alterity and Identity in Israel: The Ger in the Old Testament,* states (111): Although strangers and foreigners are mentioned in a wide range of documents (letters, administrative documents, royal inscriptions, confirmations by oath, . . . incantations, omen texts, reports of travels and other kinds of literature), no references are made to them in legal codes, except in those cases in which they are mentioned in the sections dealing with:

> the sale and purchase of *slaves*: the code of Hammurabi, for instance, mentions the "sons of another country" (see paragraphs #280–81), but these are no more than slaves of foreign extraction . . . [p. 112] the prescriptions to regulate the relationships of emigrants and *refugees*: these laws distinguished between the *free immigrant*, i.e., that who leaves his original place for personal or political reasons (Eshnunna

#30; CH #136; 30f.; Lipit Ishtar #15f.), and the *slave* (Lipit Ishtar #12–13; CH #15–20; Hittite Laws #22–24). The flight of slaves of both sexes seems to have been quite common" [and see references cited there].

[p.113] "the theme of the resident alien [is] a unique concern of the Old Testament with no parallel in the surrounding cultures" and [p. 114] "The absence of references to the stranger in the Mesopotamian laws is probably related to the feeling of superiority which was common in these cultures and which led to the archaic counter position 'us' versus 'the others.'"

We shall see that the Jewish Bible permits aliens to bring sacrifices, to participate in Israelite assemblies, and to have numerous rights.

10. In both singular and plural. The simple form of the verb appears eighty-one times. D. Kellerman, "gur; ger; geruth; meghurim," 442.

11. Not all occurrences of the verb refer to the resident alien, so only the noun will be discussed here.

12. Indeed, three times the Hebrew combination *ger vetoshav* appears, "alien and resident" (Gen. 23:4; Lev. 25:35, 47; see also Lev. 25:23; Num. 35:15; Ps. 39:13; 1 Chron. 29:15). Most scholars take this to be a hendiadys, that is, a figure of speech in which a complex idea is represented by two words connected by "and." In other words, "alien and resident" means "resident alien."

13. See Spencer, "Sojourner," 6:103.

14. For example, 2 Sam. 15:19–20. See Milgrom, *Leviticus 17–22*, 1416. *Nokhri* means "foreigner" some forty-five times in the Hebrew Bible. The same root in a different form refers thirty-six times to a foreign land and can also be used for foreign gods. B. Lang, "nkr; nekar; nokri."

15. Deut. 32:16; Isa. 17:10; Jer. 2:25; 3:13; Ps. 44:21; 81:10.

16. Exod. 30:9; Lev. 10:2; 22:12; Num. 17:11; 18:4, 7.

17. Isaiah 1:7; 25:2; Jer. 51:2,51; Ezek. 7:21; 11:9; 28:7, 10; 30:12; 31:12; Hosea 5:7; 7:9; Joel 4:17; Obad. 11; Lam. 5:2.

18. Deut. 25:5; Prov. 27:2; Job 19:15. The discussion on *zar* is based upon Snijders, "zur/zar."

19. From this point on, most of my understanding of the *ger* (unless otherwise noted) is derived from the meticulous analysis of Jacob Milgrom in his incomparable Anchor Bible commentary on Leviticus. See his "Reflections on the Biblical GER," *Leviticus 17–22*, 1416–20 (and 1493–1501).

20. The same motivation for the command *"Do not abhor the Egyptian, for you were a stranger in his land"* (Deut. 23:8). Verse 9 goes on to state, *"Children*

that are born [presumably through intermarriage with Israelites] *to them may be admitted to the congregation of the Lord in the third generation."*

21. See Tigay, *Deuteronomy*, 69 on Deut. 5:15.

22. Academic scholarship (Milgrom, *Leviticus 23–27*, 2424, and see his detailed discussion of the tithe on 2421–34, and Tigay, *Deuteronomy*, 142) understands this law in Deuteronomy as assuming the centralization of the cult in Jerusalem (compare 12:17–19), and therefore includes the Levites among the other poor elements of society (the stranger, orphan, and widow). As this centralization assumes that the local sanctuaries have been abolished, the Levites would now be deprived of the tithe they had received there (Num. 18:21–32, esp. 31). Ancient Rabbinic law (Tigay, 141), however, views all tithes as part of a single system of three obligatory tithes: Num. 18 has a "first tithe" given to the Levites (who then gave a tenth of that to the priests); Lev. 27:30–33 and Deut. 14:21–27 decree a "second tithe" eaten by the donors themselves; Deut. 14:28–29 mentions a "third tithe" for the poor.

23. See endnote 12, above. It is not clear, though, that *toshav* in Lev. 25:40 refers to the *ger*.

24. It might be possible that as Num. 9:14 would appear to relate to the Passover delayed to the second month (known as the "second" Passover—see the previous verses 10–13), the stranger may join in without undergoing circumcision. See Milgrom, *Numbers*, 70.

25. See the citations brought in Milgrom, *Leviticus 23–27*, 2205–9. However, I disagree with Milgrom's view that the text is saying, "Do not charge him interest as if he were a resident alien." Nowhere in the Torah is there an indication that it was permissible to charge interest of the resident alien. In fact, Deut. 23:21 precisely only permits charging interest of foreigners (*nokhri*), who are most probably merchants temporarily in the land. (Deuteronomy knows how to differentiate the *nokhri* from the *ger*. See 14:21.) It would be hard to reconcile either Lev. 19:33–34 or Deut. 10:18–19 with Milgrom's view here.

26. The discussion in this paragraph is in accord with Milgrom, *Leviticus 17–22*, 1417–18.

27. Milgrom, *Leviticus 17–22*, 1496.

28. Weinfeld, *Deuteronomy and the Deuteronomic School*, 230; Tigay, *Deuteronomy*, 140.

29. Milgrom, *Leviticus 17–22*, 1419.

30. Milgrom, *Leviticus 17–22*, 1419.

31. Milgrom, *Leviticus 17–22*, 1496.

32. See Tigay, *Deuteronomy*, 278.

33. One other nonlegal and noncomplimentary text in the Torah is Deut. 28:43–44. In the curses to the people if they disobey God's commandments, a statement is included which states that the *ger* will rise above the Israelite as the Israelite sinks. Further, the resident alien will be the Israelite's creditor, but not the opposite.

34. The books of Samuel bring examples of resident aliens with high social status: Doeg the Edomite, Saul's chief herdsman (1 Sam. 21:8); Zelek the Ammonite, one of David's thirty chief warriors (2 Sam. 23:37); and Uriah the Hittite (2 Sam. 11:3–13). Apparently even servants/slaves, such as Ziba (2 Sam. 9:2, 9), could own slaves and property (9:10; 19:30).

35. As in verse 6, the word *ger* does not appear here but only *toshavim*, literally, *"the residents who sojourn among you."* The fact that the text here emphasizes that these slaves come "from the nations round about you," as well as "from the children of the residents who sojourn among you," indicates that the subject is the *gerim*. On the other hand, the fact that the noun is *not* used may point to the moral difficulty that the text has in blatantly stating that the *gerim* may be bought as slaves, given the positive treatment of the *ger* elsewhere.

36. Pointed out by Milgrom, *Leviticus 23–27*, 2230–31. The ger's lack of rights will be rectified by Ezekiel (47:21–23) during the Babylonian exile.

37. Job 31:13–15 emphasize the rights to justice of male and female slaves.

38. See also Deut. 7:16, 23–24 and 20:15–18.

39. As in 1 Sam. 15:3, *"Now go attack Amalek and proscribe all that belongs to him. Spare no one, but kill alike men and women, infants and sucklings, oxen and sheep, camels and asses!"* See also in Joshua concerning Jericho in 6:21; Ai in 8:26; Dvir, Hebron, Libnah in 10:39; Hazor in 11:10–15. Nonetheless, the books of Joshua and Samuel are also literature, and it is a serious question as to whether or not they are presenting historical truth. For example, according to archaeology, Jericho was already a ruin by the time any Israelite invasion might have taken place! Furthermore, if Saul indeed had eradicated all the Amalekites, except for the king, where did the Amalekite youth come from who ended up killing him (2 Sam. 1:8, 13)? It should be noted that the *herem* was not like the genocidal acts of modern times in which the property of the victims was taken by the perpetrators. As Dru Johnson reminded me (pers. comm.), the purpose of most warfare, until recent times, was conquest, expansion of territory, and capture of booty (including movable property, slaves, and women). The *herem* prohibits any taking of booty.

40. See Tigay, *Deuteronomy*, 538nn7–8, who also mentions the Moabites (the Moabite Stone describes the "proscription"—using the same root as the Hebrew—of 7,000 Israelites). See also Moshe Greenberg, "Herem," 348.

41. Moshe Weinfeld, *Deuteronomy 1–11*, has conveniently created a side-by-side comparison of Exod. 23 and Deut. 7 on 380–82.

42. For a list of sources, see Tigay, *Deuteronomy*, 539nn13–14. See also Greenberg, "Herem," 349–50.

43. See Tigay, *Deuteronomy*, 472, who bases himself on a Hebrew study by Moshe Greenberg, and see Weinfeld, *Deuteronomy 1–11*, 384.

44. Tigay, *Deuteronomy*, 471. Greenberg, "Herem," 349, suggests that Deuteronomy could have been written down any time after Solomon.

45. Similarly, Jer. 7:31; 19:5; Ezek. 16:20–21; 23:37–39; Ps. 106:37–38; and compare 2 Kings 17:31. There has been a debate among scholars whether what is meant by the use of the terms "passing" children through the fire to the Molech or other deities or "burning" them actually constitutes child sacrifice or only a kind of dedication rite where the child is passed over the flames. However, Jer. 19:5, Ezek. 23:37–39, and Ps. 106:37–38 clearly are speaking of child sacrifice! See Wright, "Molech," and Tigay, *Deuteronomy*, 464–65. That child sacrifice was practiced in Carthage (and may have been brought there from Phoenicia) is now known from archaeological excavations. See van der Toorn, "Theology, Priests, and Worship in Canaan and Ancient Israel," 2054. Recently, see the cogent representation of Canaanite child sacrifice by Anderson and Freedman, *Micah*, 532–34.

46. See also Mal. 3:5. It may be that these warnings in protection of the resident alien influenced the Amalekite's words in 2 Sam. 1:13. The Amalekite relates to David the story of how he had killed Saul at the latter's orders when he had been mortally wounded by the Philistines. In the Amalekite's story, when Saul asks him who he is, the young man answers, *"I am an Amalekite"* (2 Sam. 1:8). The Amalekites were sworn enemies of the Israelites, whom Saul had attempted to eradicate. See 1 Sam. 15; Exod. 17:8–16; Deut. 25:17–19. After David and his men mourn Saul and Jonathan for the rest of that day (verse 12), David turns to the Amalekite and asks him, *"Where are you from?"* The Amalekite, perhaps detecting David's anger and wishing to deflect it, says, *"I am the son of a ger Amalekite"* (verse 13). His plea that he is a resident alien, and is thus deserving of mercy, falls on deaf ears as David has him executed for having killed God's anointed (verse 16).

47. Exod. 22:20–21; Deut. 10:18; 14:29; 16:11,14; 24:17, 19, 20, 21; 26:13; 27:19.

48. Lev. 19:10; 23:22; Deut. 24:14–15 (as a poor hired laborer with his Israelite counterpart).

49. The only other verse in the Hebrew Bible that combines "stranger" and "visitor" is Jer. 14:8, in which the prophet beseeches God to save His people by rhetorically asking Him, *"Why are You like a stranger in the land, like a visitor who has turned aside to sleep* [for the night]?" The idea is that, since this is God's land, He should act in its defense like the owner and not like a visitor who has no ties to it. For a similar use of the rhetorical question, "Why are You, God, not behaving as You should?" see Ps. 44:24–25.

50. However, as predicated in Deuteronomy, that ceremony—an affirmation of God's commandments and the ensuing curses for disobedience—does not list the strangers as attending! Rather, the mention in Joshua here seems to reflect what is written in Deut. 29:10 and 31:12 about the covenant ceremony held by Moses on the other side of the Jordan and the commandment to include the resident aliens in the reading of the Torah that is to take place every seventh year. The phrase of Josh. 8:33, *"stranger and citizen alike,"* on the other hand, seems to particularly pick up on Lev. 24:22, *"You shall have one law for stranger and citizen alike, for I am the Lord your God."* In other words, Josh. 8:33–35 may be indicating the viewpoint that the strangers who accompanied the Israelites in the desert, and have entered the Promised Land with them, are now full members of the nation with the responsibility of any other citizen for the fulfillment of God's law.

51. Moshe Greenberg, *Ezekiel 1–20*, 252, posits that Ezek. 14:7–8 was influenced by Lev. 17:8–9. However, the context of idolatry favors Lev. 20:2–6.

52. Most academic scholars concur that the book of Ruth was written in the fifth century BCE, which is why it appears in the last section of the Jewish Bible (the Writings), as opposed to the middle section (the Prophets), in which the book of Judges is found (the story of Ruth purports to take place during the period of the Judges).

53. Particularly in the book of Esther 2:21–23 with 6:1–3; 3:7; 4:14; 6:13; 7:7–8.

54. Chronicles may be written as late as near the end of the fourth century BCE. See the discussion by Sara Japhet, *I and II Chronicles*, 23–28.

55. See Cogan, *1 Kings*, 303 with 280. That some of "Solomon's slaves" returned to the Land after the Babylonian exile is recorded in Ezra 2:55.

56. Compare Josh 17:13; Judg. 1:19, 21, 27–35. See also the story of the Gibeonites in Joshua 9, particularly verses 22–27.

57. See Blenkinsopp, *Isaiah 1–39*, 191, 281–82. On the Chronicler's percep-

tion of the *gerim* of his time as religious proselytes, see the detailed analysis by Japhet, *The Ideology of the Book of Chronicles and Its Place in Biblical Thought*, 341–51.

58. It should be noted that Ezekiel's vision of the future Temple in chapters 40–48, within which the division of the land is placed (47:13–23), contains numerous discrepancies with the Torah. See, for example, Blenkinsopp, *Ezekiel*, 195.

59. Zimmerli, *Ezekiel 2*, 532, is of the opinion that *gerim* in verse 22 refers to the resident aliens who had joined the Israelites in the Babylonian exile as proselytes and will now return with them to the Land. However, the text does not hint that these resident aliens are a new entity, as opposed to Isa. 56:3. The latter speaks of the *"son of the foreigner who has attached himself to the Lord,"* but the word *ger* does not appear.

60. See van Houten, *The Alien in Israelite Law*, 179–83.

61. As an aside, it can be noted that the biblical usage of the noun *ger* illustrates the nonsense of the claim by some that the vast majority of the Torah was written in the Exilic and Persian periods. Frank A. Spina's article "Israelites as *geriˆm*, 'Sojourners,' in Social and Historical Context," is particularly instructive. Spina contends that since the Torah (JE) uses *gerim* in describing the Israelites *before* they took possession of Canaan, and that throughout the Bible they have been described as *gerim*, and the references in Exod., Lev., and Deut. to the Israelites as *gerim* in Egypt, *then* it is easily understood how the term can later be applied to non-Israelites after the status of the Israelites changed to being the host society. However, "if gerim first applied to non-Israelites, it is difficult to figure out how it would be later applied to Israelites" in the pre-settlement era. "Except for the pre-settlement era, there was no time when Israel, conceived as a totality, could have been called gerim. . . . If the ger-tradition were invented in the Exilic period" (when in a sense Israel did become gerim in Babylon), "then one is hard pressed to ascertain a reason as to why the Exilic literature is so silent on the subject. . . . The point is simply that if the tradition is pre-Exilic, then it must also be pre-settlement, since there is no other time when the tradition would be appropriate to Israel's pre-Exilic history or which could explain adequately the invention of the tradition." Otherwise, one has to explain how the tradition was invented as a response to exile: the JE corpus would have to be dated to the Exilic period. "Some explanation for the silence of sources on Israel's being gerim in Babylon is required . . . it is rather hard to see how Israel's 'sojourn' in Egypt could have been connected to the 'sojourn' in Babylon

without more explicit reference than we have . . . the tradition of the Exodus . . . is surely pre-Exilic, as a reading of the eighth-century prophets shows" (Spina, "Israelites as *geri^m*," 329–30).

The antiquity of the Israelite notion of protecting the stranger has been very recently attested to in extraordinary fashion by the discovery of an ostracon (writing on a potsherd) at the archaeological excavations in Khirbet Qeiyafa (possibly the biblical site of Shaarayim), above the Elah Valley in 2008. Although the writing is very difficult to read, two separate scholars, Gershon Galil and Emile Puech, have noted that the words for justice, widow, and stranger (*ger*) all appear (and possibly also orphan and poor). As these terms appear for the first time together in the Torah (with a synonym for "justice"), this ostracon may provide extremely early evidence of the existence of Torah law. Scientific dating of the ostracon in the precise place in which it was found has been very convincingly set at the end of the eleventh century or the beginning of the tenth century BCE, the time of the founding of the Israelite monarchy! See the official website of the dig, http://qeiyafa.huji.ac.il/ostracon 12_2.asp.

62. Lev. 19:10; 23:22; Deut. 24:14–15 (as a poor hired laborer with his Israelite counterpart); Ezek 22:29; Zech. 7:10 (plus widow and orphan). *Ger* appears with orphan and widow: Exod. 22:20–21; Deut. 10:18; 14:29; 16:11,14; 24:17, 19, 20, 21; 26:13; 27:19; Jer. 7:6; 22:3; Ezek 22:7; Zech. 7:10 (plus poor); Mal. 3:5; Ps. 94:6; 146:9.

63. Thus he is grouped together with the landless Levite (included with the widow and orphan) in Deut. 14:29; 16:11, 14; 26:12–13.

64. Exod. 22:20; 23:9; Lev. 19:33–34; Deut.10:18b.

65. See, recently, the admirable survey by John H. Walton, *Ancient Near Eastern Thought and the Old Testament*, 155.

66. For the variety of motivational reasons for obedience to laws in which the stranger and others are included, see van Houten, *The Alien in Israelite Law*, 166–72.

67. As opposed to the conclusion of Karel van der Toorn, *Sin and Sanction in Israel and Mesopotamia*, 16: "the attitude of Sumerians and Babylonians towards the . . . settled immigrant seems to have been similar to the one taken by the Israelites." When I questioned van der Toorn (at a private dinner in Jerusalem on May 5, 2011) on how he could make that kind of statement in light of biblical law, he admitted to me that *Sin and Sanction* was his doctorate thesis and, at the time, he was rebelling against the strict Christian upbringing that he had received in his par-

ents' home. It should be noted that van der Toorn today is not only a mature scholar with many excellent studies to his credit but also president of the University of Amsterdam. However, the kind of equating found in van der Toorn's first book frequently represents the author's agenda to judge biblical perspectives as no different from those of the ancient Near East, no matter what the textual evidence.

68. That the Torah's teaching concerning the stranger has made an impact upon the modern State of Israel (the first time in over two thousand years that the Jewish people was to have full autonomy in its own country) can be seen in the Vietnamese boat people that Israel rescued, as well as the tens of thousands of Muslim Sudanese to whom Israel afforded refuge for years. These actions go far beyond the dictates of democracy that demand, for example, the civil and religious rights given to Israel's Arab citizens. Indeed, as one of these Muslim Sudanese refugees put it, "I'd read the Bible and I knew that the Jews were good to strangers. I must go to Israel." Quoted in Gordis, *Saving Israel*, 113.

69. Since the Bible accepts the institution of slavery, it has certain similarities to Ancient Near East slavery. Like the Bible, debt servitude was known in the ancient Near East. The Hammurabi Laws (#117) requires it for a three-year period, while the Torah requires it for six (Exod. 21:2; Deut. 15:12). Monarchs did occasionally release debtors of their debt. See Weinfeld, *Social Justice in Ancient Israel and the Ancient Near East*, 152–78; Westbrook, "Social Justice in the Ancient Near East," 155–59. A major difference in the Hebrew Bible is that such debt release was required *every* seventh year, and real estate was restored every fiftieth year. On the one hand, such regulated decrees would seem to be an ethical advancement over the unpredictable debt release enactments of individual kings. On the other hand, the case has been made that these Torah and prophetic reforms created economic havoc. See Silver, "Prophets and Markets Revisited," 185–93.

70. *COS*, 2:330. Similarly, see 1 Kings 2:39–40. See also Tigay, *Deuteronomy*, 215, and the notes on p. 387.

71. These verses were included in the Declaration of the Anti-Slavery Convention held on December 4, 1833, in Philadelphia. See http://www.awe somestories.com/biographies/frederick-douglass/abolitionist-literature.

72. Clines, "Ethics as Deconstruction, and, The Ethics of Deconstruction," 78–79.

73. Propp, *Exodus 19–40*, 218, 232. At the same time, a noted exception is that one Hittite king, in requiring his provincial governors to properly

administer justice in their districts, states, "Let no [judge] take a bribe. . . . Let him do what is just. . . . And whoever has a suit, judge it for him and satisfy him (i.e., the plaintiff). If a male slave, a female slave, or a widow has a suit, judge it for them and satisfy them." See Hoffner, "Theodicy in Hittite Texts," 94.

74. Additionally, special provisions exist for the freedom given to the Hebrew debt slaves who have served out their allotted time (Deut. 15:12–15). In terms of the injury done a slave, Exod. 21:20-21 is divergent. On the one hand, verse 20 implies the death penalty for killing a slave. On the other hand, verse 21 states that if the slave lingered for a day or two after the beating and then died, no additional punishment accrues to the owner. It appears that the text here either assumes that by lingering an additional day or two, one cannot convict the owner for murder, or that the homicide was unintentional. In either case, the owner's loss of the value of the slave is seen to be sufficient punishment.

75. Tigay, *Deuteronomy*, 69. A similar idea of equality appears in Job 31:13–15, where Job states that God formed both him and his slave in the womb.

76. Fensham, "Widow," 186–87.

77. Fensham, "Widow," 187.

78. Fensham, "Widow," 188–89.

79. For a detailed chronology, see Kitchen, "Egypt, History of (Chronology)," 327–29.

80. I have been particularly aided here by the work of Harriet K. Havice, "The Concern for the Widow and the Fatherless in the Ancient Near East," who collected more relevant information on the poor and weak in Egypt, Mesopotamia, and Ugarit than I have found anywhere else. Concerning the Hittites, Hoffner brings an Old Hittite royal instructions text for judges, in which the king indicts in advance his magistrates, "you do not avenge the blood of the poor. . . . You do the wishes of the wealthy . . . and he pays you off. But you take the court fee of the poor man, and don't investigate his case!" Hoffner, "Theodicy in Hittite Texts," 94. Hoffner, there, also mentions a Hittite instruction on behalf of a poor widow.

81. Havice, "Concern," 21.

82. Havice, "Concern," 29.

83. Havice, "Concern," 31–32.

84. Havice, "Concern," 46–47.

85. Havice, "Concern," 49–50.

86. Havice, "Concern," 36–40.

87. Havice, "Concern," 43–44.

88. Havice, "Concern," 52–57. The words for "teacher" and "father" are the same, and the words for "student" and "son" are the same. Later (Nineteenth Dynasty) there is evidence that these became the instructions for the teaching of children. *Maat* not only signifies these virtues but is also the name of an Egyptian goddess. See Epsztein, *Social Justice in the Ancient Near East and the People of the Bible*, 18.

89. Havice, "Concern," 64–67. Note that the stranger, widow, and poor are combined here.

90. Havice, "Concern," 74–86.

91. Havice, "Concern," 94–95.

92. Lichtheim, *Moral Values in Ancient Egypt*, 87.

93. Leahy, "Ethnic Diversity in Ancient Egypt," 1:228–29:

> Throughout ancient times, there was a significant substratum of foreign slaves in Egypt who were engaged on royal building projects. . . . The majority were the booty of war. . . . Many arrived in Egypt through various forms of the slave trade. . . . Ramsses II did not hesitate to uproot large groups of people. . . . People enslaved in this way are individually invisible to us; they were condemned to remain at the lowest level of society and to labor their lives away in abysmal conditions on building sites or in mines and quarries of the Eastern Desert. They are often even collectively anonymous: there is no clear trace of the Hebrews in Egyptian sources.

At the same time, Leahy writes (233):

> The capacity of Egyptian society to absorb people from a wide variety of ethnic backgrounds without prejudice was one of its characteristic features. The only requirement was a willingness to integrate. Signs of ethnic tension surface only rarely, when groups actively sought to retain their ethnic character by conspicuously adhering to un-Egyptian practices or by maintaining a high profile or physical separateness.

94. Havice, "Concern," 101.

95. Havice, "Concern," 107–11.

96. Havice, "Concern," 149–63.

97. "Counsels of Wisdom," in *ANET*, 426, lines ii, 13–16.

98. Havice, "Concern," 119–24.

99. Havice, "Concern," 128–29.

100. To the widows: Hammurabi 150, 171, 172, 176–177; Middle Assyrian A

25–26, 28, 33–35, 45–46; Neo-Babylonian (ca. 700 BCE) 12–13. To the orphans: Lipit-Ishtar 24, 26–27, 31; Hammurabi 162, 173–174, 177; Middle Assyrian A 26, 28, 41; Neo-Babylonian 13, 15.

101. Havice, "Concern," 130–31.

102. Epsztein, *Social Justice*, 16.

103. Havice, "Concern," 170–71. Similarly, a Hittite text states, "to the hungry give bread . . . to the naked give clothing." See Weinfeld, *Social Justice in Ancient Israel and the Ancient Near East*, 224.

104. See Pleins, "Poor, Poverty (Old Testament)."

105. Compare Deut. 1:16.

106. See Tigay, *Deuteronomy*, 228. That the Torah's law of not taking a poor laborer's garment in debt was known to the populace appears to be proven by the Mesad Hashavyahu ostracon, dated to the reign of Josiah (late seventh century BCE), in which a reaper complains about the unjustified confiscation of his cloak (and see on Amos 2:8 below). See http://en.wikipedia.org/wiki/Mesad_Hashavyahu.

107. Tigay, *Deuteronomy*, 147.

108. Milgrom, *Leviticus 17–22*, 1628. Milgrom, who understands Leviticus 17–27 to be the product of the Holiness source (H), also sees this source as reflecting the latter half of the eighth century BCE when the family and clan structure was still strong enough in ancient Israel to provide care for the widow and orphan within those structures. However, a century later, increasing urbanization and the dispossession of small farmers by the wealthy, with the resultant consolidation of small farms into large estates, resulted in the dissolution of the family and clan structure. That situation was reflected in Deuteronomy's promulgation of laws to provide food sources for the widow and orphan—in his view. Milgrom's detailed analysis of H appears on 1319–67.

109. It is to be noted that the sabbatical law in Leviticus 25:2–7 does *not* provide for all the poor but may only be seen as providing for those for whom the householder is responsible, *"your male and female slaves, your hired laborers, and your residents who sojourn with you"* (6). It is questionable to whom "the residents" refer. Milgrom, *Leviticus 23–27*, 2160, explains that Leviticus has already provided for the general poor by the harvest laws of chapters 19 and 23.

110. Remission of debts and return of property occasionally occurred in proclamations of individual monarchs in the ancient Near East, but there was nothing comparable to the recurring requirements of the biblical sabbatical and jubilee years.

111. See also verses 46, 55.

112. Similarly, the declaration in Deut. 26:6–7.

113. Milgrom, *Leviticus 1–16*, 304–7. Milgrom notes the existence of a third century BCE Punic text that also records a concession to the indigent (304), and a similar statement in Mesopotamia, *"the widow makes her offering to you* [plural] *with cheap flour, the rich man with a lamb"* (862). It should also be noted that the half-shekel offering in Exodus 30:11–16 is the same for rich and poor (verse 15).

114. See also Josh. 17:3–6.

115. 1 Kings 17:8–24; 2 Kings 4:1–7.

116. Ps. 25:16–18; 40:18; 86:1–5.

117. Isa. 3:15; 32:6–7; Ps. 10:2, 9; 37:14; Job 24:14.

118. Zeph. 3:12; Ps. 12:6; 14:6; 35:10; Prov. 22:22–23.

119. Isa. 26:1–6-in which the people are also identified as righteous; 49:13; Ps. 18:28; 72:2.

120. Isa. 1:17; Jer. 20:13; 22:16; Ps. 72:1–2, 4, 12; Prov. 29:7; 31:9; Job 29:16; 31:21; etc.

121. Isa. 58:6–7; Ps. 132:15; Prov. 22:9; Job 31:19; etc.

122. A similar idea appears in the seventh-century BCE Hymn to Shamash (lines 41–47) in which the god intercedes on behalf of the weak to ensure justice. ANET, 388. The relatively late date of this text shows that it could not have influenced Amos or Isaiah. Geopolitically it could not have influenced Malachi either, since the hymn was found in Assyria, and Malachi lived in Persian-controlled Judah.

123. Also see Ps. 72:4; 146:7; Prov. 14:31; 22:16; 28:3.

124. Compare Job 24:4, *"They push the needy off the road."*

125. See Paul, *Amos*, 83. Compare Amos 8:6.

126. See Milgrom's cogent arguments in *Leviticus 23–27*, 2257–70.

127. As is well known, these words (with a slightly different translation) are inscribed on the Liberty Bell. The only other places, outside of this verse and Jer. 34, in which the Hebrew word for liberty, *dror*, appears are the later texts of Isa. 61:1 and Ezek. 46:17.

128. Blenkinsopp, *Ezra–Nehemiah*, 259.

129. Adelson, "The Origins of a Concept of Social Justice," 25–26.

130. Blenkinsopp, *Ezra–Nehemiah*, 259.

131. Also see Lev. 25:17, 36.

132. Havice's claim, "Concern," 229–47, that the Torah's law on behalf of the needy is often an authoritarian appeal that assumes that the hearer is an ethically incompetent actor is indefensible. No society can exist without legal requirements. The enshrinement of ethical values within a society's

law code, requiring specific actions and attitudes, is far greater evidence of the importance of those values than if they were simply left as suggestions. Consider the difference in safe driving between signs on the freeways that might read "For your own safety and that of others, the state recommends that you do not exceed 65 miles per hour" and the knowledge that one could get a severe fine for speeding (I first heard this analogy from Dennis Prager). Havice apparently has to bend over backward to prove that Israel's laws on behalf of the disadvantaged do not represent an ethical advancement over the rest of the ancient Near East.

133. Even though an individual widow may have received permission to glean in a specific field (see the Instructions of Amenemope cited above), there is no evidence that this was a societal custom.

134. See Garnsey, *Food and Society in Classical Antiquity*, *Famine and Food Supply*, and *Cities, Peasants, and Food in Classical Antiquity*, esp. 183–292. I thank Dr. Yehiel Leiter for these references. Democratic Athens created a continuous system of food distribution only in the fourth century BCE (*Famine and Food Supply*, 30, 144). Otherwise, societies had to rely on the largess of the upper classes during times of famine (*Food and Society*, 33; *Cities, Peasants, and Food*, 274).

135. I wish to thank the seminar members at the Institute for Advanced Studies (housed then at Shalem College, but now at the Herzl Institute), before whom I presented this section on the poor (June 11, 2013), for pointing this out to me. It should be noted that the concept of destruction due to immorality is not completely unknown in Mesopotamian literature. An ancient Babylonian wisdom text, "Advice to a Prince," states, "If a king does not heed justice . . . his land will be devastated. . . . If citizens of Nippur are brought before him for judgment and he accepts bribes and treats them with injustice, Enlil . . . will bring a foreign army against him." In other words, the king will be punished and may even lose his throne for his own immoral acts. Note that this text does not refer to national destruction and/or exile. Nor is it a legal text, although the king's responsibility for moral order is well known, as we have seen in chapter 2. Similarly, the Esarhaddon (king of Assyria, 680–669 BCE) inscriptions attempt to justify the destruction of Babylon (by Esarhaddon's father, Sennacherib, in 689 BCE): the Babylonians "plotted evil . . . were oppressing the weak/poor . . . they were robbing each other's property; the son was cursing his father in the street . . . then the god [Enlil/Marduk] became angry, he planned to overwhelm the land and to destroy its people." Note that the king of Assyria, after the fact, imputes

widespread moral decay to the Babylonian enemy to explain the god's decision to destroy Babylon (thus absolving his father). Although this late sentiment, at face value, accords with earlier biblical thought, this inscription is hardly comparable to the Torah's prospective legislation and admonitions or to the prophets' prophecies of doom. See Weinfeld, "Ancient Near Eastern Patterns in Prophetic Literature," 194–95.

4. The Primacy of Morality over Ritual

1. The division between church and state in American democracy would have been unknown in the ancient Near East. The integration of church and state is still characteristic of many European democracies. The queen of England, for example, is head of the Anglican Church, and in Italy, every public school classroom displays a cross.
2. Gorman, *The Ideology of Ritual*, 19.
3. Gorman, *The Ideology of Ritual*, 22.
4. Milgrom, *Leviticus 1–16*, 440–42, and see references there. On other incentives, see also 443.
5. Moshe Greenberg, "Religion: Stability and Ferment," 5:89–91.
6. Translated by S. N. Kramer, *ANET*, 573–74; Milgrom, *Leviticus 23–27*, 2442–43.
7. See Milgrom, *Leviticus 1–16*, 22–23, for the full text, and see the discussion on 24.
8. Fairman, "A Scene of the Offering of Truth in the Temple of Edfu," translation on 87. Fairman, 90, points out that this text "has obvious affinities with the texts addressed to priests that are found on the side doors leading into temples of the Graeco-Roman Period." There he quotes one such text addressed to priests of subordinate status, "Do not initiate wrongfully; do not enter when unclean; do not utter falsehood in his house; do not covet the property [of his temple]; do not tell lies; do not receive bribes; do not discriminate between a poor man and a great; . . . do not reveal what you have seen in all the mysteries of the temples." It should be noted that the fusion of moral and ritual actions is also found in Egypt in *The Book of the Dead*, chapter 125 (1550–950 BCE), in which the individual after death protests his innocence in order to persuade the divine judges to grant him life in the underworld. See *ANET*, 34–36.
9. Kaiser, *Isaiah 1–12*, 32–33, does bring evidence of this originally prophetic idea in Plato (fourth century BCE), who, in his *Laws*, IV, 716d–717a, has the Athenians declare that to engage in various rituals in communion with the gods is

superlatively fitting . . . for the good man; but for the wicked the very opposite. For the wicked man is unclean of soul, whereas the good man is clean; and from him that is defiled no good man, nor god, can ever receive gifts. Therefore the great labour that impious men spend upon the gods is in vain, but that of the pious is most profitable to them all.

10. Translated by Miriam Lichtheim, COS, 1:65, between lines 125–30. Lichtheim notes that the reading here is "loaf" as opposed to previous scholars who misread it as "character." Earlier, "Merikare" advises that one "make ample the daily offerings [because] it profits him who does it" (cited by Walton, *Ancient Near Eastern Thought*, 153).

11. Conveniently translated and edited in Martti Nissinen, *Prophets and Prophecies in the Ancient Near East*.

12. Nissinen, *Prophets and Prophecies*, 17–22. The second prophecy reads, in part, "I restored you to the throne of your father's house . . . Now hear a single word of mine: If anyone cries out to you for judgment, saying: 'I have been wronged,' be there to decide his case; answer him fairly. This is what I desire from you" (22). As in the prophecy cited in the text, the primary concern of the god is for justice, a common concept in the ancient Near East.

13. The verse, by saying, *"as the Lord your God has commanded you,"* appears to refer directly to the Ten Commandments in Exod. 20:12.

14. See Milgrom, *Leviticus 1–16*, 713, and Tigay, *Deuteronomy*, 126. Milgrom's definitive exposition of the ethics of the Torah's dietary laws appears on 704–42.

15. Similarly, see Ps. 5:5–8; also, Isa. 33:14–16; Job 31. The ethical uniqueness of the Bible here was noted by Moshe Weinfeld, "Instructions for Temple Visitors in the Bible and in Ancient Egypt."

16. As against Weinfeld, "Ancient Near Eastern Patterns in Prophetic Literature," 190, 193.

17. For the preference of the prayer of the righteous, see also Prov. 15:29.

18. On this verse, the recently deceased, much-mourned, great Assyriologist and biblical scholar Victor Avigdor Hurowitz cited the statement in the Babylonian Talmud, Sukkah 49b, "R. Elazar said: Greater is the doer of righteousness than all the sacrifices." See his Hebrew commentary, *Proverbs*, vol. 2, *Mikra LeYisrael*, 423.

19. See Fox, *Proverbs 10–31*, 691.

20. This point is well expressed by David T. Tsumura, *The First Book of Samuel*, 401. Somewhat of a similar passage to I Sam. 15:22–23 appears

in 13:8–14, which may be purposefully reminiscent of the people's anxiety in Exodus when Moses delays upon the mountain. The result in Exodus, of course, is the sin of the Golden Calf; here, the unauthorized sacrifices are seen as a reason for Saul to lose the possibility of a dynasty. Compare Exod. 32:6a with 1 Sam. 13:9; Exod. 32:21—*"What did this people do to you?"* with 1 Sam 13:11—*"What did you do?"*

21. Isaiah, Jeremiah, Ezekiel, Hosea, Joel, Amos, Obadiah, Jonah, Micah, Nahum, Habakkuk, Zephaniah, Haggai, Zechariah, and Malachi. Joshua and Samuel, in the collection of the "Former Prophets" (Joshua, Judges, 1 and 2 Samuel, and 1 and 2 Kings), are also named after prophets, but those books are primarily historical (or, better, historiosophical) works—the former about the Israelite conquest of Canaan and the latter about the rise of kingship through almost the entire reign of David.

22. This is the standard academic perspective. Some doubt exists whether or not Hosea 1–3 could be as early as the ninth century BCE. Isaiah and Micah began prophesying in the latter part of the eighth century and may have continued into the beginning of the seventh.

23. For *torah* in these prophets, in the singular or plural, see Amos 2:4; Hosea 4:6; 8:1,12; Isa. 1:10; 2:3; 5:24; 8:16; 24:5; 30:9; Mic. 4:2; compare 3:11. See Unterman, "Torah," 1083. For references to the Sinai Treaty, see Hosea 6:7; 8:1; Isa. 24:5; 33:8. Those academicians who wish to date the Pentateuch to the Exilic period or later often will claim that the above verses are later insertions to make one think that the prophets succeeded the Torah as opposed to preceding it. Thus they interpret the Bible to fit their theory by extricating all texts that contradict their perceptions. Such reasoning is not only circular but also self-fulfilling. Yehezkel Kaufmann's observation that "in the books of the Torah-group, the moral principle does not reach the level of a historically decisive factor" is still valid. He continues, "Rather than reflecting a later development of the prophetic view, the Torah-group appears to represent a historical viewpoint that has not yet attained that of prophecy. . . . The absence of this idea (the primacy of morality) is a sign, not of a stage later than prophecy, but of an earlier stage" (*The Religion of Israel*, 160).

24. It is not known if Amos was the first to so prophesy, for he recognizes a chain of genuine prophets who preceded him and who castigated the people for their sins. Why else would he say, *"for I* [God] *raised up prophets from among your sons . . . and you ordered the prophets, saying 'Don't prophesy!'"* (2:11–12). Similarly, Deut. 18:15, 18. The middle part of the verses includes *"and nazirites from among your young men . . . but*

you made the nazirites drink wine," referring to Num. 6:2–4. Amos thus shows familiarity with parts of both Numbers and Deuteronomy. The last part of verse 12 is similar to Isa. 30:10: *"who said to the seers, 'Do not see!'—to those who have visions, 'Do not show us visions of truth!'";* Jer. 11:21, *"Do not prophesy by the name of the Lord."* These words in Amos prepare the way for 3:3–8 and 7:12–13, 16. See Paul, *Amos,* 93–94.

25. Literally, "I shall not smell," that is, God will not be appeased by the sacrifices of the "solemn assemblies" on holidays.

26. All of the translations of Amos's words are taken from Paul, *Amos.*

27. See Milgrom, *Leviticus 1–16,* 482–84. For a slightly different view, see Paul, *Amos,* 193–94. In *Purity, Sacrifice, and the Temple,* Jonathan Klawans's rejection of Milgrom's position is unconvincing, since Klawans juxtaposes Jer. 7:21–22 with another verse (6:20) from a different context (i.e., not a reference to an offering specifically related to the wilderness wanderings).

28. Paul, *Amos,* 86–87.

29. Similarly, see Isa. 3:16–26.

30. For the new moon, see Num. 10:10; 28:11–15; 1 Sam. 20:5, 18, 24, 27, 34; Isa. 1:14; Ezek. 46:6; Ps. 81:4. The Sabbath, of course, is renowned in the Torah and also appears in 2 Kings 4:23 (with the new moon), Jer. 17:21–27, and Neh. 13:15–22. Other passages in which new moon and Sabbath appear together are Isa. 1:13; 66:23; Ezek. 45:17; 46:1; Hosea 2:13; Neh. 10:34; 1 Chron. 23:31. A number of these passages imply that work was forbidden on the new moon, although the Torah does not mention that prohibition.

31. Andersen and Freedman, *Amos,* 814–15.

32. Paul, *Amos,* 139.

33. Spiegel, *Amos versus Amaziah,* 43.

34. Amos 5:4–5.

35. Amos 3:14–15; 5:6; 7:8–9.

36. Compare Amos 4:6–10 with Deut. 28:21–24, 27, 38–40. See Greenberg, "Religion: Stability and Ferment," 112–13.

37. Amos 7:10; Deut. 4:27; 28:64; compare Lev. 26:30–33.

38. See the discussion in Anderson and Freedman, *Hosea,* 31–37.

39. Or "kindness," and see Macintosh, *Hosea,* 84, 234; H.-J. Zobel, "hesed," 5: 44–64. The Hebrew word *hesed* also connotes, in context, "faithfulness" and "treaty loyalty," but with an ethical thrust.

40. See Botterweck, "Yada," 5:476–77.

41. Compare 2 Sam. 3:14. See Anderson and Freedman, *Hosea,* 283.

42. Hosea 4:2 is translated here in accord with Macintosh, *Hosea,* 129.

43. Some have that anti-cultic opinion also concerning a few of the Psalms, particularly 40:7; 50:8–13; 51:18–19; 69:31–32. However, it is obvious that some of these are taken out of context: 50:14 states that one should sacrifice thanksgiving offerings, as well as fulfill one's vows to sacrifice; 51:20–21, even if an addendum, cautions against taking vss. 18–19 as anti-cultic per se; 69:30, 33–34 clarifies that the issue is that the prayers of a poor person are more important to God than the offering of large animals, i.e., God takes mercy on the poor and needy. A. A. Anderson, *The Book of Psalms*, 1:317, sensibly writes, "What is said of sacrifices is equally true of prayers, cultic songs, etc.; it is not the mere repetition of them that is acceptable to God, but rather the humble and obedient attitude which finds expression, among other things, through prayers and Psalms, and even sacrifices." See Craigie, *Psalms 1–50*, 315, who understandably sees Ps. 40:7–9 as part of the royal liturgy in which "the king is now engaged in a liturgy of supplication . . . after having faithfully performed . . . the offering of appropriate sacrifices."

44. See Macintosh's translation.

45. According to the superscription of the book in 1:1, *"in the reigns of Uzziah, Jotham, Ahaz, and Hezekiah, kings of Judah"* and Thiele's dating system. See Joseph Blenkinsopp, *Isaiah 1–39*, 105. No precise dating exists for the time of Isaiah's prophetic career.

46. Part of a longer section that covers vss. 2–31. The translation here is based on Blenkinsopp, *Isaiah 1–39*, 177–78.

47. That anonymous prophet, known as Second Isaiah, also affirms the primacy of morality over ritual; see Isa. 58:1–12.

48. Probably, Moreshet-Gat, mentioned in 1:14, a town in Judah.

49. Although the book's superscription (1:1) dates Micah from approx. 740–700 BCE, modern scholars have great difficulties in dating the time of Micah's writings. Hillers, *Micah, Hermeneia* is typical: "it is impossible to speak at any length of the life and times of Micah." See the discussion of Andersen and Freedman, *Micah*, xvii, 16–27.

50. The Hebrew word here—*pesha*—denotes a purposefully disobedient crime. In secular contexts, it refers to rebellion of a vassal to a suzerain (1 Kings 12:19; 2 Kings 1:1; 3:5, 7; 8:20, 22). See Milgrom, *Leviticus 1–16*, 1034, "the worst possible sin: open and wanton defiance of the Lord." It is this particular sin that requires the purification of the Holy of Holies on the Day of Atonement—Lev. 16:16.

51. The style of this passage is reminiscent of Deuteronomy 10:12–13, except that the immediate obligation there is to do the commandments. How-

ever, in the continuation of that passage, specific ethical duties are
required (vss. 17–19).

52. Compare 1 Kings 3:4; 8:63.

53. One of the messages of the Binding of Isaac is God's ultimate opposition
to child-sacrifice—Gen. 22:12. See also Deut. 12:31; Jer. 7:31; 19:5; Ezek.
16:20–21; 23:37–39; Ps. 106:37–38; and compare 2 Kings 17:31.

54. The only other appearance of the Hebrew root used here for "modestly"
is Prov. 11:2, in which the contrast to arrogance is explicit.

55. Mic. 2:1–2; 3:1–5, 9–11; 6:10–12 (vs. 16 may be a reference to Ahab having
Naboth killed and taking his vineyard); 7:2–6.

56. Micah 3:12; compare Jer. 26:18. See Kaufmann, 397.

57. See the exceptionally detailed analysis by Anderson and Freedman,
Micah, 413–27. However, verse 4 in Micah is an addition over Isaiah, and
vs. 5 appears to be a revision of Isa. 2:5.

58. See the prose rendition of this prophecy and its consequences in Jer. 26.
See also Jer. 6:19–20, which has similarities to the eighth century BCE
prophets. See above, in the text in the discussion of Amos, for Jer. 7:22–23.

59. For the translation here I have relied on three sources: the NJPS, Holladay, *Jeremiah 1*, and Bright, *Jeremiah*.

60. It is possible that Jer. 7:13–15 are a Jeremianic expansion on the original
prophecy, since they do not seem to give room for the possibility of
repentance that is found in verses 5–7 and 26:3–6. See Holladay, *Jeremiah 1*, 236.

61. See the story in 1 Sam. 2:11–4:22. Although specific mention of the
destruction of Shiloh does not appear, it can be assumed that the Philistines, having won the battle, would also have destroyed that cultic
center. Compare Ps. 78:59–64.

62. Jer. 17:19–27. Of course, this is one of those passages that those scholars,
who wish to deny that Jeremiah believed in the necessity of ritual, date
to the post-Babylonian exile. Those scholars are convinced that observance of the Sabbath was a post-Exilic concern, despite Jeremiah's obvious reliance on the Ten Commandments (7:9). On the authenticity of
the thoughts here, see Bright, *Jeremiah*, 120, and Brueggemann, *To Pluck
Up, to Tear Down*, 158.

63. Carroll, *Jeremiah*, 209–10.

64. Jer. 33:11, 18–22. Many academics reject vss. 14–26 on the basis of their
absence in the Septuagint. However, as that peerless scholar of the textual history of the Jewish Bible, Emanuel Tov, has stated ("The Literary
History of the Book of Jeremiah in Light of Its Textual History," 220):

Although this section has often been denied to Jeremiah . . . there is no sound reason for this skepticism. On the contrary, . . . there are several Jeremianic expressions in this section reminiscent of other passages in the book, and the argument that these represent a glossator's imitation is artificial. The burden of proof is on those who would deny this section to the prophet in whose name it has been transmitted.

65. Barton, "The Prophets and the Cult," 113, mentions the biased nineteenth-century German Protestant view of the cult in biblical religion: "There is not much doubt, for example, that Wellhausen's opposition to ritual in religion, which he regarded as a somewhat degenerate phenomenon, is linked to his liberal Protestantism." In a discussion of the prophets' rhetorical strategy, Bryan D. Bibb, "The Prophetic Critique of Ritual in Old Testament Theology," 34–35, states,

> Although Amos, Isaiah, and Jeremiah denounce the cult of Israel . . . , they surely are not calling for the elimination of ritual practice. . . . How could they envision a world without cult and ritual? Modern interpreters, who . . . live in such a world, are the ones who read into this prophetic critique of ritual a preference for a non-ritualistic religion. In actuality, this critique is simply one more aspect of the great prophetic rhetorical device, reversal . . . the prophets take something valued, assured, and settled, flip it over and use it as a club, as a way to shake up the audience and communicate their point. . . . They are not making a theological argument for the elimination of ritual practices from Israel's religion.

66. See Schmitt, "Prophecy (Preexilic Hebrew)," 5:486,

> in the ancient world and in Israel in particular, no person could conceive of worship without external expression, that is, without the rituals and actions that traditionally accompany the worship of a community or that of an individual. No one, especially before the Exile, could say that God did not require the worship in the temple as that worship had been offered from Solomon on.

Also, Alexander Rofe, *Introduction to the Prophetic Literature*, 96–97:

> Cult means service, the service of the Lord. And why would people take upon themselves to do homage to their God, sacrifice to him all that is dear to them, if it were not to express their feelings of gratitude, veneration, fear, or loyalty? And so we are in danger of misread-

ing the prophets when we do not see them in the context of their milieu. Is it feasible that the prophets envisioned a religion without cult, an amorphic creed solely fed by inner feelings?

Indeed, we see that the prophets' vision of the future is not void of acts of cult and worship. The first demand Hosea makes in his sermon of redress is the fulfillment of vows (14:3) which mostly were pledges of presenting sacrifices. Isaiah . . . bases his request for justice and modesty on the presence of the Lord God in his abode in Jerusalem . . . the future peace among the nations as deriving from a common peregrination all nations make to the House of the Lord where they are instructed in his ways (2:1–4). The cultic pilgrimage to the Temple, customary in Isaiah's days, serves as a model for his vision of the future. . . . Thus, a world devoid of any worship was inconceivable to the prophets.

What at first sight may be considered as a total rejection of worship is in fact a re-dimensioning of its significance, of its relation to other basic values. Besides, biblical poetical diction should be taken into account. For example, when in Prov. 8:10 wisdom says: 'Accept my discipline, not silver'—this sounds as a total rejection of all earthly wealth. However, what is meant is that one should prefer wisdom to riches, as is stated clearly in the second hemistich: 'Knowledge is preferable to gold'—no rejection, but a question of priorities. In this light, too, we should understand Hosea 6:6: 'For I desire goodness not sacrifice, devotion to God rather than burnt offerings.' Although goodness is preferred to sacrifice, Israel without burnt offerings is unimaginable—except for a limited period of punishment (cf. 3:4–5; 9:1–5).

See also Levine, "An Essay of Prophetic Attitudes toward Temple and Cult in Biblical Israel," 1:301: "No prophet of the classical period . . . ever explicitly advocated suspension of the formal, sacral worship of the God of Israel."

An ancient Rabbinic story seems to take Hosea 6:6 literally:

Once Rabbi Yochanan ben Zakkai was leaving Jerusalem. Rabbi Yehoshua was following him and saw the Temple in ruins (after the Roman destruction). Rabbi Yehoshua said: "Woe to us that it is destroyed! The place where the sins of Israel were atoned." He said to him: "My son, don't be distressed, we have another atonement like it.

What is it? Acts of loving-kindness, as it is written: 'It is kindness that I desire and not sacrifice.'" (Avot D'Rabbi Natan 4:5)

However, Rabbi Yochanan ben Zakkai was not repudiating ritual per se. He was just indicating that now that Jews no longer had a place to sacrifice, acts of kindness would be a substitute. All rituals that could still be performed without the Temple remained in force.

67. Moshe Greenberg-in an introductory course to the religion of the Jewish Bible (at the Hebrew University of Jerusalem, early 1970s).
68. Paul, "Prophets and Prophecy," 1161, 1172–73. It is still the best encyclopedic article on prophecy in the Jewish Bible. See also Clements, *Prophecy and Covenant*, 95:

> it is clear that what these prophets rejected was not the cult as such, for its own sake, but the cult which had become divorced from righteousness and obedience to Yahweh. The very fact that the prophetic criticisms stress righteousness and justice over against the offering of sacrifices points to the relative, rather than the absolute, nature of their opposition to the worship of the sanctuaries. . . . they opposed the cult which they found because it no longer expressed the ethical nature of true Yahwism.

Similarly, Rainer Albertz, *A History of Israelite Religion in the Old Testament Period*, 1:171,

> Amos, Micah, and Isaiah fundamentally reject the cultic practice of their time because it covers up social injustice and misery in society. . . . The prophetic polemic is not directed against sacrifice or against cultic worship of God as such . . . but against a worship which is no longer matched by any ethical service of God in everyday life.

Terry L. Fenton, "Israelite Prophecy: Characteristics of the First Protest Movement," claims of the prophetic message that "this is the first record we have of criticism directed against a monarchy or central government (over a period of centuries and by a succession of men sharing broadly the same views) without the intent to oust the current ruler or change the form of government. It sought to correct, not to replace" (138). Perhaps that is so because the prophets are speaking not only to the governing authorities but to all the people. Ultimately, in the aftermath of the Roman destruction of the Temple, ancient Rabbinic literature (Avot

D'Rabbi Nathan 4:5) would conceive of ethics as replacing the sacrificial ritual (see the end on note 66).

69. A paraphrase of Paul, "Prophets and Prophecy," 1172–73. In "The Prophet versus Priest Antagonism Hypothesis: Its History and Origin," 208, Ziony Zevit says of the prophets:

> Had they been opposed to the cult on principle, . . . they would have had to address those who promoted and administered the system. But they expressed no principled objections to the cult and no principled antagonism against those charged with overseeing and maintaining it. An argument could be made that for many of the prophets the temple cult was conceived as a graceful gift from YHWH to Israel and that conception clarifies their statements (Isa. 2:2–3; Mic. 4:1–2). Jeremiah declared in the temple: "Improve your ways and I will cause you to dwell in this place" (Jer. 7:3). The post-exilic prophets certainly seem concerned that the cult not only functioned, but functioned well (Hag. 1:7–8; Mal. 1:6–2:9).

70. For example, Josh. 23:8, 16; 24:20; Judg. 2:11–15; 3:7–8; 1 Sam. 12:9–10; 2 Kings 17:6–18; 21:1–15.

71. Y. Kaufmann, *The Religion of Israel*, 366; Paul, "Prophets and Prophecy," 1174.

5. The Requirement of "Return"

1. Lambert, *Babylonian Wisdom Literature*, 14. Much of the thinking in the following paragraphs derives from Lambert's excellent article in BWL, "Introductory Essay: The Development of Thought and Literature in Ancient Mesopotamia," 1–21.

2. John H. Walton, *Ancient Near Eastern Thought and the Old Testament*, 144–45, quoting the *Counsels of Wisdom*, a Kassite period text, although it may be a copy originating in the Old Babylonian period.

3. Lambert, BWL, 15.

4. Known from nine copies in the library of Ashurbanipal (seventh century BCE); Lambert, BWL, 26.

5. The quotations below are taken from ANET, 597. A number of commonalities exist between this text and the *Prayer of Lamentation to Ishtar*, ANET, 383–85, from the library of Ashurbanipal. See also the Sumerian *Man and His God*, COS, 1:573–74 (perhaps early second millennium BCE).

6. BWL, 16.

7. BWL, 16. Similarly, in a Late Babylonian text:

Line 1, "Ea, Shamash and Marduk, what are my iniquities?"
Line 16, "Release and remove the iniquities of my father and mother!"
Line 29, "My iniquities are many: I know not what I did."
Line 148, "I have continually committed iniquities, known and unknown."

8. Copies were found in Ashurbanipal's library and other Assyrian and Babylonian cities. This paragraph summarizes BWL, 63–65.
9. BWL, 16–17.
10. BWL,. 148–49.
11. COS, 1:526–31; see Gane, *Cult and Character*, 358–62.
12. COS, 1:418–19.
13. See Singer, *Hittite Prayers*. I thank Prof. Ada Taggar-Cohen for drawing my attention to this work. Aside from the individual prayers, see Singer's introduction, 5–11.
14. John H. Walton, *Ancient Israelite Literature in Its Cultural Context*, 185, cf. 184–85. See also Mowinckel, *The Psalms in Israel's Worship*, 2:183; cited by Walton, 152, who states that confession in Babylonia was

> a consequence of the conception of sin being much more arbitrary in Babylonia and less ethically oriented [than in Israel]. Behind it lies the idea that the deity is arbitrary: what is right in the eyes of man may be evil in the eyes of the god and vice versa: man can never know what outraged the god—or some god—and why he is so angry. That is why he confesses his sinfulness without any attempt at particularization.

15. See COS, 1:404–17.
16. ANET, 391–92, ll.19–33, 51–58. Van der Toorn, *Sin and Sanction*, 94–95, agrees that the petitioner does not know what sin he has committed, and therefore ignorance becomes a reason why he should be exonerated, for "His imperfections are inherent in his nature . . . [and] the actual sin is a mystery." However, the penitent still has to confess his guilt because to be human is to err in ways which one does not know might offend the gods. Van der Toorn brings several other examples of confession of unspecified sins (130–37), including those to Shamash, the god of justice, even though the *Shamash Hymn* delineates specific crimes and good deeds, such as various frauds and honest judgment. It is odd that Milgrom, *Cult and Conscience*, 107, thinks that the type of general confession found in the *Prayer to Every God* is comparable to the specific delineation of sins found in the *Plague Prayers of Mursilis*.
17. Milgrom, "Cult and Conscience," 132–33.

18. Milgrom, "Cult and Conscience," 22, 28–31.
19. Milgrom, "Cult and Conscience," 106–7; ANET, 395–96. In reality, the king is confessing the sins of his father, which he has inherited; see Singer, *Hittite Prayers*, 59, 62.
20. This is a rare text in the ancient Near East because it offers reparation.
21. Walton, *Ancient Israelite Literature*, 155, citing Lambert, *Journal of Near Eastern Studies* 33 (1974): 137–44. Similarly, part of the *Ritual for the Repair of a Temple*, ANET, Text A, 339, l.17 (from Uruk in the Seleucid Period, probably a copy of an older text), "On a favorable day, the king shall purify and cleanse himself and call out the admission of sin to the gods Anu, Enlil, and Ea. . . . You shall cause the king to *speak* the (special) poems of appeasement of these (deities)"; compare 340, l.24. "The admission of sin" presumably referred to the king's allowing the temple to suffer disrepair.
22. Milgrom, *Cult and Conscience*, 115. Italics in the text are Milgrom's. For the similarities (and differences) to the Torah's laws, see the next section in the text. In column IV of the Hittite *Instructions for Temple Personnel*, a few examples occur of confession before apprehension for violation of sancta. In these cases, the transgressor is subject to a life-or-death ordeal. See Milgrom, *Cult and Conscience*, 29–35. I thank Prof. Ada Taggar-Cohen for focusing my attention on this text.
23. Lichtheim, *Ancient Egyptian Literature*, 2:110. The theme of the god having mercy on the sinner appears in two other texts (105–9), including the "Votive Stela of Nebre with Hymn to Amen-Re" (106–7):

> Though the servant was disposed to do evil,
> The Lord is disposed to forgive.
> The Lord of Thebes spends not a whole day in anger,
> His wrath passes in a moment, none remains.
> His breath comes back to us in mercy.

This selection has much in common with Isa. 54:7–8, although geography and time preclude direct influence. One can only say that in these passages the mid-second millennium BCE Egyptian and the sixth-century BCE Judean worshiper have similar feelings and appreciation of the Deity.
24. http://en.wikipedia.org/wiki/Maat#42_Negative_Confessions_.28papyrus_of _Ani.29. For a brief discussion of *maat* and the magical aspects of this ritual, see chapter 3 above. Note that in Egyptian literature (usually in mortuary contexts), a few petitions do contain general confessions of sin. See Dalglish, *Psalm Fifty-One: In the Light of Ancient Near Eastern Patternism*, 96.

25. *ANET*, 331–34, from tablets dating to the Seleucid (Hellenistic) period, but acknowledged as going back to a "much earlier time."

26. Gane, *Cult and Character*, 368.

27. Gane, *Cult and Character*, 369.

28. See Gane, *Cult and Character*, 373n77. How Milgrom, *Leviticus 1–16*, 25, can call the Babylonian king's speech a "confession" is inexplicable. Protestations of innocence also occur in some biblical prayers; see—by individuals—Ps. 7:4–6; 17:1–5; 26; 59:2–5; 131:1 (compare Jer. 15:17); by the people—Ps. 44:18–23 (here, the Psalmist is so convinced of the people's innocence that he accuses God of ignoring their unjust sufferings!—vss. 24–27). In some of these texts, internal pain may be understood as God "examining" the innocent. In these texts, however, such claims of blamelessness may be uttered because the Israelite knows what God expects of him, unlike Mesopotamians. Similarly, Job, too, will deny his guilt (e.g., Job 31, and in vs. 35 he will even challenge God to inform him of his sin). On the other hand, Adam and Eve's denial of guilt by claiming lack of responsibility (Gen. 3:12–13) is only, apparently, done out of fear or shame (see vss. 8, 10, there); compare Cain, Gen. 4:9.

29. The Greco-Roman world is beyond the purview of this study. Although it seems that the situation in Greek and Roman literature was somewhat different, repentance was still not yet seen as a moral obligation. According to David Konstan, *Before Forgiveness: The Origins of a Moral Idea*, forgiveness is "a bilateral process involving a confession of wrongdoing, evidence of sincere repentance, and a change of heart or moral perspective on the part of the offender, together with a comparable alteration in the forgiver, by which she or he consents to forego vengeance on the basis precisely of the change in the offender" (21). Konstan claims that "remorse and change of heart do not enter into the strategies for anger appeasement in classical literature" (63). Rather, Konstan shows that renewing a relationship relies on denial of guilt (77) or on the self-effacement of the wrongdoer who pleads with the injured person to ignore the past offense (81). Konstan's comments on the Hebrew Bible (in chapter 4 of his book) are somewhat inconsistent and quite incomplete. Konstan does cite Lev. 4:13–20 (99–100); mentions 4:27; 5:1–26—where "one must first compensate the person one has deceived or harmed"; Num. 15:22–29; 30:3–15 (100). Thus he concludes that "the representation of forgiveness in the Hebrew Bible falls short of the full modern conception: . . . it is for the most part God who forgives, rather than human beings, but also that the kind of offense that requires

forgiveness is a generalized rejection of the Lord, as opposed to particular wrongs committed against a fellow being." On the other hand, he
continues, "Because of what constitutes genuine worship in the Jewish
tradition is ethical in nature, a return to God's commandments certainly
entails moral reform." Nonetheless, he states, "But the emphasis on the
orientation to God tends to endow wrongdoing with the quality of sinfulness as a state or spiritual condition, as opposed to a specific act of
wrongdoing." Given the details in the biblical text, that statement is not
supported. Further, he does not deal with the prophets, nor the Adam
and Eve story as it appears in the Bible, nor with the Joseph story prior
to the later addendum in Gen. 50:17–20. Laurel Fulkerson, *No Regrets:
Remorse in Classical Antiquity* argues that:

> remorse in the ancient world was normally not expressed by high-
> status individuals, but by their inferiors, notably women, the young,
> and subjects of tyrants, nor was it redemptive, but often served to
> show defect of character. Through a series of examples, especially
> poetic, historical, and philosophical texts, this book demonstrates
> this was so because of the very high value placed on consistency of
> character in the ancient world. High-status men, in particular, faced
> constant challenges to their position, and maintaining at least the
> appearance of uniformity was essential to their successful function-
> ing. The redemptive aspects of remorse, of learning from one's mis-
> takes, were thus nearly absent in the ancient world. (From the
> publisher's blurb; see http://ukcatalogue.oup.com/product
> /9780199668892.do.)

30. Milgrom, *Cult and Conscience*, 120n441, cites the examples of Pharaoh
of the Exodus in Exod. 9:27 and 10:16 (although these resemble ancient
Near East confessions); the people to stop the plague of the fiery
serpents—Num. 21:7; and Balaam in 22:34. On 119, he mentions
David—2 Sam. 12:13 and 24:10; Ahab—1 Kings 21:27; Josiah—2 Kings
22:11–13, 18–20. One may further add Pharaoh (the incident with
Sarah)—Gen. 12:19; Abimelech—Gen. 20:5; Judah and Tamar—Gen.
38:26; Pharaoh's chief cupbearer—Gen. 41:9; Joseph's brothers—42:21
(compare 44:16); Saul—1 Sam. 15:24, 30; Hezekiah—2 Kings 18:14; compare 2 Chron. 12:6–7, 12—Rehoboam; 32:26—Hezekiah; 33:12–13, 19,
23—Manasseh (in Chronicles, the verb "humbled [himself]" probably
alludes to contrition—compare Lev. 26:41). As in the ancient Near East,
the corporate personality of the king as representative of the people

means that the king's sin can cause tragedy to strike the people and his confession can stop or avoid such suffering.

In the case of David's acknowledging his sin (vis-à-vis Bathsheba and Uriah), the message is the ability of repentance to mitigate the punishment, for he is not killed. At the same time, since one of the results of David's compounded sin (adultery plus homicide) is the death of Uriah, the power of repentance is limited, since the taking of life can only be compensated for by another life—the newborn's death is decreed (see the section on law in chapter 2 above; see Uriel Simon, *Reading Prophetic Narratives*, 102). This is a text that certainly runs counter to modern ethical sensibilities (and contradicts Deut. 24:16!).

It is also conceivable that a key element in the Garden of Eden story is the *lack* of confession. According to the "rules," the only penalty that the man and woman should have incurred upon eating the forbidden fruit was mortality (Gen. 2:17). Why then are they punished additionally by difficulty in producing food from the ground and pain in childbirth (3:16–19)? Perhaps it is because they did not confess their crime when they were faced with it, but instead passed the buck (3:9–13).

31. Milgrom, *Cult and Conscience*, 120, mentions confessionary intercession by Moses at the Golden Calf (Exod. 32:30–31; 34:9; Samuel–1 Sam. 7:3–6; 12:19–20; see also 12:10). Such intercession is also found in the prophecies of Jeremiah—Jer. 3:22–25 (compare Hosea 14:3–4); 14:7, 20 (compare 15:1; Ps. 99:6); 31:18–19 (compare 31:9a; on the connection between Jer. 3:22–25 and 31:18–19, see Unterman, *From Repentance*, 34–35, 51–52). On the worship of foreign gods, which the people know is a sin and then show contrition, see Judg. 2:1–5; 10:10–16. Confessionary intercession in the Bible may be similar to confession recited on behalf of the penitent by the priest in the ancient Near East; indeed, some texts "expressly order the priest to recite the confession" (Milgrom, *Cult and Conscience*, 107). However, Mesopotamian intercession was much more complex than simply having the priest serve as a mediator between the suppliant and the angry god. Intercession was often effected by a combination of rituals—prayer, sacrifices, and music—and praying to another deity (or deities), and even having family members pray to intercede with the god who needed to be appeased. See Gabbay, *Pacifying the Hearts of the Gods*, who notes that although "personal distress" is "the result of sin, even though the particular sin may be unknown, the land's destruction is not connected to the deeds or sins of humanity" in certain types of laments. "The Word of Enlil is even said to have hurt inno-

cent children: 'The young people (who) had no sin!'" (24). Further, in many litanies, gods respond to accusations of destruction by passing the responsibility to their divine ancestors: "How could you have destroyed . . . ? I did not do it! My father made me do it!" (59–62). The overarching goal of such rituals was simply to calm down the angry god so that he would cause the destruction to cease.

32. For example, in the Egyptian story of *The Eloquent Peasant*, the official does not say that he was wrong not to believe the peasant, nor does the older brother admit that he was wrong in *The Tale of the Two Brothers* (also Egyptian). In the Akkadian *Gilgamesh Epic*, neither Ea nor Enlil admit doing wrong. An exception appears to be the Ugaritic *Tale of Aqhat* in which the goddess Anat shows remorse for killing Aqhat (*ANET*, 153, Aqht B-C, ll. 39–41 through l. 19). One of the most vexing issues in biblical theology revolves around whether or not God regrets or shows remorse. Verbs such as "confess, admit," "humbled himself," "repent" (the spiritual use of the Hebrew root *shin, vav, vet*; contrast Jer. 4:28 where God does *not* regret bringing, or relent from His punishment), or "feel guilty" are *never* applied to God. However, a verb (from the root *nun, het, mem*) that has been variously translated as "become remorseful, repent of something, regret, be sorry, feel sorrow or sympathy, find comfort, be comforted" or "an alteration of Yahweh's decision, recant, change his mind" in the *niph'al* (normally, passive) conjugation (H. Simian-Yofre, "*nhm*," 342–43) appears over twenty times (Simian-Yofre, 343–47). To these definitions, one can add "relent" (344). It should be noted that of all such meanings, concerning humans only Jer. 8:6 and 31:19 clearly refers to an element of repentance. Even the idiom that uses this verbal form with God as the subject and the object is "concerning the evil" does not per se indicate regret, for it may refer to God simply responding to the human reaction to His conditional promise, as in Jer. 18:7–10, "I will decide differently about the good or evil that I thought to bring upon them"; the Hebrew noun for evil sometimes refers to divine punishment. Even in those texts in which this verb refers to God not or never doing it (1 Sam. 15:29; compare Num. 23:19; Hosea 12:9), it is not clear whether "regret" or "change his mind" is the meaning. Thus due to the complexity of the problem, no attempt will be made herein to come to a conclusion about whether or not any biblical texts actually refer to God's own repentance, even though one such text might be Gen. 6:6–7 (compare verses 12–13), where God, with deep sadness, appears to regret creating humanity. However, even there, one cannot conclude that God

repents of doing evil. Rather, the more logical conclusion is that God intended that humanity should behave morally, and He regrets creating them since *they* chose to do evil. (Of course, the human exception is Noah, which is why he and his family are saved.)

33. Rashi comments that "the owner of the debt (God) has found an occasion to demand payment." See also the commentary of E. A. Speiser, *Genesis*.

34. The question remains as to whether or not Joseph has fully forgiven his brothers. True, in Gen. 45:4–8, he lets them off the hook by declaring and repeating that it was all a Divine plan: *"Now do not be distressed or reproach yourselves because you sold me hither; it was to save life that God sent me ahead of you"* (vs. 5). However, many years later, when their aged father Jacob dies, the brothers fear that Joseph will now take vengeance upon them (50:15): *"What if Joseph stills bears a grudge against us and pays us back for all the wrong that we did him!"* So,

> they sent this message to Joseph, *"Before his death your father left this instruction: So shall you say to Joseph, 'Forgive, I urge you, the offense and guilt of your brothers who treated you so harshly.' Therefore, please forgive the offense of the servants of the God of your father."* And Joseph cried as they spoke to him (vss. 16–17).

The brother's request for forgiveness (both in their own words and in the words they most probably put into their father's mouth) indicates that they, at least, still have doubts about whether or not Joseph has forgiven them. They even offer to be his slaves (vs. 18). His tears, though, may well signify that he has forgiven them, and that he is sad that they still harbor such suspicions—to the point that they feel desperate enough to invoke, as it were, their father's plea! Joseph must be aware that they are lying about their father's words, for if Jacob had indeed found out about his sons' treachery, it would have been remarked on in his blessings (49:2–27; compare vss. 4–8 there). In any case, Joseph not only reiterates that this was all God's beneficial plan (vs. 20), but he reassures them that he will take care of them and their children (vs. 21). At the end of the book, he even trusts them with his remains (vs. 25).

35. http://www.jewishvirtuallibrary.org/jsource/Judaism/repentence.html. I thank Shalom Paul for pointing me in this direction and for referring me to the work of Nechama Leibowitz (*Studies in Bereshit [Genesis]*, 462–69). It is possible that Maimonides here alludes to Judah's refusal to again have intercourse with Tamar (38:26). Of course, the true reason that Judah does not have intercourse with Tamar again may be simply

that she is forbidden to him, since she is his daughter-in-law who also had been promised in levirate marriage.

36. Perhaps it was Judah's own experience with Tamar that had triggered his transformation.

37. Most of the material in this section derives from Jacob Milgrom's meticulous analysis of the relevant texts in Leviticus and Numbers, first published in his trailblazing article, "The Priestly Doctrine of Repentance"; additional discussion appears in his commentary, *Leviticus 1–16*.

38. See the note on theodicy—the vindication of God in the face of seemingly unwarranted evil—at the end of this chapter.

39. For a detailed description and explanation, see Milgrom, *Leviticus 1–16*, 1009–84.

40. Milgrom, *Leviticus 1–16*, 254–61.

41. Milgrom, *Leviticus,* 30–31.

42. 2 Sam. 12:6—the precise sentence pronounced by David on the thief (before David realizes that Nathan has told him a parable).

43. A thief was not imprisoned in the Jewish Bible, but was required to work off his debt—an example of debt-slavery.

44. Milgrom's translation, Milgrom, *Leviticus,* 57. Herein, "YHWH" has been replaced by "the Lord," the verse numbers have been removed, "dissembled" has been replaced by "dealt deceitfully" (NJPS), and the translation has been put into italics.

45. Again, Milgrom's translation; see Milgrom's *Numbers,* 34–35 including the notes. A similar passage is Lev. 5:1–19 concerning a variety of improper ethical and cultic behaviors, all in which a person feels guilty (sometimes due to the realization that one did something wrong) and is then able to take advantage of the effect of repentance.

46. Compare the laws of redemption of consecrated property and objects requiring a one-fifth surcharge—Lev. 27:9–31, particularly vss. 13, 15, 19, 27, 31.

47. Milgrom, *Leviticus: A Book of Ritual and Ethics*, 57–58, notes that this point was emphasized by the Tanaitic rabbis in Mishnah Yoma 8:9: "For those transgressions that are between a person and God, Yom Kippur atones, but for those transgressions that are between man and his fellow man, Yom Kippur does not provide atonement until he pacifies his fellow man." Similarly, Matt. 5:23–24 (New English Bible): "If when you bring your gift to the altar, you suddenly remember that your brother has a grievance against you, leave your gift where it is before the altar. First go make peace with your brother, and only then come back and offer your gift."

48. Based upon Milgrom, *Leviticus*, 60. Frank H. Gorman, "Pagans and Priests: Critical Reflections on Method," challenges the way Milgrom compares particularly Leviticus to ancient Near Eastern materials, including criticizing Milgrom's emphasis on the distinction between the demonic forces purged by Babylonian priests from the sanctuary, as opposed to the impurities created by humans in the sanctuary as understood in Leviticus (99; Gorman's primary focus is on what constitutes symbolism). However, aside from his opinion that "forgiveness" in Lev. 5 is mechanistic (98), he does not deal with the material and concepts that have been covered here. Concerning his opinion that "Forgiveness is the guaranteed result of enactment . . . , and it is not based on an existential decision of Yahweh . . . at the moment of enactment," the obvious question is, "How does Gorman know that?" The text says "he shall be forgiven," or "it shall be forgiven him," but by whom? Since the speaker throughout this section is God (4:1; 5:14, 20), then, minimally, God is saying, "By this procedure, I decree that the sinner shall be forgiven," that is, God is the one who forgives. Gorman's assumption is wrong. Further, see Kselman, "Forgiveness (OT)," 831, who states, "'and it shall be forgiven him [by the deity]' . . . a divine passive, and so the agent effecting forgiveness is God, through the intercession of the priest; the passive verb makes the point that forgiveness does not inhere in the priestly rites, but in the action of God."

49. Milgrom, *Numbers*, 397.

50. Unterman, *From Repentance*, 11. The term "covenantal" in reference to *shuv* used in this way was coined by William Holladay, *The Root šûbh in the Old Testament*, 116–57. Fabry, "*Shuv*," 468, states that the "covenantal usage" appears in an Aramaic Sefire treaty between Barga'yah and Matti'el (eighth century BCE), leading apostates back into their status of service and loyalty.

51. See Milgrom, *Cult and Conscience*, 121–22, who refers to Holladay's figures. In prophetic books: twenty-three times among three eighth-century BCE prophets (Amos, Hosea, Isaiah), twenty-seven times in Jeremiah (late seventh century, early sixth century), twenty-three times in Ezekiel (sixth century), and twelve times in the late-Exilic or post-Exilic prophets (Second Isaiah, Haggai, Zechariah, Malachi; late sixth century, early fifth century). Additionally, *shuv* in this sense appears four times in Deut. 4 and 30; seven times in the historiographic books of Joshua through Kings—once in 1 Samuel and six times in Kings; nineteen times in the Kethuvim (Psalms, Lam., Job, Dan., Neh., Chron.).

52. However, the prophets also occasionally use other terms in speaking about religious repentance, although much less frequently: "seek (God)"—the roots *bqsh* and *drsh*. The former appears in Hosea 3:5, parallel to *shuv*; 5:15 (cf. vs. 6); 7:10, parallel to *shuv*; Jer. 29:13; 50:4; Zeph. 2:3; compare Deut. 4:29 (*shuv* is in vs. 30); 2 Chron. 7:14 (with *shuv*); 15:4 (with *shuv*). The latter is found in Hosea 10:12; Amos 5:4–6 (compare vs. 15); Isa. 9:12 (with *shuv*); Jer. 29:13 (with *bqsh*); Isa. 55:6 (compare vs. 7; Second Isaiah); compare Deut. 4:29 (with *bqsh*); Ps. 14:2 = 53:3; 77:3; 78:34 (with *shuv*). For those who do *not* "seek" God in this sense, see Isa. 31:1 (*drsh*); Jer. 10:21(*drsh*); Zeph. 1:6 (*drsh, bqsh*). A rare root used for "contrition" is *nchm* in Jer. 31:19, "after I turned away (from God), I felt regret."

53. Most of the information in this section relies on Unterman, *From Repentance*, particularly 32–38, 47–53. For the words of the people (placed in their mouths by the prophet) as a response to 3:12–13, see verses 21–25 (*From Repentance*, 33, 36).

54. Unterman, *From Repentance*, 1, 32–33, 184n25. Note the beginning of verses 11 and 12, "The Lord said to me. . . . Go and call out these words."

55. See also Isa. 1:16–17, 19; 30:15; 31:6; 44:22; 55:6–7; 58:6–10, 13 (Unterman, *From Repentance*, on Second Isaiah, 173–74); Jer. 3:14, 22; 4:1–2, 3–4, 14; 7:3–6; 15:19 (to the prophet!); 18:7–11; 21:12; 22:3–5; 25:4–7; 26:3–6, 13; 35:15; Ezek. 3:16–21; 14:6–11; 18:30–32; 33:10–20; Hosea 5:15; 14:2–5; Joel 2:12–13; Amos 5:4–6, 14–15; Jon. 3:2–10; Zeph. 2:1–3; Zech. 1:2–6; Mal. 3:7. See Raitt, *A Theology of Exile*, 37–39.

56. The Hebrew word is *hasid*. The first letter in Hebrew is a guttural from the same root as *hesed*. As an activity identifying God, see Jer. 9:23.

57. Similarly, although in a non-repentance context, see Isa. 54:7–8.

58. Heschel, *The Prophets*, 298.

59. From the verb *yada*, "know".

60. Similarly, Jer. 14:20; 31:19.

61. For the connection of this passage to Jeremiah 3, see Unterman, *From Repentance*, 53.

62. From the root *pesha*. In secular usage, it refers to a rebellion of a vassal against his suzerain, such as in 1 Kings 12:19; 2 Kings 1:1; 3:5. In religious terms, as deliberately disobeying God, it appears in Lev. 16:16, 21; Isa. 1:2; 43:27; Jer. 2:8; 33:8; Mic. 1:5. See Milgrom, *Leviticus 1–16*, 1034.

63. This is also the conclusion of Michael Fishbane's superior Hebrew article, "Teshuva," 961.

64. Courts often met at the gate of a town.

65. See Jer. 25:4–5. The sanctuary at Shiloh had been destroyed in the distant past.

66. A possible exception is Ahab's acts of repentance in 1 Kings 21:27–29 (I thank Marvin Sweeney for reminding me of these verses), but God's acceptance only delays the punishment upon his dynasty, i.e., it is a *political* punishment. For an extremely similar passage, compare 2 Kings 22:19–20 (compare vs. 11)—on the good king, Josiah!

67. Unterman, *From Repentance*, 12, quote. Once the punishment of exile is inevitable or has already occurred, one finds a few passages in which repentance only relates to the survival of the individual, such as Ezek. 3:16–21; 18; 33:10–20— *From Repentance*,168. In some prophecies, such as Jer. 3:12–13, repentance is also required in exile before God will effect restoration. The issue of repentance in exile will be investigated more properly in chapter 6. I wish to thank Dru Johnson, Marvin Sweeney, and Yair Zakovitch for pointing out some lack of clarity in the original writing of this paragraph, which I hope I have now corrected.

68. Rabbinic literature will maintain the importance of compensating the victim *before* God will accept the people's repentance; see Mishnah Yoma 8:9.

69. Compare Isa. 1:16–19; Ezek. 18:29–32; Hosea 14:2–9; Joel 2:12–13; Amos 5:4, 6, 14–15; Jon. 3:1–10.

70. Milgrom, "The Priestly Doctrine," 201–4. Milgrom has shown conclusively that all the Pentateuchal material on repentance was written prior to that of the prophetic understanding and therefore dates from no later than the First Temple period. See Milgrom's arguments in *Leviticus 1–16*, 376–78.

71. See, for ex., Josh. 24:20; Judg. 2:1–4,10–23; 1 Sam. 7:3–4 (prophetic-type repentance!); 12:8–25; 2 Kings 17:7–23; Neh. 9 (a summary of biblical history until that time!). I thank Yair Zakovitch for reminding me of this fact.

72. I thank Yair Zakovitch, Marvin Sweeney, Dru Johnson, and philosopher Simon May for urging me to write this excursus, and for their comments—some of which I have tried to address here. It should be noted that the topic of theodicy in the Jewish Bible has generated an enormous literature over the ages—far too much to bring in this brief synopsis.

73. Isa. 45:7 has often been seen to be anomalous: "*I form light and create darkness, I make weal and create woe, I the Lord do all these things.*" The Hebrew word for "weal" is *shalom* ("peace, welfare, prosperity," when it happens naturally or as a blessing from God) and that for "woe" is the classical biblical word for "bad" or "evil," *ra* (in either masculine or feminine). Shalom Paul, *Isaiah 40–66*, 257–58, makes several important observations: (a) the common interpretation that this verse is an

attempt to counteract the divine duality in Zoroastrianism is most probably incorrect, since we do not know if Cyrus (see vs. 1) was a Zoroastrian, and nowhere in the biblical text is that religion alluded to, nor is any Persian deity mentioned; (b) by stating that God "creates darkness," the verse is polemicizing against the view in Gen. 1:2 that darkness was *not* created by God (i.e., that darkness was there before God began creation). Rather, the verse is saying that God created both light and darkness; (c) *ra* in this verse does *not* mean evil, because it is contrasted not with *tov* ("good") but with *shalom* ("peace, welfare"). What is the opposite of *shalom*? War or disaster! So Amos 3:6, *"When a ram's horn is sounded in a city, do the people not tremble* [in fear]*? Can disaster-ra'ah beset a city, and God has not caused it?"* See also Jer. 18:8, 11. As the verses in Jeremiah illustrate, the Hebrew word for evil can also mean disastrous punishment for evil behavior. Thus in the context of Isa. 45:7, as a contrast for "peace," it makes much more sense to understand *ra* as "disaster" or "disastrous punishment" rather than "evil."

74. Similarly, Jer. 13:23; 17:1, 9; Lam. 3:38–39; Eccl. 7:20.

75. The hiddenness of God (or God's face) is a motif that appears a number of times in the Hebrew Bible, often as an expression of this unhappy bewilderment, or as punishment for disobedience: Deut. 31:17, 18; 32:20; Isa. 8:17; 45:15 (in a positive sense); 54:8; 59:2; 64:6; Jer. 33:5; Ezek. 39:23, 24, 29; Mic. 3:4; Ps. 10:11 (what the wicked thinks); 13:2; 22:25 (a denial that God hid His face from Israel); 27:9; 30:8; 51:11 (a plea to God to ignore sins); 69:18; 88:15; 89:47; 102:3; 104:29; 143:7; Job 13:24; 34:29. Indeed, the Scroll of Esther can be viewed as a response to the seeming hiddenness of God. I thank Rabbi Raymond Apple for urging me to address this motif.

76. Similarly, see Laato and de Moor, *Theodicy in the World of the Bible,* viii, xxi–xxv, and these articles: Loprieno, "Theodicy in Ancient Egyptian Texts," 27–56; van der Toorn, "Theodicy in Akkadian Literature," 57–89; Hoffner, "Theodicy in Hittite Texts," 90–107; de Moor, "Theodicy in the Texts of Ugarit," 108–50. At the same time, anybody who reads these articles will note that a multiplicity of views exist throughout the ancient Near East polytheisms and even within individual civilizations. For example, in the Hoffner article on the Hittites, 96, he brings an exceptional text, "He/she (some deity) it is who always vindicates just men, but chops down evil men like trees" and on 97, "from the Hittite adaption of a Mesopotamian hymn to the Sun-god: 'You alone, O just one, always show mercy. You alone attend to prayer. . . . To you alone the just person is dear, and you vindicate him/her.'" A characteristic of Ugaritic

myths in de Moor's article seems to be the "limited power" of the gods (121; compare 132).

77. Also, Ps. 10:7–8; 13:2; 35:19–20.

78. Also, Ps. 9:19–21; 10:17–18; 13:6; 25:18–22; 27:14. Compare Mowinckel, *The Psalms in Israel's Worship*, 1:216.

79. Compare Ps. 11:5; Job 1–2.

80. Similar to the sin-offerings on behalf of the people on each holiday at the sanctuary (in Leviticus and Numbers), on the assumption that the people may have sinned.

81. The literature on theodicy in Job is vast. To illustrate the scholarly debate on Job 38–42, it is worthwhile comparing the following interpretations by two superior scholars: Edward L. Greenstein, "The Problem of Evil in Job," 353–62; and Michael V. Fox, "God's Answer and Job's Response."

82. Following Fox's translation of Job's last sentence (except that I interpret "repent on"—the "on" not to be taken literally, but to be understood as it normally is with the verb *nun, het, mem*—"concerning, about"), Fox, "God's Answer and Job's Response , 19–20, and Fox's understanding of the purpose of the Divine speech, 21–23.

83. Ecclesiastes may have been influenced by general Greek philosophical thought.

84. B.T. Kiddushin 39b; compare Saadia Gaon , *The Book of Beliefs and Opinions*, 213–14.

85. The Mishnah is the primarily legal collection of the Tanaim—the early rabbis who flourished during the late Second Temple period until the beginning of the third century CE.

6. The Establishment of Hope

1. Philistia was the habitation of the Philistines in the coastal plain in southern Canaan. The area known as Canaan or the Land of Israel was first called Palestine by a few Greek authors starting with Herodotus (fifth century BCE), but did not become the official name of the area until the Romans created the province "Syria Palaestina" following the defeat of the Bar Kochba (Jewish) Revolt in 135 CE—perhaps to suppress the Jewish connection to the land. Thus to use "Palestine" as a reference to the Land of Israel in the biblical period is an anachronism.

2. Eschatology comes from the Greek word *eschatos*, meaning "last, ulti-mate, end"—beliefs about the end of history. In the Hebrew Bible, the phrase "the days to come" or "the days that will come afterwards" have often been translated incorrectly as "the last days," that is, the end of his-

tory. It really refers to a future time of permanent redemption or restoration, when the God-Israel covenantal relationship will be ensured. History will thus continue far into the future, but it will be a positive one. That is how the term "eschatology" is used here.

3. The texts here are taken from two sources, ANET, 455–63, trans. S. N. Kramer, and Jacobsen, *The Harps That Once . . .*, 447–74.

4. Compare Ps. 44:18–19, 27; Lam. 4:22a; 5:21.

5. Sumerian civilization ended, and Ur never captured its previous grandeur, but it did survive for another 1,500 years.

6. The poetic texts here are also taken from two sources, ANET, 611–19, trans. S. N. Kramer; Michalowski, *The Lamentation over the Destruction of Sumer and Ur*, 37–69.

7. Jacobsen, *The Harps That Once . . .*, 476–77.

8. Isin was reestablished after the fall of Sumerian civilization and continued to exist until the end of the second millennium BCE.

9. Michael V. Fox, pers. comm., January 28, 2015; Lichtheim, *Ancient Egyptian Literature*, 1:149–50, re: *The Admonitions of Ipuwer* (see COS, trans. Nili Shupak, 1:93–98; dates to Eighteenth or Nineteenth Dynasty, ca. 1580–1200 BCE, 93) are not brought here due to the scholarly debate about the meaning of the text (see Shupak, 97n34).

10. COS, trans. Nili Shupak, 1:106–10.

11. COS, 109n34.

12. The two goddesses of Upper and Lower Egypt. See COS, 109n36.

13. The contrasts here are between the two Egyptian words *ma'at* and *isfet,* which mean "order" and "chaos," the archetypical Egyptian "right" and "wrong." See Lichtheim, *Ancient Egyptian Literature*, 1:145.

14. This included building a line of fortresses to defend the eastern border from invasion by foreign forces. COS, trans. Nili Shupak, 1:109 and 110n38.

15. Compare Isa. 9:3–6; Mic. 5:3–5; Zech. 9:10.

16. W. W. Hallo, "Akkadian Apcalypses," notes their "*pretended* predictions" (235). Martti Nissenen, "Neither Prophecies nor Apocalyses," affirms (quoting A. K. Grayson) that their purpose is to "justify a current idea or institution or to forecast future doom for a hated enemy" (134–35). See also Clifford, "The Roots of Apocalypticism in Near Eastern Myth," 1:12–14.

17. From Neujahr, *Predicting the Past*, 46.

18. Neujahr, *Predicting the Past*, 49.

19. In reality, these were forced deportations of the idol representing successful attacks on Babylon. See Neujahr, *Predicting the Past*, 38.

20. Using both COS, 1:481, and Neujahr, *Predicting the Past*, 31–34.

21. Neujahr, *Predicting the Past,* 39–41.
22. Clifford, "The Roots of Apocalypticism," 12. For Text A, see ANET, 607. For the mention of twelve kings, and which ones were favorable, see Longman, "Fictional Akkadian Royal Autobiography," 358–60.
23. Clifford, "The Roots of Apocalypticism," 13. For a convincing analysis, see Neujahr, *Predicting the Past,* 63–67.
24. S. Kaufmann, "Prediction, Prophecy, and Apocalypse," 223–25.
25. Kaufmann, "Prediction, Prophecy, and Apocalypse," 225. Moshe Weinfeld, *Social Justice in Ancient Israel and the Ancient Near East,* 58, quotes the same sixth-century BCE text as does Kaufmann, but insists that it refers to the Babylonian king doing justice and righteousness, and sees in it a similar vision to Isa. 9:6 and 2 Sam. 8:15. On 59, Weinfeld states that, likewise, in Egyptian drawings, the base of the king's throne "is shaped like the hieroglyph for *ma'at,* a concept which expresses the value of justice and righteousness in ancient Egypt" and compares it to Ps. 89:15. However, any ethics contained in *ma'at* are subservient to the overall ideal of a harmonious and constant social order.

    There are such few texts that support Weinfeld's contention that biblical prophecies of redemption draw on ancient Near Eastern material that he has to resort to Virgil's Fourth Eclogue (69–72; first century BCE) and a text from the Sybilline Oracles (68–69; second through sixth centuries CE), and then claim that, even though no evidence exists, they are rooted in Ancient Near East traditions, despite the fact that he admits that the Sybilline oracles are "clearly influenced by Israelite prophecy" (68).

    On 67n34, he refers to his own article (Moshe Weinfeld, "Mesopotamian Eschatological Prophecies"; I thank Shalom Paul for this reference) which mentions the *Shulgi Prophecy.*
26. Hanson, "Jewish Apocalyptic against Its Near Eastern Environment," *Revue Biblique* 78 (1971): 38–39, cited by Walton, *Ancient Israelite Literature,* 122.
27. Gese, "The Idea of History in the Ancient Near East and the Old Testament," *Journal for Theology and the Church* 2 (1965): 53, cited by Walton, *Ancient Israelite Literature,* 123.
28. Walton, *Ancient Israelite Literature,* 314: "When people of the ancient Near East thought about the future on earth, they thought of it as unchanging—there is no better world coming, even though they would have hoped for more comfortable conditions." David L. Petersen, "Eschatology (OT)," 2:576, states categorically that "no evidence from Ancient Near East civilization attests the level of eschatological expecta-

tion which we find in Israel." In "Prediction, Prophecy, and Apocalypse," 226, on the *Uruk Prophecy* Stephen Kaufmann states, "To my knowledge no one has yet succeeded in discovering any kind of eschatology in Akkadian literature. Indeed, the Mesopotamian idea of the ideal future would seem to be (for those in power, at least) nothing more than an indefinite continuation of the status quo; witness the last two lines of our new Uruk text: 'He will exercise authority and kingship in Uruk, his dynasty will stand forever. The kings of Uruk will exercise authority like the gods.'" Kaufmann then concludes, 228, "That apocalyptic achieved the popularity that it did in Jewish life of the Second Temple period, while Akkadian 'prophecy' . . . was never more than a totally marginal offshoot from the mainstream of Mesopotamian literature, reveals a great deal about some of the fundamental differences in the intellectual concerns and assumptions of these two societies."

29. It is not accidental that most of this material reflects two distinct threats of destruction and exile: Assyria against North Israel—final destruction and exile realized in 722 BCE, and Babylonia against Judah—–realized in 586 BCE.

30. Unterman, "Redemption (OT)," 650–52; other socio-legal contexts described there are cultic offerings, the firstborn, marriage to the wife of a deceased relative, the owner of a goring ox, the "blood redeemer," and ransom (using the root *k-p-r*).

31. Unterman, "Redemption (OT)," 651–52; Num. 35:12–28; Deut. 19:4–6, 11–13; Josh. 20; 2 Sam. 14:11; compare Judg. 8:18–21 with 1 Kings 16:11; 2 Sam. 3:27; 13:28–29.

32. Unterman, "Redemption (OT)," 652; Deut. 7:8; 9:26; 13:6; 15:5; 21:8; 24:18; 2 Sam. 7:23 paralleled by 1 Chron. 17:21; Mic. 6:4; Ps. 74:2; 77:16; 78:35, 42; 106:10; 111:9; Neh. 1:10.

33. Unterman, "Redemption (OT)," 652–53; Hosea 7:13; 13:14; Isa. 1:27; Mic. 4:10; Jer. 31:11; 50:34; Isa. 35:9, 10 (=51:11); 41:14; 43:1 (compare vs. 3), 14; 44:6, 22–24; 47:4; 48:17, 20; 49:7, 26; 50:2; 51:10; 52:3, 9; 54:5, 8; 59:20; 60:16; 62:12; 63:4, 9, 16; Zech. 10:8; Ps. 107:2.

34. Unterman, "Redemption (OT)," 653; compare Isa. 49:25–26; 51:9–11; 59:16–20.

35. Unterman, "The Social-Legal Origin for the Image of God as Redeemer *go'el* of Israel," 405n13. It is possible that this chapter was delivered by the prophet after the people had returned to the land under Persian rule and were living in depressed conditions. See Paul, *Isaiah 40–66*, 11, 321.

36. Other examples: Isaiah 40:1–2; Psalm 126:1.

37. Other examples: Hosea 11:10–11; Jer. 30:3.

38. Other examples: Jer. 31:12; Isaiah 65:21; Ezek. 36:8, 11.

39. See also Lev. 26:3–4, 10, and Deut. 28:5, 8, 11–12.

40. Other examples: Isaiah 2:2, 4 (compare Judg. 3:2), and 11:9; Ezek. 37:25–26.

41. Compare Deut. 28:7.

42. Even though this passage predicts the renewal of the Davidic dynasty over the northern kingdom of Israel, its lack of mention of a Davidic heir shows its primitiveness as a messianic concept, thereby attesting to its early date. Even Hosea (3:5) is more developed. The rebuilding of the "fallen booth of David" refers to the reestablishment of the united monarchy of David and Solomon over both North and South.

43. Jesse is the father of David. This is a prophecy about a scion of the line of David.

44. Also, Jer. 33:15–17, 19–22, 26, in which Jeremiah depicts an entire line of kings who are descendants of David.

45. "To tend them" means in justice and kindness, as opposed to the previous "shepherds" who exploited the people (verses 3–16). See also, Ezek. 34:24; 37:24–25; Zech. 12:8. Note that Zechariah 9–14 have long been seen by academic scholarship as a later addition to Zechariah. Meyers and Meyers, *Zechariah 9–14*, 26–29, assign these chapters to the fifth century BCE. The late sixth-century BCE prophets of the returnees to Zion under Persia, Haggai and Zechariah (Ezra 5:1–2; 6:14), prophesy about Zerubbabel (Hag. 1:1, 12–14; 2:1–5, 20–23; Zech. 4:1–14) as the hoped-for messianic king of the line of David (compare 1 Chron. 3:17–19; grandson of Jeconiah). Zerubbabel is the appointed Persian governor (compare Ezra 2:1–2; 3:1–5:2; Neh. 12:1).

46. These prophecies are also known as "messianic" prophecies. The Hebrew word upon which the English "messiah" is based means "anointed." In the Jewish Bible, only two types of individuals were anointed—the king and the high priest. Perhaps the first prophetic verse to intimate such a future society is Hosea 2:21.

47. See Paul R. Raabe, *Obadiah*, 268–70, 272–73. See also Isa. 1:26, which resembles Obad. 21, as does Isa. 24:23. Could Isa. 1:26 be a later prophecy?

48. For the following, see Paul, *Isaiah 40–66*, 22: "Contrary to the general belief in the future reinstatement of a Davidic scion upon the throne, the prophet unequivocally states that 'the enduring loyalty promised to David' shall be transferred to the nation as a whole (55:3–4) and that God alone shall rule over them (41:21; 43:15; 44:6; 52:7)." See also Paul's comments on 437–39.

49. 2 Sam. 7:16; 23:5; Ps. 89:4–5, 25, 29. Second Isaiah, in effect, is providing an answer to the complaint in Ps. 89:50.

50. All of Ezekiel, chapters 40–48, is a prophecy of the future service in the Temple in Jerusalem! See also Isa. 2:1–4 // Mic. 4:1–3, the centrality of the Temple, and Isa. 27:13; Second Isaiah—Isa. 56:3–7 (on the strangers who attach themselves to the Lord; compare 60:7; 66:20–23); compare 44:28. Marvin Sweeney pointed out to me that Ezekiel's prophecy of the new Temple in chapters 40–48 may represent a fulfillment of Josiah's reforms.

51. It is true that neither Isaiah 2 nor Micah 4 mentions sacrifices and that the texts focus on following God's "paths" and judgment of the nations. However, it is difficult to imagine a prophet conceiving of the Temple existing without the presence of sacrifices, too. Ps. 122 also mentions "going to the House of the Lord" (vs. 2) and how the tribes went there to be judged (vss. 4–5). It is, however, unimaginable that the Psalmist would have thought that he was portraying a Temple without sacrificial offerings.

52. See also 66:18b–21.

53. On Haggai's and Zechariah's prophecies: Hag. 1:7–2:9; Zech. 3:6–7; 4:8–10; Ezra 5:1–2; 6:14. On the witness of historiography: Ezra 1:1–11; 2:68–69; 3:1–4:4, 24–6:22; compare 2 Chron. 36:22–23.

54. A parallel passage is Jer. 32:38–40. For other Jeremiah redemption passages speaking of God's covenant with Israel, see 33:20–26; 50:5. Ezek. 36:26–28 adapts Jeremiah's New Covenant prophecy and substitutes "laws" and "statutes" for "torah." He accepts Jeremiah's teaching that God will ensure that the people sin no more (Ezek. 36:27).

55. Unterman, *From Repentance*, 107–10.

56. Hosea 2:20; Ezek. 16:59–62; 34:24–25; 37:26–27; Isa. 42:6; 49:8; 54:10; 55:3; 56:4, 6; 59:21; 61:8.

57. See also vss.11–13 there and Deut. 28:9–10, 13.

58. But compare Ps. 37:31.

59. Lev. 10:11; Deut. 17:8–11; 33:8–10; Hag. 2:11–13.

60. That the covenant between God and Israel remained in effect through the very end of the writing of the Hebrew Bible is evidenced by Daniel 11, apparently written at the time of persecutions by Antiochus Epiphanes in 167 BCE, for it speaks of the "holy covenant" that the righteous of the people maintain, vs. 32, "He [Antiochus] *will flatter with smooth words those who act wickedly toward the covenant, but the people devoted to their God will stand firm.*"

61. Based on Milgrom's translation, *Leviticus 22–27*, 2273–74, except that Milgrom interprets the people's repentance as conditional. The text, however, gives no indication of that. On the contrary, it seems that the people's repentance here is guaranteed, and see below on Deut. 4 and 30. Further, Milgrom views vss. 43–44 as late and puts the tenses of the verbs in the past. Even if his dating is correct, the switch of tenses makes no sense for an editor who is trying to interweave these verses here, so the tense should remain in the future. He also translates "ancients" in vs. 45, instead of the literal translation "first ones," which can also simply mean "former" and, therefore, can refer to the previous generation. Nonetheless, that interpretation ("former") is also problematic because vs. 45 purports to be part of the speech of God to Moses at the Tent of Meeting (as does the entire book, Lev. 1:1) at the foot of Mt. Sinai (26:46; 27:34), implying that this verse was written at a later date. However, several Jewish medieval commentators noted that the text is referring to the future exiles. Therefore, for those exiles, the Sinai covenant was made with a "former" generation.

On 2364–65, Milgrom dates vss. 40–42, 45 not later than the eighth century BCE and cogently argues against those who see these verses as later. One of his proofs is the lack of the usage of the verb *shuv* in relationship to repentance, which indicates that the first four books of the Torah were written before eighth-century BCE prophetic concepts of repentance became the norm.

62. Based upon Moshe Weinfeld's translation, *Deuteronomy 1–11*, 194, but translating the text the way it is written, and not interpreting it in vs. 29 as "if" the people will search for God in exile.

63. Here, too, as in Leviticus, the people's abandoning (here, "forgetting") the covenant (4:23) has its reversal in that God "will not forget" it. See Weinfeld, *Deuteronomy*, 207.

64. Alexander Rofe, "The Covenant in the Land of Moab (DT 28:69–30:20)," 312, makes a good argument for attaching Deut. 30:1–10 to the end of Deut. 28.

65. If restoration is intimated in Lev. 26 and Deut. 4, why is it not explicitly stated? Methodologically, it is always difficult to ascertain why something is *not* in a text. Proper literary analysis only examines what *is* in the text. Given that caveat, it is possible that the reason Lev. 26 and Deut. 4 do not explicitly mention redemption is for the same reason that redemption is not mentioned at the end of 2 Kings 25 or the placement of a nearly identical copy of 2 Kings 25 at the end of the Book of Jeremiah—because restoration had not yet occurred (restoration in the

latter two cases in terms of the exiles who returned from Babylon after it was conquered by Persia). That does not mean that Lev. 26 and Deut. 4 were written just before the Persian restoration in the sixth century BCE. As Milgrom pointed out, the passage in Lev. 26 was written before the prophetic terminology on repentance became the norm. Furthermore, Deut. 4:29–31 has affinities with the eighth-century BCE prophet Hosea (Weinfeld, *Deuteronomy 1–11*, 218), and even Deut. 30 (if it was indeed moved from its original context at the end of Deut. 28) might only look to the imagined exile to Egypt!—Deut. 28:68 (note also how Deut. 30:9b reverses Deut. 28:63).

A similar text to the passages in Lev. 26 and Deut. 4 is the end of Solomon's speech at the dedication of the Temple—1 Kings 8:44–53. That passage also speaks of the people repenting in exile (vs. 48), but there God's reaction is to ensure that their captors are merciful to them (vs. 50). In other words, 1 Kings 8:44–53 dovetails with the description of the elevation of Jehoiachin by the king of Babylon in 2 Kings 25:27–30. However, 1 Kings 8:44–53 might be earlier than the final redaction of Kings. See Unterman, *From Repentance*, 72–74.

66. This point was noted by Milgrom, *Leviticus 1–16*, 377, also in contrast to the Book of Kings—see, for example, 2 Kings 17:13 and 23:25. See also 1 Sam. 7:3. Milgrom also points out there that *shuv* in any kind of other spiritual sense in the Torah appears only twice—as apostasy (!) in the phrase "turning away from" following God; see Num. 14:43 and 32:15 (both of which Milgrom attributes to JE, and the second one also to P). Milgrom also observed there that this usage is identical to Josh. 22:16, 18, 23, 29 and 1 Sam. 15:11.

67. Most of the material on the relationship between repentance and redemption in the rest of this chapter is taken from Unterman, "Redemption (OT)," 653–54, and *From Repentance*.

68. The agricultural image is apparently of one sifting fine grain where the pebbles remain in the sieve—that is, the sinners are caught.

69. The translation of Anderson and Freedman, *Hosea*, 291.

70. Admah and Zeboiim were demolished together with Sodom and Gemorrah (Deut. 29:22).

71. See Jacob Milgrom, "Did Isaiah Prophesy during the Reign of Uzziah?" 169, concerning repentance as a condition of redemption. Compare also Isa. 1:27. It is an unresolved question whether repentance would be done by those who survived in the land only, or also those who returned from afar. Isa. 11:11–16 does not speak of repentance.

72. Mic. 2:12–13; 4:1–8; 5:1–8; 7:18–20.
73. The translation is primarily based upon Andersen and Freedman, *Micah,* 594–99.
74. Exod. 15:11; Jer. 49:19; 50:44; Isa. 44:7; Ps. 35:10; 71:19; 77:14; 89:9; 113:5; Job 36:22 (conveniently listed in Anderson and Freedman, *Micah,* 597).
75. Compare Anderson and Freedman, *Micah,* 596.
76. Jer. 3:6; see also Jer. 1:2.
77. The full passage is Jer. 3:6–13, 19–4:2. See also the parallel passage in 31:2–9, 15–22 (Unterman, *From Repentance,* 25–53).
78. The prophecy is directed to the northern tribes exiled by the Assyrians in 722 BCE.
79. A bloodless affair. Babylon briefly besieged Jerusalem in 597 BCE, but Jehoiachin and his courtiers quickly surrendered (2 Kings 24:8–17).
80. The parallel passage is 29:10–14. Unterman, *From Repentance to Redemption,* 55–87.
81. That is, "I will give them a heart that will be obedient to Me."
82. See Jer. 32:1–2 and the prophecy of redemption in vv. 36–44 (vss. 42–44 refer back to vv. 6–8, 15, 25). Vv. 36–44 are a parallel prophecy to 31:27–37. On these parallel prophecies, see Unterman, *From Repentance,* 90–116.
83. A reference to the days to come when God will bring back the exiles, who will recognize the justness of God's punishment (verses 27–29)—a time just preceding the giving of the new covenant.
84. This passage actually is part of a literary unit that stretches from vs. 27 through vs. 37.
85. Jeremiah had been taken in chains with the exiles as far as Ramah (a few miles north of Jerusalem) before he was released (40:1–6).
86. Compare Jer. 33:25–26, *"Thus says the Lord: 'As surely as I have established My covenant with day and night—the laws of heaven and earth—so I will never reject the offspring of Jacob and David My servant.'"*
87. See also 32:40; 33:6–11, 26; 50:17–19.
88. Ezek. 1:1 starts with the words *"In the thirtieth year,"* but no information is given which indicates the referent for that number. Verse 2 correlates that thirtieth year with the fifth year of the Jehoiachin exile, i.e., 593 BCE.
89. Although he does state that repentance is required for the *individual* to continue to live. Ezek. 3:16–21; 18; 33:10–20.
90. Based on the translation of Moshe Greenberg, *Ezekiel 1–20,* 186.
91. See also Ezek. 6:8–10; 16:53–63; 39:26; 43:10–11, and compare 37:23. For 36:31–32, see below in the text.
92. See also Jer. 24:7. Ezek. 18:31 tells the people to make themselves "a new

heart and a new spirit." That is a precondition of redemption only for the members of the people to continue to live.

93. See the previous verses, 20–21. A somewhat similar passage, but with more concern for the people, is 39:25–28 (particularly vss. 25 and 28). Baruch J. Schwartz, "Ezekiel's Dim View of Israel's Restoration," claims that Ezekiel's prophecies of restoration are not prophecies of redemption because they are not expressions of God's love for Israel, that is, they contain no consolation or salvation, but that restoration—with the people's self-loathing, which Schwartz sees as permanent—is a part of the punishment! Further, Schwartz states that God in these prophecies only cares about His name, not about Israel. I believe that Schwartz has exaggerated the situation in Ezekiel. Chapter 36:5–12, a prophecy addressed to the Land of Israel, emphasizes God's coming punishment of the nations around the Land of Israel and the future fruitfulness of the Land for the sake of "My people" (vss. 8, 12, compare vss. 10–11). Further, vss. 33–38 (particularly 37) describe acts that God will do also for the sake of the people. See also 34:11–31; 37:11–13, 21–28; 39:22–29. Indeed, 39:25 mentions God's mercy upon Israel, but Schwartz rejects that verse as secondary (53, which is too easy a method to do away with texts that are problematic for one's thesis). Schwartz's claim that the people's self-loathing (once restored to the land) is permanent is unproven: no statements of permanence accrue to it, as opposed to, for example, God's promise to never again hide His face from His people (39:28), His permanent covenant of peace/friendship (37:26), His promise that the people will abide in the Land forever (37:25), and so forth. Similarly, Schwartz's statement (51n27) that "I will be your God and you shall be My people" is "a one-sided declaration of resolve by YHWH to have the Israelites as his servants so that he can have a people to rule" is indefensible. See the immediate contexts of 34:24 (compare 34:30–31); 36:28; 37:23, 27.

94. See also Ezek. 37; 39:25, 28.

95. It should be noted that a scholarly debate exists between (a) those who think that the prophecies in 40–48 were spoken while the prophet was in exile, while chapters 49–66 were said after he had accompanied the people who came back to the land (after the declaration of Cyrus in 539 BCE), and (b) those who deem 49–55 to also be Exilic.

96. The arguments of Menahem Haran, *Between Former (Prophecies) and Later (Prophecies)*, and Paul, *Isaiah 40–66*, that all of chapters 40–66 (and 34–35) were written by one prophet who was in exile with the

people and then accompanied those who returned are convincing (although many scholars hold that the words of two prophets are found here; 40–55, 56–66); see Paul, *Isaiah 40–66*, 4–12, 321. If at least chapters 56–66 were written in Jerusalem, why does the prophet speak prophecies of redemption there? Because (a) not all the exiles have returned, and (b) many of the older prophecies about the future redemption inside the land have yet to be fulfilled.

97. Paul, *Isaiah 40–66*, 23–24, lists God's attributes and descriptions of His relations to Israel which are cited in the following text. The translations here are based on his.

98. See Gruber, "The Motherhood of God in Second Isaiah." Compare Isa. 45:11.

99. See also vs. 5, and 62:5.

100. Isa. 49:26; 60:16.

101. Isa. 41:14, 16, 20; 43:3, 14; etc.—over ten occurrences.

102. Isa. 43:11–13; 45:15, 17, 21; etc.—over twenty occurrences.

103. Isa. 41:10, 13–14; 44:2; 49:8; 50:7, 9.

104. Isa. 41:8–9; 42:1; 43:10, 20; etc.—over ten occurrences.

105. Isa. 43:1, 7, 15; 44:2, 21, 24; 45:11; 49:8; 64:7. Israel is even *"the people I formed for Myself"* (43:21).

106. Prophecies against foreign nations are an entire literary genre in academic biblical studies. Even though some of these prophecies, as here, are related to prophecies of redemption, a detailed analysis would take the current work too far afield.

107. A confession is found in Isa. 53:4–6, one of the Servant Songs, but there is no evidence that it is tied to redemption.

108. It is not a coincidence that the ancient rabbis chose these verses to be the essence of the prophetic reading during the morning service on Yom Kippur.

109. Isa. 59:1–8 is another rebuke, followed by the people's confession, vss. 9–13. Verse 20 concludes with a statement that only those who repent from rebellious acts will be redeemed in the new Zion: *"He shall come as a redeemer to Zion, to those in Jacob who turn back from rebellious transgression"* (compare 1:27). The people's confession reappears in 64:4b-6 (compare 63:17) as a prelude to a plea to God to react to the devastation of Jerusalem and the Temple (vss. 7–11). Finally, in 65:1–7, 11–12, 14–15 (parts); 66:3–6, 14c–18a, 24, God rebukes those who are either idolaters or severe cultic violators and sentences them to death for their abominations, while in the rest of those chapters God promises His bounty to those who are loyal to Him.

110. Many scholars think that these words were appended to the book by a later author.

111. The meaning here is not repentance, as some have thought, but "causing the heart of x to turn to y," as in Ezra 6:22.

112. Verses 23–24 may very well be based upon 1 Kings 19:19–21 in which Elijah, who is on a mission from God to eliminate the Baal from Israel, delays his assignment so that Elisha may go and say a proper farewell to his parents. In effect, he turns Elisha's request into his own command. The phrase *"What have I done to you?"* must be interpreted as meaning, "What bad thing do you think I have done to you?" Every time the interrogative "what?" appears with the verb "do" in the past tense in biblical Hebrew (with or without an object), it always refers to a negative act, real or imagined. When Elisha asks permission from Elijah to say good-bye to his parents, it implies that Elijah could say "yes" or "no." Elijah's response means, "What bad thing have I done to you to make you think that I could say 'no' to a child who wishes to fulfill the commandment, 'Honor thy father and the mother'?" If for Elijah, the mission of God must be delayed for that simple, ethical commandment, for Malachi, the mission of God cannot be accomplished without reconciliation between children and parents.

113. Unterman, "Redemption (OT)," 654, and *From Repentance,* 178–79.

114. Bright, *Covenant and Promise,* 21–22.

115. The previous verses in 2 Chronicles 36, verses 20–21, also attribute the duration of the exile to Jeremiah's prophecy!

Conclusion

1. Shinan and Zakovitch, *From Gods to God,* 1. The quote is by Yair Zakovitch (pers. comm.).

2. Deuteronomy 4 has other examples of self-awareness of the uniqueness of God's relationship to Israel; see verses 5–7, 19–20, 32–40.

Bibliography

Adelson, Howard L. "The Origins of a Concept of Social Justice." In *Social Justice in the Ancient World*, ed. K. D. Irani and Morris Silver, 25–38. Westport CT: Greenwood, 1995.

Albertz, Rainer. *A History of Israelite Religion in the Old Testament Period.* Vol. 1. Trans. John Bowden. London: SCM, 1994.

Ancient Near Eastern Texts Relating to the Old Testament. 3rd ed. with supplement. Edited by James Pritchard. Princeton: Princeton University Press, 1969.

Anderson, A. A. *The Book of Psalms.* In vol. 1 of *New Century Bible.* London: Oliphants, 1972.

Anderson, Francis I., and David N. Freedman. *Amos.* Anchor Bible. New York: Doubleday, 1989.

———. *Hosea.* Anchor Bible. Garden City NY: Doubleday, 1980.

———. *Micah.* Anchor Bible. New York: Doubleday, 2000.

Arnold, Bill T., and David B. Weisberg. "A Centennial Review of Friedrich Delitzsch's 'Babel und Bibel' Lectures." *Journal of Biblical Literature* 121 (2002): 441–57.

Assman, Jon. "Monotheism and Polytheism." In *Religions of the Ancient World: A Guide,* ed. Sarah Iles Johnston, 17–31. Cambridge MA: Belknap Press of Harvard University, 2004.

Baines, John. "Society, Morality, and Religious Practice." In *Religion in Ancient Egypt: Gods, Myths, and Personal Practice,* ed. Byron E. Shafer, 123–200. London: Routledge, 1991.

Barton, John. "The Prophets and the Cult." In *Temple and Worship in Biblical Israel,* ed. John Day, 111–22. London: T & T Clark, 2005.

Beckman, Gary. *Hittite Diplomatic Texts.* 2nd ed. SBL Writings from the Ancient World series, vol. 7. Atlanta: Scholars, 1999.

Berman, Joshua. *Created Equal: How the Bible Broke with Ancient Political Thought.* Oxford: Oxford University Press, 2008.

Bibb, Bryan D. "The Prophetic Critique of Ritual in Old Testament Theology." In *The Priests in the Prophets,* ed. Lester L. Grabbe and Alice Ogden Bellis, 31–43. London: T & T Clark International, 2004.

Blenkinsopp, Joseph. *Ezekiel.* Louisville: John Knox, 1990.

———. *Ezra–Nehemiah.* Philadelphia: Westminster, 1988.

———. *Isaiah 1–39.* Anchor Bible. New York: Doubleday, 2000.

Botterweck, G. Johannes. "Yada . . ." In *Theological Dictionary of the Old Testament,* 5: 448–81.

Bright, John. *Covenant and Promise.* London: SCM, 1977.

———. *Jeremiah.* Anchor Bible. Garden City NY: Doubleday, 1965.

Brueggemann, Walter. *To Pluck Up, to Tear Down: A Commentary on Jeremiah 1–25.* Grand Rapids MI: Willima B. Eerdmans, 1988.

Carroll, Robert P. *Jeremiah.* Old Testament Library. London: SCM, 1986.

Chan, Wing-tsit. "Confucian Thought: Foundations of the Tradition." In *The Encyclopedia of Religion,* ed. Mircea Eliade, 4: 15–24. New York: Macmillan, 1987.

Clements, Ronald. *Prophecy and Covenant.* London: SCM, 1965.

Clifford, Richard J. "The Roots of Apocalypticism in Near Eastern Myth." In *The Encyclopedia of Apocalypticism,* ed. John J. Collins, 1: 3–38. New York: Continuum, 2000.

Clines, David J. A. "Ethics as Deconstruction, and, The Ethics of Deconstruction." In *The Bible in Ethics: The Second Sheffield Colloquium,* ed. J. W. Rogerson et al., 77–106. Journal for the Study of the Old Testament supplement series 207. Sheffield: Sheffield Academic, 1995.

Cogan, Mordechai. *1 Kings.* Anchor Bible. New York: Doubleday, 2000.

The Context of Scripture: Canonical Compositions, Monumental Inscriptions, and Archival Documents from the Biblical World, ed. William W. Hallo. 3 vols. Leiden: Brill, 1997–2002.

Craigie, Peter C. *Psalms 1–50, Word Biblical Commentary.* Waco TX: Word Books, 1983.

Crenshaw, James L. *Education in Ancient Israel: Across the Deadening Silence.*
Anchor Bible Reference Library. New York: Doubleday, 1998.

——. "Education in Ancient Israel." *JBL* 104 (1985): 601–15.

Curtis, Edward M. "Man as the Image of God in Genesis in the Light of
Ancient Near Eastern Parallels." PhD dissertation, University of Pennsylvania, 1984.

Dalglish, Edward R. *Psalm Fifty-One: In the Light of Ancient Near Eastern
Patternism.* Leiden: E. J. Brill, 1962.

de Moor, Johannes C. "Theodicy in the Texts of Ugarit." In *Theodicy in the
World of the Bible,* ed. Antti Laato and Johannes C. de Moor, 108–50.
Leiden: Brill, 2003.

Eichler, Barry L. "Examples of Restatement in the Laws of Hammurabi." In
*Mishneh Torah: Studies in Deuteronomy and Its Cultural Environment in
Honor of Jeffrey H. Tigay,* ed. Nili Sacher Fox, David A. Glatt-Gilad, and
Michael J. Williams, 365–400. Winona Lake IN: Eisenbrauns, 2009.

Epsztein, Leon. *Social Justice in the Ancient Near East and the People of the
Bible.* Trans. John Bowden. London: SCM, 1986.

Fabry, Heinz-Josef. "*Shuv.*" In *Theological Dictionary of the Old Testament,*
ed. G. Johannes Botterweck et al., trans. Douglas W. Stott, 14: 461–522.
Grand Rapids MI: William B. Eerdmans, 2004.

Fairman, H. W. "A Scene of the Offering of Truth in the Temple of Edfu."
Mitteilungen des deutschen Archaologischen Instituts Abteilung Kairo 16
(1958): 86–92.

Fensham, F. Charles. "Father and Son as Terminology for Treaty and Covenant." In *Near Eastern Studies in Honor of William Foxwell Albright,* ed.
Hans Goedicke, 121–35. Baltimore: Johns Hopkins University Press, 1971.

——. "Widow, Orphan, and the Poor in Ancient Near Eastern Legal and
Wisdom Literature." *Journal of Near Eastern Studies* 21 (1962): 129–39.
Reprinted in *Essential Papers on Israel and the Ancient Near East,* 176–
92. New York: New York University, 1991.

Fenton, Terry L. "Israelite Prophecy: Characteristics of the First Protest Movement." In *The Elusive Prophet,* ed. J. C. De Moor, 129–41. Leiden: Brill, 2001.

Finkelstein, Jacob J. "Bible and Babel: A Comparative Study of the Hebrew
and Babylonian Religious Spirit." *Commentary* 26 (November 1958): 431–
44. Reprinted in *Essential Papers on Israel and the Ancient Near East,* ed.
Frederick E. Greenspahn, 355–80. New York: New York University, 1991.

Fishbane, Michael. "Teshuva." In *Encyclopedia Mikrait,* 8: 949–62. Hebrew.
Jerusalem: Bialik, 1982.

Fox, Michael V. "God's Answer and Job's Response." *Biblica* 94 (2013): 1–23.

——— . *Proverbs 1–9*. Anchor Bible. New York: Doubleday, 2000.

——— . *Proverbs 10–31*. Anchor Bible. New Haven: Yale University Press, 2009.

Fulkerson, Laurel. *No Regrets: Remorse in Classical Antiquity*. Oxford: Oxford University Press, 2013.

Frymer-Kensky, Tikva. "The Atrahasis Epic and Its Significance for Our Understanding of Genesis 1–9." *Biblical Archaeologist* 40, no. 4 (December 1977): 147–55.

——— . *Studies in Bible and Feminist Criticism*. Philadelphia: Jewish Publication Society, 2006.

Gabbay, Uri. *Pacifying the Hearts of the Gods: Sumerian Emesal Prayers of the First Millenium BC*. Wiesbaden: Harrassowitz, 2014.

Gane, Roy E. *Cult and Character*. Winona Lake IN: Eisenbrauns, 2005.

Garnsey, Peter. *Cities, Peasants, and Food in Classical Antiquity: Essays in Social and Economic History*. Ed. W. Scheidel. Cambridge: Cambridge University Press, 1998.

——— . *Famine and Food Supply in the Graeco-Roman World: Responses to Risk and Crisis*. Cambridge: Cambridge University Press, 1988.

——— . *Food and Society in Classical Antiquity*. Cambridge: Cambridge University Press, 1999.

Goetze, A., and S. Levy. "Fragment of the Gilgamesh Epic from Megiddo." *Atiqot: Journal of the Israel Department of Antiquities* 2 (1959): 121–28.

Gordis, Daniel. *Saving Israel: How the Jewish People Can Win a War That May Never End*. Hoboken NJ: John Wiley and Sons, 2009.

Gorman, Frank H., Jr. *The Ideology of Ritual: Space, Time, and Status in the Priestly Theology*. Journal for the Study of the Old Testament supplement series 91. Worcester: Sheffield Academic, 1990.

——— . "Pagans and Priests: Critical Reflections on Method." In *Perspectives on Purity and Purification in the Bible*, ed. Baruch J. Schwartz et al., 96–110. New York: T & T Clark, 2008.

Greenberg, Irving. *The Jewish Way*. New York: Summit, 1988.

Greenberg, Moshe. "The Biblical Grounding of Human Value." Samuel Friedland Lectures, 1960–1966, 39–52. New York: Jewish Theological Seminary of America, 1967.

——— . *Ezekiel 1–20*. Anchor Bible. New York: Doubleday, 1983.

——— . "Herem." In *Encyclopedia Judaica* 8: 44–50. Jerusalem: Keter, 1972.

——— . "More Reflections on Biblical Criminal Law." In *Studies in Bible, Scripta Hierosolymitana XXXI*, ed. Sara Japhet, 1–17. Jerusalem: Magnes, 1986.

——— . "Religion: Stability and Ferment." In *The Age of the Monarchies: Cul-*

ture and Society, ed. Abraham Malamat, *The World History of the Jewish People*, 5: 79–123. Jerusalem: Masada, 1979.

———. "Some Postulates of Biblical Criminal Law." In *Studies in Bible and Jewish Religion: Yehezkel Kaufmann Jubilee Volume*, ed. Menahem Haran, 5–28. Jerusalem: Magnes, 1960.

———. "Three Conceptions of the Torah in Hebrew Scriptures." In *Studies in the Bible and Jewish Thought*, 11–24. Philadelphia: Jewish Publication Society, 1995.

Greenstein, Edward L. "Biblical Law." In *Back to the Sources*, ed. Barry W. Holtz, 83–103. New York: Summit, 1984.

———. "The Problem of Evil in Job." In *Mishneh Todah*, ed. N. S. Fox, D. A. Glatt-Gilead, and M. J. Williams, 333–62. Winona Lake IN: Eisenbrauns, 2009.

Gruber, Mayer I. "The Motherhood of God in Second Isaiah." *Revue Biblique* 90 (1983): 351–59.

Hallo, William W. "Akkadian Apocalypses." *Israel Exploration Journal* 16 (1966): 231–42.

———. "Ancient Near Eastern Texts and Their Relevance for Biblical Exegesis." In *The Context of Scripture*, 1: xxv.

———. *The Context of Scripture: Canonical Compositions, Monumental Inscriptions, and Archival Documents from the Biblical World*. 3 vols. Leiden: Brill, 1997–2002.

Haran, Menahem. *Between Former (Prophecies) and Later (Prophecies)*. Hebrew. Jerusalem: Magnes, 1963.

Hasel, Gerhard F. "Sabbath." In *Anchor Bible Dictionary*, ed. David N. Freedman, 5: 849–51. New York: Doubleday, 1992.

Havice, Harriet K. "The Concern for the Widow and the Fatherless in the Ancient Near East: A Case Study in Old Testament Ethics." PhD dissertation, Yale University, 1978.

Heidel, Alexander. *The Babylonian Genesis*. 2nd ed. Chicago: University of Chicago Press, 1951.

———. *The Gilgamesh Epic and Old Testament Parallels*. 2nd ed. Chicago: University of Chicago Press, 1949.

Heschel, Abraham Joshua. *The Prophets*. Philadelphia: Jewish Publication Society, 1962.

Hillers, Delbert R. *Micah*. Hermeneia. Philadelphia: Fortress, 1984.

Hoffner, Harry A., Jr. "Theodicy in Hittite Texts." In *Theodicy in the World of the Bible*, ed. Antti Laato and Johannes C. de Moor, 90–107. Leiden: Brill, 2003.

Holladay, William L. *Jeremiah 1: A Commentary on the Book of the Prophet Jeremiah, Chapters 1–25*. Hermeneia. Philadelphia: Fortress, 1986.

——. *The Root šûbh in the Old Testament*. Leiden: Brill, 1958.

Hurowitz, Victor Avigdor. *Proverbs*, vol. 2, *Mikra LeYisrael*. Hebrew. Jerusalem: Magnes, 2012.

Jacobsen, Thorkild. *The Harps That Once . . .* New Haven: Yale University Press, 1987.

——. *Treasures of Darkness*. New Haven: Yale University Press, 1976.

Japhet, Sara. *I and II Chronicles*. Old Testament Library. London: SCM, 1993.

——. *The Ideology of the Book of Chronicles and Its Place in Biblical Thought*. Frankfurt am Main: Peter Lang, 1989.

JPS Hebrew-English Tanakh. 2nd ed. Philadelphia: Jewish Publication Society, 1999.

Kaiser, Otto. *Isaiah 1–12*. Old Testament Library. 2nd ed. Trans. John Bowden. Philadelphia: Westminster, 1983.

Kaufmann, Stephen A. "Prediction, Prophecy, and Apocalypse in the Light of New Akkadian Texts." In *Proceedings of the Sixth World Congress of Jewish Studies*, 1: 221–28. Jerusalem: World Union of Jewish Studies, 1977.

Kaufmann, Yehezkel. *The Religion of Israel*. Trans. and abridged Moshe Greenberg. Chicago: University of Chicago Press, 1960.

Kellerman, D. "gur; ger; geruth; meghurim." In *Theological Dictionary of the Old Testament*, ed. G. Johannes Botterweck and Helmer Ringgren, 2: 439–49. Grand Rapids MI: William B. Eerdmans, 1975.

Kidd, Jose E. Ramirez. *Alterity and Identity in Israel: The Ger in the Old Testament*. Beihefte zur Zeitschrift für die alttestamentliche Wissenschaft 283. Berlin: Walter de Gruyter, 1999.

Kitchen, K. A. "Egypt, History of (Chronology)." In *Anchor Bible Dictionary* 2: 321–31. New Haven: Yale University Press, 1992.

——. *On the Reliability of the Old Testament*. Grand Rapids MI: William B. Eerdmans, 2003.

Klawans, Jonathan. *Purity, Sacrifice, and the Temple*. Oxford: Oxford University Press, 2006.

Klein, Jacob. "A New Look at the Theological Background of the Mesopotamian and Biblical Flood Stories." In *A Common Cultural Heritage: Studies in Mesopotamia and the Biblical World in Honor of Barry L. Eichler*, ed. G. Frame et al., 151–76. Bethesda MD: CDL, 2011.

Konstan, David. *Before Forgiveness: The Origins of a Moral Idea*. Cambridge: Cambridge University Press, 2010.

Kselman, John S. "Forgiveness (OT)." In *Anchor Bible Dictionary*, 2: 831–33.

Laato, Antti, and Johannes C. de Moor, eds. *Theodicy in the World of the Bible.* Leiden: Brill, 2003.

Lambert, W. G. *Babylonian Wisdom Literature.* Oxford: Oxford University Press, 1960.

——— . "Mesopotamian Creation Stories." In *Imagining Creation,* ed. M. J. Geller and M. Schipper, 15–59. Institute of Jewish Studies in Judaica 5. Leiden: Brill, 2008. As cited in http://www.ancient.eu/article/225/.

Lang, B. "nkr; nekar; nokri." *Theological Dictionary of the Old Testament,* 9: 423–31. Grand Rapids MI: William B. Eerdmans, 1998.

Larsen, Mogens Trolle. "The 'Babel/Bible' Controversy and Its Aftermath." In *Civilizations of the Ancient Near East,* ed. Jack M. Sasson, 1: 95–106. Peabody MA: Hendrickson, 2000.

Leahy, Anthony. "Ethnic Diversity in Ancient Egypt." In *Civilizations of the Ancient Near East,* ed. Jack M. Sasson, 1: 225–34. New York: Scribner, 1995.

Leibowitz, Nehama. *Studies in Bereshit (Genesis).* 4th rev. ed. Trans. and adapted Aryeh Newman. Jerusalem: World Zionist Organization, 1981.

Lemaire, Andre. "Education." In *Anchor Bible Dictionary,* 2: 305–12. New York: Doubleday, 1992.

Levine, Baruch A. "An Essay of Prophetic Attitudes toward Temple and Cult in Biblical Israel." In *In Pursuit of Meaning,* vol. 1. Winona Lake IN: Eisenbrauns, 2011.

Lichtheim, Miriam. *Ancient Egyptian Literature.* 2 vols. Berkeley: University of California Press, 1976.

——— . *Moral Values in Ancient Egypt.* Orbis Biblicus et Orientalis 155. Fribourg, Switzerland: University Press; Gottingen: Vanderhoeck and Ruprecht, 1997.

Liedke, G., and C. Peterson. "*tora* Instruction." In *Theological Lexicon of the Old Testament,* ed. Ernst Jenni and Claus Westermann, trans. Mark E. Biddle, 3: 1415–22. Peabody MA: Hendrickson, 1997.

Loewenstamm, Samuel. "Beloved Is Man in That He Was Created in the Image." Hebrew. *Tarbiz* 27 (1957): 1–2. English translation in Loewenstamm, *Comparative Studies in Biblical and Ancient Oriental Literature,* AOAT 204 (1980): 48–50.

Longman, Tremper, III. "Fictional Akkadian Royal Autobiography." PhD dissertation, Yale University, 1983. Ann Arbor: University Microfilms International.

Lopez, Garcia, and H.-J. Fabry. "*Tora* instruction, teaching." In *Theological Dictionary of the Old Testament,* ed. G. Johannes Botterweck et al., trans. David E. Green, 15: 609–46. Grand Rapids MI: William B. Eerdmans, 2006.

Loprieno, Antonio. "Theodicy in Ancient Egyptian Texts." In *Theodicy in the World of the Bible,* ed. Antti Laato and Johannes C. de Moor, 27–56. Leiden: Brill, 2003.

Macintosh, A. A. *Hosea.* International Critical Commentary. Edinburgh: T & T Clark, 1997.

Mendenhall, George E. "Covenant Forms in Israelite Tradition." *Biblical Archaeologist* 17 (September 1954): 50–76.

Mendenhall, George E., and Gary A. Herion. "Covenant." In *Anchor Bible Dictionary,* ed. David N. Freedman, 1: 1179–1201. New York: Doubleday, 1992.

Meyers, Carol L., and Eric M. Meyers. *Zechariah 9–14.* Anchor Bible. New York: Doubleday, 1993.

Michalowski, Piotr. *The Lamentation over the Destruction of Sumer and Ur.* Winona Lake IN: Eisenbrauns, 1989.

Milgrom, Jacob. *Cult and Conscience: The ASHAM and the Priestly Doctrine of Repentance.* Leiden: E. J. Brill, 1976.

———. "Did Isaiah Prophesy during the Reign of Uzziah?" *Vetus Testamentum* 14 (1969): 164–82.

———. *Leviticus: A Book of Ritual and Ethics.* Continental Commentary. Minneapolis: Fortress, 2004.

———. *Leviticus 1–16.* Anchor Bible. New York: Doubleday, 1991.

———. *Leviticus 17–22.* Anchor Bible. New York: Doubleday, 2000.

———. *Leviticus 23–27.* Anchor Bible. New York: Doubleday, 2001.

———. *Numbers.* Philadelphia: Jewish Publication Society, 1990.

———. "The Priestly Doctrine of Repentance." *Revue Biblique* 82 (1975): 186–205. Reprinted in Milgrom's *Studies in Cultic Theology and Terminology,* 47–66 plus addenda. Leiden: E. J. Brill, 1983.

Mowinckel, Sigmund. *The Psalms in Israel's Worship.* 2 vols. Trans. D. R. Ap-Thomas. 1951; reprint, Oxford: Basil Blackwell, 1962, 1967.

Nel, Philip J. "The Concept of 'Father' in the Wisdom Literature of the Ancient Near East." *Journal of Northwest Semitic Languages* 5 (1977): 53–66.

Neujahr, Matthew. *Predicting the Past in the Ancient Near East.* Providence RI: Brown Judaic Studies, 2012.

Nissinen, Martti. "Neither Prophecies nor Apocalyses: The Akkadian Literary Predictive Texts." In *Knowing the End from the Beginning: The Prophetic, the Apocalyptic, and Their Relationships,* ed. Lester L. Grabbe and Robert D. Haak, 134–48. London: T & T Clark International, 2003.

———. *Prophets and Prophecies in the Ancient Near East.* Writings from the Ancient World 12. Atlanta: Society of Biblical Literature, 2003.

Olyan, Saul M. *Rites and Rank: Hierarchy in Biblical Representations of Cult.* Princeton NJ: Princeton University Press, 2000.

Paul, Shalom. "Adoption Formulae: A Study of Cuneiform and Biblical Legal Clauses." *Maarav* 2 (1979–80): 173–85.

———. *Amos.* Hermeneia. Minneapolis: Fortress Press, 1991.

———. "Biblical Law." In *The Jewish Bible,* ed. Carol Hupping, 69–75. Philadelphia: Jewish Publication Society, 2008.

———. *Isaiah 40–66.* Grand Rapids MI: William B. Eerdmans, 2012.

———. "Prophets and Prophecy." In *Encyclopedia Judaica,* 13: 1150–75. Jerusalem: Keter, 1971.

———. *Studies in the Book of the Covenant in the Light of Cuneiform and Biblical Law.* VT supplement 18. Leiden: Brill, 1970; reprint, 2006.

Paulus, Susanne. "Foreigners under Foreign Rulers: The Case of Kassite Babylonia." In *The Foreigner and the Law: Perspectives from the Hebrew Bible and the Ancient Near East,* ed. R. Achenbach, R. Albertz, and J. Wohrle, 1–15. Wiesbaden: Harrassowitz, 2011.

Petersen, David L. "Eschatology (OT)." In *Anchor Bible Dictionary*, ed. David N. Freedman, 2: 575–79. New York: Doubleday, 1992.

Pleins, J. David. "Poor, Poverty (Old Testament)." In *Anchor Bible Dictionary*, 5: 402–14. New York: Doubleday, 1992.

Propp, William C. *Exodus 1–18.* Anchor Bible. New York: Doubleday, 1999.

———. *Exodus 19–40.* Anchor Bible. New York: Doubleday, 2006.

Raabe, Paul R. *Obadiah.* Anchor Bible. New York: Doubleday, 1996.

Raitt, Thomas M. *A Theology of Exile.* Philadelphia: Fortress, 1977.

Robertson, John F. "Temples and Sanctuaries—Mesopotamia." In *Anchor Bible Dictionary*, ed. David N. Freedman, 6: 369–76. New York: Doubleday, 1992.

Rofe, Alexander. "The Covenant in the Land of Moab (DT 28:69–30:20)." In *Das Deuteronomium,* ed. Norbert Lohfink, 310–20. Leuven: Leuven University Press, 1985.

———. *Introduction to the Prophetic Literature.* Sheffield: Sheffield Academic, 1997.

Roth, Martha T. *Law Collections from Mesopotamia and Asia Minor.* 2nd ed. SBL Writings from the Ancient World Series, vol. 6. Atlanta: Scholars, 1997.

Saadia Gaon. *The Book of Beliefs and Opinions.* Trans. Samuel Rosenblatt. New Haven: Yale University Press, 1948.

Sarna, Nahum. *The JPS Torah Commentary: Genesis.* Philadelphia: Jewish Publication Society, 1989.

Schiffman, Lawrence H. "Priests." In *Harper's Bible Dictionary*, ed. Paul J. Achtemeier, 821–23. San Francisco: Harper and Row, 1985.

Schmitt, John J. "Prophecy (Preexilic Hebrew)." In *Anchor Bible Dictionary*, 5: 482–89. New York: Doubleday, 1992.

Schwartz, Baruch J. "Ezekiel's Dim View of Israel's Restoration." In *The Book of Ezekiel: Theological and Anthropological Perspectives*, ed. Margaret S. Odell and John T. Strong, 43–67. Atlanta: Society of Biblical Literature, 2000.

———. "Israel's Holiness: The Torah Traditions." In *Purity and Holiness: The Heritage of Leviticus,* 47–59. Jewish and Christian Perspectives series, vol. 2. Leiden: Brill, 2000.

Shetter, Tony L. "Genesis 1–2 in Light of Ancient Egyptian Creation Myths." Dallas Theological Seminary, 2005. http://bible.org/article/genesis-1-2-light-ancient-egyptian-creation-myths.

Shinan, Avigdor, and Yair Zakovitch. *From Gods to God*. Trans. Valerie Zakovitch. Philadelphia: Jewish Publication Society/University of Nebraska Press, 2012.

Silver, Morris. "Prophets and Markets Revisited." In *Social Justice in the Ancient World,* ed. K. D. Irani and Morris Silver, 179–98. Westport CT: Greenwood, 1995.

Simian-Yofre, H. "*nhm.*" In *Theological Dictionary of the Old Testament*, ed. G. Johannes Botterweck et al., trans. David E. Green, 9: 340–55. Grand Rapids MI: William B. Eerdmans, 1998.

Singer, Itamar. *Hittite Prayers*. Atlanta: Society of Biblical Literature, 2002.

Snijders, L. A. "zur/zar." In *Theological Dictionary of the Old Testament*, 4: 52–58. Grand Rapids MI: William B. Eerdmans, 1980.

Soloveitchik, Joseph B. "The Lonely Man of Faith." *Tradition* 7, no. 2 (Summer 1965): 5–67.

Speiser, E. A. *Genesis*. Anchor Bible. Garden City NY: Doubleday, 1964.

Spencer, John R. "Sojourner." In *Anchor Bible Dictionary*, 6: 103–4. New York: Doubleday, 1992.

Spiegel, Shalom. *Amos versus Amaziah*. New York: Jewish Theological Seminary, 1957.

Spina, Frank A. "Israelites as *geri^m,* 'Sojourners,' in Social and Historical Context." In *The Word of the Lord Shall Go Forth: Essays in Honor of David Noel Freedman*, ed. Carol L. Meyers and M. O'Connor, 321–35. Winona Lake IN: Eisenbrauns, 1983.

Talmon, Shemaryahu. "The 'Comparative Method' in Biblical Interpretation—Principles and Problems." In *Essential Papers on Israel and the Ancient*

Near East, 381–419. New York: New York University, 1991. Reprinted from *Supplements to Vetus Testamentum* 29 (1977): 320–56.

Telushkin, Joseph. *Biblical Literacy.* New York: William Morrow, 1997.

Tigay, Jeffrey. *The JPS Commentary: Deuteronomy.* Philadelphia: Jewish Publication Society, 1996.

———. "On Evaluating Claims of Literary Borrowing." In *The Tablet and the Scroll: Near Eastern Studies in Honor of William W. Hallo*, ed. Mark E. Cohen, D. C. Snell, and D. B. Weisberg, 250–55. Bethesda MD: CDL, 1993.

Tov, Emanuel. "The Literary History of the Book of Jeremiah in Light of Its Textual History." In *Empirical Models of Biblical Criticism*, ed. Jeff Tigay, 212–37. Philadelphia: University of Pennsylvania Press, 1985.

Tsumura, David T. *The First Book of Samuel: The New International Commentary on the Old Testament.* Grand Rapids MI: William B. Eerdmans, 2007.

Unterman, Jeremiah. "Covenant." In *Harper's Bible Dictionary*, ed. Paul J. Achtemeier, 190–92. San Francisco: Harper and Row, 1985.

———. "Firstborn, first fruits, firstling." In *Harper's Bible Dictionary*, 310.

———. *From Repentance to Redemption: Jeremiah's Thought in Transition.* Journal for the Study of the Old Testament supplement series 54. Sheffield: JSOT, 1987.

———. "Providing for the Poor, the Widow, and the Orphan: A Social and Religious Ethical Revolution in the Hebrew Bible." In *Religion and Poverty, Global Humanities: Studies in Histories, Cultures, and Societies*, ed. Frank Jacobs, 91–111. Berlin: Neofelis, 2015.

———. "Redemption (OT)." In *Anchor Bible Dictionary*, ed. David N. Freedman, 5: 650–54. New York: Doubleday, 1992.

———. "The Social-Legal Origin for the Image of God as Redeemer *go'el* of Israel." In *Pomegranates and Golden Bells: Studies in Biblical, Jewish, and Near Eastern Ritual, Law, and Literature in Honor of Jacob Milgrom*, ed. David P. Wright, David N. Freedman, and Avi Hurvitz, 399–405. Winona Lake IN: Eisenbrauns, 1995.

———. "Torah." In *Harper's Bible Dictionary*, ed. Paul J. Achtemeier, 1083–84. San Francisco: Harper & Row, 1985.

Uriel, Simon. *Reading Prophetic Narratives.* Translated by Lenn J. Schramm. Bloomington: Indiana University Press, 1997.

van der Toorn, Karel. *Sin and Sanction in Israel and Mesopotamia: A Comparative Study.* Van Gorcum: Netherlands, 1985.

———. "Theodicy in Akkadian Literature." In *Theodicy in the World of the Bible*, ed. Antti Laato and Johannes C. de Moor, 57–89. Leiden: Brill, 2003.

————. "Theology, Priests, and Worship in Canaan and Ancient Israel." In *Civilizations of the Ancient Near East,* ed. Jack M. Sasson, 3: 2043–58. New York: Scribner's, 1995.

van Houten, Christiana. *The Alien in Israelite Law.* Journal for the Study of the Old Testament supplement series 107. Sheffield: JSOT, 1991.

Vargyas, Peter. "Immigration into Ugarit." In *Immigration and Emigration within the Ancient Near East,* ed. K. van Lerberghe and A. Schoors, 395–402. Festschrift E. Lipinski, Orientalia Lovaniensia Analecta 65. Leuven: Peeters, 1995.

Walton, John H. *Ancient Israelite Literature in Its Cultural Context.* Grand Rapids MI: Zondervan, 1989.

————. *Ancient Near Eastern Thought and the Old Testament.* Grand Rapids MI: Baker Academic, 2006.

Ward, William A. "Temples and Sanctuaries—Egypt." In *Anchor Bible Dictionary,* ed. David N. Freedman, 6: 369–72. New York: Doubleday, 1992.

Weinfeld, Moshe. "Ancient Near Eastern Patterns in Prophetic Literature." *Vetus Testamentum* 27 (1977): 178–95.

————. *Deuteronomy and the Deuteronomic School.* Oxford: Clarendon, 1972.

————. *Deuteronomy 1–11.* Anchor Bible. New York: Doubleday, 1991.

————. "Instructions for Temple Visitors in the Bible and in Ancient Egypt." In *Egyptological Studies, Scripta Hierosolymitana 28,* ed. Sarah Israelit-Groll, 224–50. Jerusalem: Magnes, 1982.

————. "Judge and Officer in Ancient Israel and the Ancient Near East." *Israel Oriental Studies* 7 (1977): 65–88.

————. "Mesopotamian Eschatological Prophecies." Hebrew. *Shnaton* 3 (1978): 263–76.

————. *Social Justice in Ancient Israel and the Ancient Near East.* 2nd ed. Jerusalem: Magnes Press, 2000.

Westbrook, Raymond. "Punishments and Crimes." In *Anchor Bible Dictionary,* ed. David N. Freedman, 5: 546–56. New York: Doubleday, 1992.

————. "Social Justice in the Ancient Near East." In *Social Justice in the Ancient World,* ed. K. D. Irani and Morris Silver, 149–64. Westport CT: Greenwood, 1995.

Wilson, J. A. "Authority and Law in Ancient Egypt." *Journal of the American Oriental Society,* supplement to 40, no. 1 (1954): 1–7.

Wright, David P. "Holiness (OT)." In *Anchor Bible Dictionary,* ed. David N. Freedman, 3: 237–49. New York: Doubleday, 1992.

————. "Molech." In *Harper's Bible Dictionary,* 646. San Francisco: Harper and Row, 1985.

Zevit, Ziony. "A Phoenician Inscription and Biblical Covenant Theology." *Israel Exploration Journal* 27 (1977): 110–18.

———. "The Prophet versus Priest Antagonism Hypothesis: Its History and Origin." In *The Priests in the Prophets*, ed. Lester L. Grabbe and Alice Ogden Bellis, 189–217. London: T & T Clark International, 2004.

Zimmerli, Walther. *Ezekiel 2*. Hermeneia. Trans. James D. Martin. Philadelphia: Fortress, 1983.

Zobel, H.-J. "hesed." In *Theological Dictionary of the Old Testament*, 5: 44–64. Grand Rapids MI: William B. Eerdmans, 1986.

Subject Index

Abraham, 45, 195n41, 197n61

"abuse," prohibitions against the stranger, widow, orphan, poor, 47, 57, 61, 79

Adad, 90

Admah, 161, 246n70

adoption, 191n4

adultery, 116, 120

"Advice to a Prince," 216–17n135

Akhenaten, xix

Alalakh treaty #2, 63

Amalekites, 95, 206n39, 207n46

Ameny, 146–47

Amos: disadvantaged people, 78–79; ethics and ritual, 96–99, 219–20nn24–25; redemption, 153–54, 161, 174, 246n68; return to God, 130

anachronistic terminology, xxiv, 239n1

animal sacrifices, 17, 123–24

anointed ones, 243n46

antisemitism, 202n3

apodictic style, 22–23, 32, 194n29

Apsu, 2–3, 4

Aristotle, xix

Ark of the Covenant, 17

Asa, 138

Assyria, 162, 242n29; laws of, 19, 25, 27, 28, 70, 193n19, 197n59; texts from, 148, 188n21; treaties of, 191n5

Assyriology, 183n3

Athens, 43–44, 216n134

Atrahasis epic, 8, 189n23

Awel-Marduk, 149

Babylon, 163, 170, 216–17n135, 247n79

Babylonia: confession in, 227n14; creation epic of, 2–7, 29, 185n4,

Index of Hebrew Bible Passages

In the JPS Essential Judaism Series

*Justice for All: How the Jewish
Bible Revolutionized Ethics*
Jeremiah Unterman

*Thinking about the Torah: A
Philosopher Reads the Bible*
Kenneth Seeskin

To order or obtain more information on these or other Jewish
Publication Society titles, visit
jps.org.